ALTERNATIVE DESIGNS OF HUMAN ORGANISATIONS

NITISH R DE

Alternative Designs
of
Human Organisations

FOREWORD BY FRED E EMERY

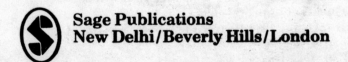

Sage Publications
New Delhi/Beverly Hills/London

First published in 1984 by

SAGE Publications India Pvt Ltd
C 236 Defence Colony
New Delhi 110 024

SAGE Publications Inc
275 South Beverly Drive
Beverly Hills, California 90212

SAGE Publications Ltd
28 Banner Street
London EC1Y 8QE, England

Published by Tejeshwar Singh for Sage Publications India Pvt Ltd, phototypeset at Southend Typographics, Pondicherry, and printed at Pearl Offset Press, New Delhi.

Library of Congress Cataloging in Publication Data

De, Nitish R. (Nitish Ranjan), 1927-
    Alternative designs of human organisations.

    Includes indexes.
    1. Management—India—Employee participation.
    2. Quality of work life—India.   I. Title
HD5660.15D4   1984   658.3'152'0954   84-15024
ISBN 0-8039-9480-X
ISBN 0-8039-9481-8 (pbk.)

For my wife,

GAUTAMA

whose on-going contributions to
enriching our shared lives
have led me to explore the quality of life
in human organisations

Contents

Foreword

We have here, for the first time, a balanced overview of one of the most extensive *programs* of workplace democratisation that has yet occurred in the world. Many more individual instances of work democratisation have turned up in other countries (e.g., Sweden), but they have not resulted from a single unified program with clearly identifiable leadership. The only comparable programs are the Norwegian Industrial Democracy Project of the sixties and the Australian program of the seventies, centred around the Centre for Continuing Education, Australian National University. However, Norway and Australia are small, culturally homogeneous 'first world' countries with mature and stable social systems and a long tradition of pursuing liberal democratic/social democratic ideals. Nitish De is reporting from India, a vast third world country, with all that that entails, plus great cultural heterogeneity and a unique caste system.

At the same time as people in the USA were trying but failing to put together such a program, that is post-1972, Nitish De was able to persuade the Central Government of India to modify its legislation and to establish the National Labour Institute (NLI). From this base De proceeded to successfully carry through this massive program and, incidentally, provide the liveliest international forum for discussion of these matters—the *Bulletin of the NLI*.

The starkness of the contrast between the Indian experience and the experience of USA (with its fabulous pool of MBAs and social science Ph.Ds) cannot be blurred by pointing to differences of scale; the Indian industrial enterprises with which De worked were very large by any international standard and very modern.

The real difference lies where Nitish De puts it, that is in the recognition that the so-called 'bottom line' encompasses not only goods and services that have been profitably produced but also the people that the work has produced. It is indisputable that people are transformed by the work in which they engage, whether they be managers or 'mere cleaners', and that the transformation is not always in their best interest. The individual enterprise, public or private, is always tempted to blot over this part of the bottom line. However, it is in the national interest that work should produce strong, reliant and self-regarding people. Amongst the leaders of India's nationalised industries, BHEL, Nitish De found people who could accept this challenge, at least after the Central Government had given its public sanctioning, and Nitish De and his colleagues had argued that it could be done without risking loss of efficiency and return to capital. Within India the contrast is with the multinationals. Some of these, like Shell and ICI, were leaders in work democratisation in Britain, Australia and Canada and were acquainted, at first hand, with the NLI program. They made no response in the seventies.

In the USA the national interest in work democratisation was not publicly established. For a brief moment, with the release of the O'Toole Commission Report in 1974, it seemed that this interest would be sanctioned. However, the then president of the USA shrugged it off, in public. Also, unlike in Norway and Australia, it was just not possible to get alternative sanctioning from centralised trade union and employee federations—effective ones did not exist.

It is my judgement, based on some personal experience of each of these programs, that when all of the many theories of diffusion are boiled down, this sanctioning of a national interest in work democratisation is critical for the speed, scale and depth of diffusion. In the absence of such sanctioning diffusion will be laborious and fragmentary, and frequently divisive. It will be divisive when motives for work redesign are sought for in narrower sub-group interests—e.g., as an attempt to keep out unions or to pare away managerial prerogatives.

The willingness to nationally sanction such demands on employers certainly seems to presuppose a shift in cultural values. However, I think De has shown that that does not entail 'modernisation' of third world traditional cultures along US lines. The cultural shift that made it possible for politicians and managers to even consider the possibility of efficient non-authoritarian workplaces was a different cultural shift. It is the world-wide cultural shift that emerged in the sixties—a reassertion of human dignity and the challenge to all traditional hierarchies. The USA has not exactly been a leader in bridging this broadening gap, although in many ways it seems that their Presidency is being used as the last institutional barricade to any accommodation.

The implications of this study go far beyond the demonstration that some Indian managers and social scientists can match the world in managerial innovation. For third world countries like India, that are starved for local capital and unwilling to pay the price that is exacted for an uninterrupted inflow of foreign capital, this report should spark off some optimism. Democratisation of work is shown, once again, to reduce the demand for capital, it vastly enhances the scope for skill training on the job (giving a much needed multiplier effect to the technical college systems) and it vastly enhances the flow of technical and product innovations from the shop floor. The demonstrated potentials for the administrative sector are no less impressive. What De and his colleagues achieved in banking, insurance, taxation and the post office offers the only hope I know of for reversing the universal trend toward bloated white collar staffs and their budgets. The improvements in administration also make it more likely that legislative policies will be translated into practice and, by giving effective service, reduce the need to bribe and corrupt the administrators.

A veritable rash of scholars in the USA are now broadcasting their discovery that nothing less than a 'socio-technical revolution' is needed if their country is to regain world leadership. Nitish De has gone far beyond these abstract and programmatic declarations to present a set of very concrete demonstrations of what can be done to bring about that socio-technical revolution in India, as she is today, with all her warts and tribulations. This work abolishes any academic notion that there is a natural succession of steps through which national economies must pass in order to achieve 'advanced industrialisation' and hence to be in the happy situation of the USA of confronting 'post-industrialism'.

According to these academics, usually US citizens, the third world was condemned to go through the same process of industrialisation as the first world countries. This was a bitter process of recruiting and domesticating an industrial workforce. It was a long process. Arkwright, one of the foremost designers of the British factory system, was convinced that domestication was achieved only when the children of the first generation followed their parents into the factories. The strains imposed on the social structure and cultural web of a society were immense. The process split a society with class divisions and class hatreds; it created a mass of unskilled, unpropertied workers who had been rendered incapable of entering the market with products of their own making; it perpetuated and magnified all manner of ethnic, sex, age and religious divisions within the workforce (and hence in society); and led to trade union movements that had to obstinately fight against just about all technological change.

Since petro-dollars started to flood the world we have had at least seven clear examples of what it means to hasten down the historical road to progress. The 'Newly Industrialised Countries' (the NICs) include Taiwan, South Korea, Hongkong, Philippines, Singapore and Brazil. They threw their doors open to the petro-dollars that were being re-cycled by the private banks and sped down the road of industrialisation. In each case a harshly repressive, dictatorial regime has been a prerequisite and in each case a potentially explosive workforce has emerged. In each case a lopsided economy has emerged that is essentially an appendage to the economies of the metropolitan countries. With the continuing depression of those central economies the NICs are deprived of the very markets they were created to serve and hence are deprived of the income needed to serve their massive debts. Returning their unemployed workers to whence they came looks like being an insoluble problem.

From independence, India has very deliberately chosen to avoid this path and the pitfalls it holds for any democracy. They chose the so-called Soviet path of heavy industry and an elite workforce of skilled personnel, under Indian Government management and subject to some degree of *national* economic planning. It was hoped that by proceeding in this manner India would retain greater control over its destiny and avoid the de-stabilising effects of early industrial capitalism. Apart from such technically backward sectors as coal mining the strategy has probably succeeded. However, as Nitish De spells out, this strategy has not prevented the growth of divisions between the workforce and management and the growth of inefficiency and lethargy. In the western tradition this situation would call for a tightening of the screws (scientifically, of course, a la McKinsey) and de-nationalising of the BHEL. The program described here proves that there is an alternative path to advanced industrialisation that requires neither further de-humanisation of work nor a retreat to 'capitalist planning'.

The alternative described by De offers the possibility that industrialisation, instead of being a major source of social instability, may act as a major integrative force, much as the Indian army is for such a hetero-geneous society. Instead of de-skilling or narrowly specialising skills the program led to multi-skilling; instead of tightening lines of authority and responsibility in true McKinsey style the program gave much of the authority for co-ordination to those whose work was co-ordinated. The observed results were that:

(*a*) idle time was drastically reduced without resorting to any speed-up; it was simply a matter of the operators being able to themselves determine how they co-ordinated their efforts.

(*b*) there was a greater multiplier effect from each skilled person on the job. In effect each work-site was a technical college.

(c) the 'gap at the bottom of the executive chain' (Wilfred Brown, 1958) was markedly reduced:
  (i) there was no longer a role for unskilled labour, *per se*.
  (ii) the role of foremen as the NCOs of industry was rendered increasingly redundant.
  (iii) at Tiruchirapalli they showed how the channels to management or independent entrepreneurship could be opened up to operators. Foremanship was no longer the only place to go, nor the last promotion.

(d) relations on the job became task-related, over-riding the distinctions of caste, etc., that persisted in the labour market.

(e) there was the beginning of a recognition that unions could be constructively involved in technological innovation to the benefit of their members. Their members acted as if this was not in question.

For Indian society these changes could only be beneficial. The only hitch for a democratic India would seem to be that the increase in efficiency would reduce the number of employees required to do the work that is now being done. This is likely to be an absurdly short period of adjustment. Investment plans are made with a view to the future price of products and services that could be marketed. If significant economies are evident in the current operations then it is easy to plan for expanded production, whether it be for export or import-substitution. The De program shows where such economies can be achieved and lays the ground for expanded reproduction.

I would be seriously in default of my duties as a 'foreword writer' if I failed to emphasise, not just mention, the manner in which the program of work-redesign proceeded. It was not a blue-print, as it might seem from my retrospective remarks. Nitish De and his colleagues challenged the principles underlying current management practices and put forward new principles, backing their arguments, of course, with evidence from existing demonstrations. The actual socio-technical analysis and redesign was in each case eventually worked out by the people who had been operating the system and would be working the new one. The process of analysis and redesign was used so that the potential co-producers could test out the conditions of mutual trust and mutual respect. In the sixties we used to regard the problem of mutual trust as primary. In fact, I only moved to develop the method of 'participative design workshops' in 1972 because I sensed that an adequate latitude of trust then existed in the Australian industrial relations. However, I now doubt that. I think the hub of the matter is mutual respect. When, in Norway, we brought forward *our* studiously thought-out plans for socio-technical redesign and allowed the workers to vote on them *we* made the question of trust the foremost issue. In each instance our designs were patently fairer and more liberating than existing management practices but we had done the same thing that management was always doing—we scorned their knowledge. We learnt the hard way. De and his colleagues did the wise thing and learnt from the mistakes of others.

This issue of respecting the learnings of others is the focus of the next two sections of the book.

The National Labour Institute extended its work to rural labour. It could hardly do otherwise because for all of the great strides in heavy industry India remains the land of more than three hundred thousand villages. Only one of the NLI rural projects is discussed, but it is discussed against the background of four other very diverse efforts to improve conditions at the village level. What is clearly brought out is that multi-skilling, as in the factories and the Maharashtra rural project, is nowhere near being an adequate solution, and knowledge gained on the job is nowhere near providing an adequate explanation of the complex economic, legal, administrative and cultural web that enmeshes the condition of rural labour. The practical focus of even the participative redesign workshops was too narrow for the purposes of the village camps the NLI organised. For the NLI to teach the villagers about their predicament was rejected by Nitish De as self-defeating—the very process of teaching would rub the noses of the villagers in their ignorance and reinforce the belief that only the educated classes had power. Instead De reached out to the work being done by Paulo Freire in West Africa and the work being done on the 'search conference'.

Although these approaches had emerged in markedly different settings, the third world and first world respectively, De grasped the way that they converged on his problem. Both shared the epistemological position that knowledge is gained by a process of 'perceptual differentiation', i.e., by looking harder, looking closer, looking around, looking behind, and not by 'perceptual enrichment', i.e., by abstracting, conceptualising and making logical inferences. The traditional educational paradigm, to which continuing educators usually subscribe, confuses processes that aid the recording and parroting of knowledge with gaining of knowledge. This so-called enrichment is certainly denied to the uneducated but gaining knowledge, perceptual differentiation, is not. The ignorance of the individual villagers is that which arises from having severely circumscribed fields of vision, not from being uneducated nor from lack of wit. In pooling and sharing their perceptions they are able to come to knowledge that would be unattainable for the silent individual. If they come to trust their newly gained and shared knowledge they can start to look at things in ways they never considered or dared to do; they can start looking for things that were previously over their horizon. With the Chipko study De gives a beautiful and moving instance of such a growth in consciousness. I think this is the sort of process that Freire's 'consciousness raising' and the 'search conference' could help. The alternatives, as De indicates in his case studies, are unattractive or rather like 'Waiting for Lefty'.

The final chapters on global planning and meta-ideals indicate both the perspective and motive for the practical programs in the factories, offices and villages. The scholarship shown in these chapters is profound. However, it is for the author but a tool, like a telescope to the eye of a sea-captain. Nitish De knows full well where his feet are planted; he has no illusions about the puny nature of the craft he has launched, relative to the vast turbulent sea of third world villages, but he has one eye fixed on the dim and distant shore. Of channels through the reefs and of safe anchorages he knows nothing and does not pretend to know. That distant shore is the same as some of us in the first world countries have been eyeing from afar, e.g., Schumacher, Goldsmith, Rozak, Freire, Illych, *not*, mind you, the Daniel Bells and the Herman Kahns. I am not sure, however, that he pays enough heed to the off-shore wind that over the past decade has, with increasing strength, driven us back almost beyond sight of land. Soon, so it would seem, the over-riding consideration will be to stay afloat, not where we are heading. De's reply to this is, in his last chapter, that when you are out of sight of land, but still afloat, your most important possession is your compass. For us, in our societies and organisations, the only thing that can serve as a compass are our shared values and ideals. Choosing between positive ends can be politically charged but it is child's play compared with choosing between sacrifices to be made. It is the latter choices that test the commitment to shared values and ideals.

The world economy has gone into another of its tail-spins and all the important choices now seem to be choices between sacrifices.

In the 1930s, we went through a time like that which we are now entering. From Hamburg to Athens all pretence to a national consensus on values and ideals was swept aside. It was almost as if those nations that had no economic fat had nothing else to bind together their nations than dictatorship and naked force. Is that to be our fate, yet again?

Over the past decade of the petro-dollar the world banking community has made no bones about its preference for military dictatorships. This is probably not for ideological reasons but simply because the stability of such states is usually under-written by the USA or the USSR. What seems to be really different this time is the absence of such powerful polarising forces as the 1930s movements toward communism and fascism, and the absence of any possible 'colonial empire' solution of the sort that fired the maverick, 'have not' nations of that era, Germany, Italy and Japan. It is hard to realise just how much stability has been achieved through the virtual elimination of colonialism and the emergence of the EEC. The one terrible threat that looms over this relatively stabilised world system is the possibility that the balance of power between the USA and the USSR may be seriously disturbed by the inability of one of them to cope with the current economic crisis. However, this is something that can be seen as it develops—it would stimulate the Europeans to arbitrate a new world order rather than see Europe as a nuclear battlefield. A new world order would only be more stable if it was along such lines as envisaged by the Brandt North–South Commission.

Nitish De is not in the realm of wishful thinking with his long list of current agenda items nor his perception of the reality of the meta-ideal of *Samaj-Siddhi*. The most difficult half of the Brandt proposals has already been accomplished. It happened without inter-governmental planning and almost without notice of the overall process. We have woken up today to the fact that in the past decade of the petro-dollars a massive transfer of resources from the North to the South has already taken place. The willy-nilly way this took place has created a stupendous debt problem—in January 1983, 25 countries were behind in debt payments and the list continues to grow (for comparison with the thirties, 27 were behind by 1936). Ironically this is the best guarantee that work will be commenced on putting into place the rest of the Brandt Program—and De's.

Fred E. Emery

Wharton School
University of Pennsylvania
June 1984

Acknowledgements

The book reflects the privileges and opportunities ungrudgingly offered to me by numerous organisations and their employees in India and abroad. Engaged in action-research programmes, I have benefited from the concrete experiences and reflections of working people. But for their continuing interest in and support to the projects the book would not have seen the light of day. I cannot adequately express my debt to them.

I have been fortunate in sharing my thoughts, including doubts, with many colleagues in India and abroad. I have gained from these fruitful interactions while crystallising and clarifying my thoughts and ideas. In particular, I wish to name Fred and Merrelyn Emery, whose interest and encouragement have sustained me in my efforts throughout the period 1974 to 1983.

I would like to name five persons who have stood by me as close associates in the completion of the book. Arunendu Banerjee assisted me as an earnest colleague from when the first draft was prepared in 1974 till the finalisation of the book. His patience, meticulous attention to a clumsily written manuscript and unfaltering devotion by putting long hours of work cannot be compensated in any manner. My son, Subasish, systematically provided me with notes, papers, books and monographs from my personal library whenever I sought his assistance. Sunil Dhawan helped me considerably in compiling figures and tables. Jatinder Singh and Kanwaljit Singh helped by typing out some chapters which I acknowledge with gratitude.

Chandigarh   NITISH R. DE

Prologue

We now move towards the terminal decades of an eventful century. Human experiences, during this century, have offered a momentous kaleidoscope: two global conflicts with far-reaching politico-economic consequences; exponential scientific and technological advancement and chilling, mega-dimensional human misery and deprivation. Simultaneously, human societies have been transformed into organisational entities. The formal structures dominate human lives from the cradle to the grave. They also determine the destiny of those humans who constitute the non-formal sector and otherwise exist at the periphery of civilisation.

We concern ourselves with the organisational reality, the experiences of life in the organisational space. Our search leads us inevitably to the reckoning of what we confront. As illustration of what we find, two examples will suffice. Kanter and Stein (1979) document people's experiences with contemporary work places in the USA: obsession with power at the top, career concern at the middle and estranged, embattled existence at the bottom. Skullduggery and decadence are not rare organisational phenomena. As if not to be outflanked, the working class regimes offer us Haraszti's (1977) confrontation with a socialist production system in Hungary. The 'efficient' system with its guardians engages human labour as inputs of production. Rigorous piece-rates have been devised as the primary motivator of work commitment. Supervisors provide the superstructure of enforced discipline. Managers and experts contribute the brain power of work. The upshot of the system is a display of work-evasive conduct with all the subtleties of human ingenuity and yet the joy of social labour is reflected in the creation of *homers*. The sensitive author, a milling machine operator, expresses himself this way:

By making homers we win back power over the machine and our freedom from the machine; skill is subordinated to a sense of beauty. However insignificant the object, its form of creation is artistic. This is all the more so because (mainly to avoid the reproach of theft) homers are rarely made with expensive, showy or semi-finished materials. They are created out of junk from useless scraps of iron, from left-overs, and this ensures that their beauty comes first and foremost from the labour itself ....

Before we commit ourselves to a search for structural symmetries and their obverse in the first and the second worlds, we may mention in passing that the quality of life as embodied in an organisational system poses a similar dilemma in the third world. Let us compare Punjab, a prosperous state in India with Kerala, one of the poorest. Punjab produces four times the food it consumes. Kerala is always a deficit state dependent on imports from surplus zones. Punjab has sustained an annual economic growth rate of 6 per cent per annum over a decade. Kerala has maintained 2 per cent; barely keeping pace with its population increase. Per capita annual income growth rate is 0.2 per cent in Kerala against Punjab's 3 per cent. The average farm holding in Kerala is half-hectare with a per capita annual income of Rs. 1,100 against Punjab's Rs. 2,300. In Punjab only 10 per cent of the farmers have holdings below one hectare against Kerala's 90 per cent. Kerala has a population density of 654 per sq. km., more than twice that of Punjab. Against Punjab's irrigation facilities at 80 per cent, Kerala's is a paltry 6 per cent. Kerala's per capita food intake stands at 1,600 calories against Punjab's 2,700. On the accepted norms of development, the two states contrast sharply.

However, on the Physical Quality of Life Index (PQLI) worked out on the basis of infant mortality, literacy and expectation of life at birth, Kerala, with 100 as the index, is at the top in India. Punjab gets 60 marks. The country's most prosperous district, Ludhiana in Punjab, sustains 25 per cent of its population living below the poverty line while the state's average is one-third of its population. The PQLI for women in Punjab is 45 against Kerala's 93. 6 per cent of the total work force in Punjab is child labour against Kerala's 2 per cent. Kerala's literacy rate is 70 per cent while it is 40 per cent in Punjab. 'Enslavement' of immigrant farm labour, a practice prevalent in Punjab, is a rare phenomenon in Kerala (*The Statesman*, 1982).

All this may lead to the tentative conclusion that equity and social justice have by-passed public policy in Punjab and less so in Kerala. Public policies are the products of public institutions and public forums and we may legitimately enquire whether alternative models of public institutions exist in these two states. We are thus led to seek what there is in the organisation system that unleashes impressive prosperity as well as mounting human misery before we attempt to resolve the contradictions.

What strikes us as significant are three interlinked issues in organisational life. One is the problem of alienation. Marx (and Engels) in *The Economic and Philosophic Manuscripts of 1844, The Holy Family, The German Ideology, Grundrisse* and *Capital,* have deliberated upon the human phenomenon of alienation originating from the logic of production relations. Novack (1976) has summed up the Marxian stand in these words:

> The antagonistic relation of production injures the workers in many ways. (1) He is estranged from his own body which must be maintained as a physical subject, not because it is part of himself, but so that it can function as an element of the productive process. (2) He is estranged from nature since natural objects with all their variety, not as means for his self-satisfaction or cultural fulfilment, but merely as material means for profitable production. (3) He is estranged from his own peculiar essence as a human being because his special traits and abilities are not needed, used or developed by his economic activities which degrade him to the level of a more physical force. (4) Finally, he is separated from his fellow human beings, 'where man is opposed to himself, he also stands opposed to other men'.

In Marxian analysis, there is a distinction between concrete labour and abstract labour. While one produces use value, the other contributes to the economics of exchange value. Work in the latter sense thus becomes the product of saleable labour which earns money to procure goods and services from an ever-expanding consumer society. With the modernisation of the production system, increased leisure time is devoted to the commercialised leisure industry. Alienated labour is not confined to the workers. The logic of the system spreads it to the supervisory and managerial groups also. There are other dimensions of alienation—social and psychological. Seeman (1972) observes in mass-society such forms of alienation as powerlessness, meaninglessness, value isolation, self-estrangement and social isolation emanating from the structural trends of impersonality, rationality (sans emotionality), heterogeneous complexity, mobility (uprootedness) and enlargement of scale (large size of corporate sector). Keniston (1972) identifies primarily the numerous psychological dimensions of alienation in society. The phenomenon of alienation, which predates the industrial society, is not confined to the capitalist world. The socialist world is not free from alienated forms of behaviour—

as evidenced in the USSR and the People's democracies (Bahro, 1978; Yanowitch, 1979).

Apart from what Marx has postulated as the determinants of alienation inherent in the structure and motivation of work organisations, we shall find the second interlinked element in the way the human beings are organised as work units. The logic on which the division of labour is based contributes to alienated work behaviour. The traditional division of labour—vertical and horizontal—creates a hierarchy of functionaries, segmented and constrained responsibility, antagonistic relations, deprives employees from the opportunities of continuing education, thus creating an organisational leviathan which fosters a culture of manipulating potentially productive human beings into impersonal tools of activity. People may thus fall prey to subservience or subversion in their work life. Democratisation of work life remains an abiding illusion. It seems that in the capitalist as well as in the socialist regimes work systems are organised under the logic that whether an individual or social entity, human labour as a process is treated similarly in that its organisation is to be based on the principle of efficiency. And that the dictates of efficiency offer a unique, unalterable form of the organising process—the micro-division of labour.

Why is this phenomenon so immutable across the systems? Some response can be provided by the third characteristic: the organisational hierarchy which provides the rationale for the hierarchy of power, privilege and knowledge. Marx indicted the capitalist world for fashioning the political, social and economic mechanisms to exploit, demean and alienate labour power. Bahro (1978), Heller (1976), Markus and Hegedus (1976), all citizens of the eastern bloc of Socialist countries, have unequivocally articulated the dysfunctions of the party–governmental elitist bureaucracy as a symbol of an organisational society where members of the productive labour force continue to suffer from anonymous existence and denial of what Marx visualised as 'man's self-esteem, his sense of freedom, ... (a) community of men that can fulfil their highest needs' (quoted in Hampton, 1981). While discussing the advancement in the structuring of work organisations in GDR, Hanspach, *et al* (1979) discuss about work-place hygiene factors but not democratisation of work. In the USSR, Dovba, *et al* (1979) mention the existence of worker autonomy and semi-autonomous work group functioning (work brigades) but their data on the characteristics of job content in weaving mills indicate that the control and decision-taking roles repose in the supervisory cadre. Gvishiani (1972) justifiably criticises the manipulative management 'schools' of thought of the bourgeois society but his Marxist–Leninist correct practices of designing human organisations have not been explicitly stated from which one can comprehend the elements of an alternative model.

The elitism of the bureaucratic, hierarchical work structure, Emery (1981) points out, may, through the medium of democratic practice, create 'an elite of multi-skilled workers, highly rewarded employees against a back-drop of large scale unemployment and multitude of short-term, part-time jobs in service industries.' Emery, understandably, refers to the state of contemporary capitalist crisis. What, however, is at stake is the more fundamental dichotomy between mental and manual labour, thinking and doing, objective conceptualisation and concrete performance. The rationale for organisation design is premised on this third principle of the hierarchy of knowledge—social as well as scientific, leading to the reality of organisational power of the experts, of the party ideologues, of the technocrat–bureaucrats, of the professional managers, and as Marcuse (Woddis, 1972) believes, of the labour aristocracy. It is thus no surprise, as Trevor Williams (1982) has mentioned, that the innovation in work organisations are prone to suffer from the encapsulation disability.

This tyranny of the elite caste in designing and fostering a hierarchic, power-skewed system is not confined to the first world. We may offer an example from Vietnam. During the formative years of struggle for liberation and simultaneous system-transformation, Ho Chi Minh offered four recommendations and five interdictions to party cadre (the elite in the perception of the village peasants).

Recommendations

1. To help the population in their daily work; husking and milling rice, fetching water and firewood, looking after the children.
2. To get acquainted with local customs and habits, to respect strictly all 'taboos' observed in the region and by the family with whom one is staying.
3. To learn the local dialect, to teach the people to sing, read and write, to win their sympathy and, little by little, to conduct revolutionary propaganda.
4. To win the population's confidence and support through one's correct attitude and good discipline.

Interdictions

I. Not to cause any damage to the crops and fields, not to deface or impair the population's furniture and household articles.
II. Not to insist on buying or borrowing what people do not want to sell or lend.

III. Not to forget one's promises.
IV. Not to violate local customs, habits and religious beliefs.
 V. Not to divulge any secrets (Hodgkin, 1981).

After the country has purged itself of colonialism and embarked on the path of system-transformation, Ho Chi Minh's advice to the party functionaries to de-elitise themselves so as to close the ranks between them and the people in order to create a climate for participation culture seems to have been abandoned. What Ho Chi Minh wanted was cultural mutuality as opposed to cultural domination. A strong voice of protest has recently come from a veteran party intellectual, Nguyen Khac Vien (Quinn-Judge, 1982) who mentions that the current leadership of the nation has set up an inefficient system resulting in erroneous organisational policy and a policy to promote persons with mediocre qualities to key positions. Persons with a creative urge who could offer diverse constructive views have been passed over while the elites, given to opportunism and crude flattery, have been installed in the positions of power. The socialist transformation process has thus regressed into what Marx had cautioned against with his insightful lessons derived from the western organisational society.

Such organisational betrayal may also emerge in Cuba (Sohr, 1982) where inflow of foreign capital to the tune of 49 per cent in joint enterprises was announced as a policy decision. Along with capital inflow would enter the western organisational logic with its experts-based cultural domination which might betray the enthusiasts of revolution who believed in the logic of alternative organisation culture (Zeitlin, 1972).

There is, thus, an organisational crisis in all the three worlds where the design principles have been built on micro division of labour, dichotomy between mental and manual work, dysfunctional, skewed distribution of power with the elites occupying the higher positions endowed with the monopoly of knowledge and expertise.

Given this hard and harsh assessment, one has to seek alternative design principles to overcome the tragedy of alienative labour and the contradictions that exist between the routine of work-life and the potential of the quality of enriched life. It is necessary to pay attention to the liberation of work as Burns, *et al* (1979) have mentioned in the context of organisational and institutional designs.

To quote:

A major task for both social theory and practice, we are suggesting, is to explore and try to develop more holistic approaches toward work and work life. This would entail, above all, giving consideration to economic, technological, socio-political and cultural factors and their dynamic interrelationships, which shape and reshape work conditions and work experiences.

In the first world social realities are treated as fragments, each to be dealt with on the basis of limited programmes and reforms. A common thread does not run through in a world with divided enclaves. In the second world the supra-structure of the bureaucracy ensures that the totality of the system dominates over the unique properties and the concrete realities of the sub-systems. There is thus unconnectedness on the one side and a tight control on the other side.

Be that as it may, the challenge lies in overcoming the current conflict in the redesign principles. Gorz (1965) has expressed the contradiction in the following words:

> The problem for big management is to harmonise two contradictory insights: the necessity of developing human capabilities, imposed by the modern processes of production and the political necessity of ensuring that this kind of development of capabilities does not bring in its wake any augmentation of the independence of the individual, provoking him to challenge the present condition of labour and distribution of power.

To overcome this existing contradiction in the work system design it is necessary to appreciate that a reductionist logic holds sway over the design parameters. Conversion of this logic into what Ackoff (1981) calls the expansionist logic so as to install alternative design principles is a challenge to education—to develop a new paradigm of educational philosophy (Emery, 1981). Education should aim at practice of freedom so that human beings can become social units of productive labour through a process of 'learning to learn' even in the precinct of the educational institutions. The debureaucratisation and dealienation efforts might initially concentrate on the education system itself. The practice of freedom should become the *weltanschauung* of a new educational paradigm. The theory of educational organisation should be embedded in the practice of liberation as reflected in its daily functioning. The acid test of ideas and principles lies in their historical grounding in concrete and specific fulfilment as made out by Gramsci (Salamini, 1981).

Referring to the context, as earlier mentioned, one may seriously consider the need for an economic system which has been compared to a space-ship. The space-ship economy, as Boulding (1966) mentions, is designed to minimise the levels of production and consumption necessary to maintain the desired levels of physical and mental health. It is energy conserving compared to the cowboy economy which is energy dispersing. An organisation system is to be built on such principles as can overcome the reckless, wanton exploitation of resources—human and material— thereby negating the logic of the traditional forms of power-concentrated organisation system.

In the context of the overwhelming might of corporate society in the first world and the bureaucratic hegemony of the second world where organisations reflect the sovereign power of institutional mega-structures, it may be worth our while to opt for a cooperative sector of activities designed along egalitarian lines. There is increasing evidence that the cooperative movement is gaining steady ground in France, Italy and the UK as a response to the collapse of private enterprise system (Logan, 1982). The Mondragon experiment (Bradley, *et al*, 1981) offers an alter- native model for social labour, creative motivation and alternative control systems based on horizontal monitoring and vertical trust relationship. There is further evidence in the Mondragon case that manual labour has been accepted as healthy of which one need not be ashamed (Flassati, 1981). It may, however, be mentioned that we do not wish to romanticise the virtues of worker ownership enterprises. There are empirical evidences (Russell, *et al*, 1979) which indicate that starting with enthusiasm and egalitarian values such companies may turn out to be hierarchical and vertical control-system oriented. What is being suggested, however, is that it is possible to initiate and sustain alternative work systems on cooperation philosophy. There is scope to reflect on the Mondragon experience in the context of the culture of the Basque provinces of Northern Spain.

Lastly, all attempts at system transformation as opposed to system maintenance will unleash values, defined as preferred outcomes, which will carry the seeds of some ideals. The initial fervour reflected in trans- forming a system keeping the ideals in view can be converted into stabilised norms of conduct, healthy social relationships and non-exploitative work systems. Just as there is a possibility of insipient ideals to degenerate into repressive forces, there lies a prospect of managing the transition phase of politico-social transformation in a productive manner. It is offered as a suggestion that the key mediating variable during the transition phase is to intervene in redesigning micro-system of work organisations. Experi- ences of the socialist countries indicate that the overwhelming concern of overhauling the macro-system of society ended up in ultra-bureaucratised elite-run state and this has happened, on account of, among other reasons, the failure to intervene in refashioning the micro-work-systems in the field of education, art and economy so as to assert the genuine human values as reflected, running as a common theme, in the writings of Karl Marx. After evaluating the numerous organisational models in practice, Davies (1980) finds that the most likely productive candidate is the democratic-participative design. Needless to mention, however, that this alternative design will draw upon itself the opposition from the traditional systems from the first, second and third worlds.

I

ALTERNATIVE DESIGN PURSUIT

Introduction

The three chapters incorporated in this section offer glimpses of some alternative design principles. The principles as reflected in the cases are not immutable. But the values inspiring those principles are.

Chapter 1 is a report on the work redesign projects carried out in India and reflections on these projects emanating from the accumulated experiences. On productivity criteria, the projects carried out in industrial, commercial and service organisations have recorded overall improvements. Work-hygiene factors have improved. The grass-roots employees have responded positively to work-related issues. The hiatus between thinking and doing processes have been reduced, though not eliminated. There are limited signs of progress towards quality of work-life. The limitations of the experiments have also been identified. The 'new music' has not caught on. There are endogenous and exogenous forces which militate against the spread effect.

Chapter 2 is a study of rural development agencies. We have sought to pin-point the forces which influence and shape the designs of such organisations. The crucial elements identified in the study are the organising and mobilising dynamics. These organisations are avowedly committed to the poorest strata of the rural society. Attempts have been made to distil the characteristics of the structural properties of these human corporations from their functioning as reflected in the processes of organising and mobilising. One can derive some aspects of the alternative design criteria from some of these cases.

Chapter 3 engages itself, somewhat explicitly, to the value premises behind the design principles. Drawing a distinction between an organisation and an institution on the premises of a purposeful system, an attempt has been made to identify two intervention methods to move an organisation towards an institution. These process strategies are based on a new educational paradigm. While the search conference experiences emanate from the first world, the conscientisation process owes its origin and spread to the third world countries. There are, however, convergent elements in them. There is a conscious effort to eliminate the barrier between concept-based knowledge and gut-level knowledge, thereby facilitating the way to the practice of freedom.

1

A Review of the Work-System Redesign Efforts in India

To crush, to annihilate a man utterly, to inflict on him the most terrible punishments so that the most ferocious murderer would shudder at it and dread it beforehand, one need only give work of an absolutely, completely useless and irrational character.

Dostoevski
(O'Toole, 1974)

This chapter seeks to review the work carried out in India, however scanty and limited, with a view to ushering in alternative forms of work organisation. Based on the review some reflections will be recorded as to the prospects and limitations of the new forms of work organisations.

The phrase, *new forms of work organisation*, may be clarified in the very beginning. The more traditional form and yet the most prevalent is the bureaucratic form of work organisation with which the names of Max Weber and Frederick W. Taylor are associated. Stated in broad terms, the sociologist in Weber provided the basic rationale for an efficient hierarchical, impersonal work organisation and the technician in Taylor highlighted the significance of the machine system and its work organisation as an answer to ensuring efficiency. Both of them, therefore, converged on the philosophy of efficiency on which premise a form of organisation had been conceived, which, with the ascent of industrial culture and proliferation of government machinery in manpower and activities, assumed almost a universal character known as the 'bureaucratic form' of organisation.

The reaction to this organisational milieu dramatically expressed by Dostoevski, has been poignantly depicted in Charles Chaplin's *Modern Times* and Sinclair Lewis' *Babbit*. The alternative to bureaucratic ethos took the form of human relations approach and, later on, human resources approach. Elton Mayo emphasised one aspect which was further strengthened by the work of Kurt Lewin. Group dynamics started taking roots as a way of organisation culture in which trust formation, team building, collaborative decision-making and group norm setting assumed new content and meaning. It sowed the seed of challenge to a hierarchical form of organisation.

The second major breakthrough came with the work of Trist and Bamforth (1951) and others at Tavistock Institute on the basis of their experience in the British coal industry. This work initiated a new approach, based on Lewin's work, known as the socio-technical systems approach conceptualised by Emery and Trist (Emery, 1959; Emery and Trist, 1960).

Essentially, the socio-technical approach is anchored to the open systems theory on the one hand and the ambience of technical system and socio-psychological dimensions on the other. The theory assumed significance on account of longitudinal action research in the coal industry as reflected in the works of Herbst (1962) and Trist, *et al* (1963).

What started in England took deeper roots, first in Norway and, then, in Sweden. It assumed a new name 'industrial democracy'. In different kinds of technology, successful action research work led to new forms of viable work organisation in both the countries (Emery and Thorsrud, 1975; Herbst, 1974; Jenkins, 1974; Klein, 1976A, etc.). The movement proceeded further to the continent and North America (Davis and Cherns, 1975; O'Toole, 1973).

The essential thrust of this worldwide movement, which has also found a place in the Pacific region—Australia and Japan for example—is that technology, sophisticated or otherwise, can be made appropriate for autonomous group working not simply to extract efficiency from employees and raise productivity but also to offer a viable and meaningful medium of activity for working men and women. It is just not job enlargement or enrichment nor is it a movement built on nostalgia for the bygone days of craftsmanship. The ideal is to convert technology into a purposeful tool in the hands of common men and women who are to handle it. 'Humanisation of work' is not an adequate expression of what it stands for but it does convey the spirit of what is being sought. Among the basic objectives of the movement, the significant ones are (*i*) to debureaucratise the work system and (*ii*) to harness what science and technology can offer to the best advantage of humanity through non-elitist participation in the processing of technology as instruments of production.

The origin of the socio-technical systems approach leading to industrial democracy and then to the quality of work-life movement resulting in serious search for alternative forms of human organisation was not confined to only action researchers in the early 1950s. J.D. Bernal, writing in mid-1950s urged fellow scientists to find a more democratic method of organising laboratories for work that would motivate people to give their very best. In 1960, Dennis Gabor wrote that the industrial system was moving towards the role when its task would be not so much to provide people with goods as with satisfying jobs (Low, 1976). The real challenge, it seems to the designers of new forms of human organisation, lies in what Theodore Roszak wrote in 1971, 'our nearly single-minded commitment to the objective mood of consciousness had led us not to the promised new Jerusalem but to the technocratic trap' (Low, 1976).

Early Indian Experience

It is not very widely known that while action-research in new forms of work organisation was in progress in the British coal industry, Rice (1958) initiated a similar experiment in a cotton textile manufacturing group in Ahmedabad in 1953. Socio-technical systems approach was introduced after a diagnostic study in a participative form in four loomsheds—two automatic and two non-automatic—in the Calico Mills and the Jubilee Mills. In one automatic loomshed, a block of 64 looms was organised with appropriate composition of work group while the boundary functions were taken over by the supervisory personnel. The results of the action research were documented by Rice in terms of productivity as well as worker involvement. In one non-automatic loomshed, the powerlooms were organised in a cluster of 40 looms and similar work groups were constituted which, the evaluation indicated, could perform the inter-dependent tasks forging inter-dependent work relationships. The evaluation further revealed that the 'whole' task approach to formation of work groups, which is a basic tenet of the socio-technical approach, resulted in substantially increased earnings for the workers. Although the cost of production was somewhat higher, this was more than compensated by higher output and, what is more significant, the damages were lower by 59 per cent.

There was a follow-up study of Rice's pioneering work by Miller (1975) which indicated that out of the four original work locations utilising the group system of work, only in one, a non-automatic loomshed, had the work organisation and levels of performance remained unchanged over a 16-year period. In the other loomsheds, the new forms of work system mostly disappeared. The evaluation indicated that, among other reasons, the setback was caused by the inability to maintain the boundary conditions in terms of readjustment to changing technology and changing tastes of customers for products. In fact, the inability to appreciate the demands of the turbulent environment resulted in some form of regression.

The findings are, therefore, a mixed bag. There is a success story as well as a failure story. One issue that inevitably arises out of such evaluation findings is the issue of cultural relevance and relativity. Foy and Gadon (1976) in comparing the approach to worker participation in decision-making in three countries—Sweden, Britain and the USA—refer to the tradition of industrial relations culture based on the larger social context. They indicate that the trend towards cooperation between employees and employers in the three countries can be explained in terms of differential elements of cultural tradition.

This issue has relevance for India as well. Van Groenou (1976), while discussing the sociology of work in India, mentions that the Indian workers do not experience any form of participation in the decision-making process, whether it is in the arena of politics, or work situation, or trade union activities. They also feel that decision-making is centralised in the hands of the managerial group and one reason adduced is that workers are disqualified through their lack of education. There is a suggestion that the Indian workers are more interested in job security, redressal of individual grievances at work, good pay and working conditions and not in substantive decision-making powers. Tandon, *et al* (1980) have documented the fact that the rank-and-file members of trade unions do not enjoy any worthwhile decision-making status.

The findings on Indian managerial values (Haire, *et al*, 1966; Smith, *et al*, 1972; England, 1975) indicate that Indian managers give high importance to security and esteem needs and low importance to self-actualisation need. They are sensitive about status and they believe in group-based participative decision-making but have little faith in the capacity of their subordinates for taking initiative and responsibility. They are convinced that managers have to compromise ethics and morals in order to accomplish a task and, on the whole, they are reluctant to share power. They put a premium on prestige, dignity, power, individuality, obedience, loyalty and organisational stability (as opposed to change).

It may also be relevant to mention here that, if one maintains the distinction made by Milton Singer between text and context of Indian religio-philosophical writings of ancient and mediaeval period, the concept of physical labour has received, by and large, low status in the nexus of the socio-economic reality of the caste system. According to *Vasisthasmriti, Gautam-Dharmsutra, Apastamba Dharmashastra* and *Yajnavalkyasmriti* (the probable dates of these texts are between 600 B.C. and A.D. 300), the unskilled worker (called the Shudra) was destined to suffer from social and other disabilities. He was forbidden to amass wealth by his toil, according to *Manusmriti*, and if he saved something from his earnings, such savings could be used for the support and benefit of the people of higher castes. His life was equated with that of a dog, a frog and a rat (Saran, 1957). This orientation towards manual labour sanctified, as it were, by the caste system with the weight of tradition for over 2,000 years, would certainly be a major force to contend with in creating polyarchical, cooperative and democratic forms of work organisation.

At the same time, one should take into account the secular tradition in the Hindu way of life. The co-existence of the *Lokayata* tradition (Chattopadhyaya, 1973, 1975, 1976) did militate against the contempt shown for the lower castes and manual labour. The concept of *Karma* as the determinant of status and privileges in this world leading to a rationale for the caste-ridden *status quo* was challenged by Carvaka. The subsequent materialist philosophers such as Payasi made a contribution, although indirectly, to the dignity of labour by the materialistic and this-worldly outlook of life. Similarly, the concept of Ganapati, the god of the common man (who has been decried by the traditional law-giver Manu), the concept of Gauri and Tantrik practices, all, more or less emanating from the tradition of tribal culture, did contribute to an orientation towards this-worldliness and the necessity of work-culture as a value. Even some of the contemporary actors on the Indian scene, Ram Mohan Roy, Vivekanand, Tagore and Gandhi, in a way rejected the absolute monism of Sankara; *Karmayoga*—action—was highlighted by them in spite of their orientation towards higher spiritual values.

Thus, there is a parallel tradition of acceptance of work not only as a reality but as something that is essential and desirable. The mediaeval mystics (Sen, 1961), both Hindus and Muslims, propounded the concept of universal man in terms of equality, irrespective of caste, creed and religion, and de-elitisation of religious rites and privileges. In the process, they also contributed to the thought that simply because of the low status work performed by a person he should not be looked upon as a lowly creature. Thus, the other-worldly and the oppressive character of the socio-economic caste structure of Indian society were buttressed by this-worldly egalitarian, work-oriented attitudes. That work is not a vice but a desirable virtue has been reflected in the Jain philosophy and its counterpart in South India, giving an impetus to trading communities.

There is, indeed, a need to mention this tradition of attitude to work in India because it also parallels the Western tradition (Yankelovich, 1974). The early Greeks regarded work as a curse which sentiment was also echoed by the Hebrews. With the Christian values, the concept of work started acquiring a less negative connotation; nonetheless, in the writings of St. Thomas Aquinas inherent value was not attributed to work itself. With the advent of Protestantism, Martin Luther and then Calvin, synchronising with the rise of mercantilism, the concept of work acquired a more positive value, even though closely linked with the profit motive. So, in Western thought, a negative attitude to work gradually got transformed into a positive orientation, although the parasitic culture retained its pockets of isolated existence, particularly among the rentiers. Similarly, it is postulated that traditionalism, a fatalistic orientation to life and other-worldliness of Hindu ideals co-existing with social and cultural inequalities need not necessarily be treated as of such great magnitude that quality of work-life movement cannot become a reality in India.

Revival Movement: 1973–74

Van Groenou (1976) lamented that the work of Rice was not replicated in India. It is true that Ken Rice's work in Ahmedabad did not have the diffusion effect in the Sarabhai group of companies where it started in the cotton textile mills nor did it evoke adequate interest in Indian industries. The social scientists too did not pick up the threads to initiate more pilot-project type experiments in diverse fields. The lessons of the Ahmedabad experiment lingered on in a dormant state, till a workshop was organised in 1973 in Calcutta by Nitish De and his colleagues where Fred and Merrelyn Emery were invited from Australia. The workshop was attended by senior managers and trade union leaders from some of the major public enterprises and one government department. Fred Emery, in addition, gave several seminars and held discussions with managers in Calcutta and Delhi. The response to the workshop was favourable and at least two organisations showed an interest in undertaking pilot projects on work redesign as a way of overcoming employee apathy to work.

In July 1974, the National Labour Institute was set up as an autonomous body in New Delhi where industrial democracy was taken up as a priority programme by the action-research-oriented professional staff. A series of workshops were planned from October 1974 and, in the course of two years, twenty-three seminars/workshops and programmes were organised in different parts of the country which were attended by over 1,150 government administrators, industrial managers and trade union leaders.

The thrust of these activities was to develop a dialogue on the current status of working life for blue and white collar workers, young managers and people at the higher echelons, in the context of the prevailing technology of work systems vis-à-vis employee motivation. Carefully selected cases were presented from similar situations. Initially, the top decision-makers from industries were invited. Their response was, understandably, mixed—guarded to open. Simultaneously, enterprise-based and industry-based trade union leaders were invited to these pro-grammes and the search conference method was utilised to develop, based on their experiences, viable alternative forms of work organisation for industrial as well as trade union organisations. The relevance of debureaucratising organisation culture was examined. Strategies for action were deliberated on. The early efforts in the latter part of 1974 led to specific invitations from some of the major industrial and government organisations to start action-research projects on industrial democracy in early 1975.

The projects that had started received a further impetus when six simultaneous workshops were held in April 1976, with the active partici-pation of eleven international experts drawn from Europe, Australia and Japan. These workshops were attended by, in some cases, exclusive interest groups like banking and insurance, and, in some cases, by mixed groups such as managers from different industries and their counterparts, the trade union leaders. On the whole, the seed that was sown in December 1973, started taking roots in early 1975 through the efforts, primarily of the National Labour Institute, in different types of work systems including government bureaucracies.

Simultaneously, efforts were initiated to develop a network in India involving resource persons from the academic world and industrial enter-prises so that these resource persons could initiate action in their own spheres of influence and also be made available to others. This initiative has yielded positive results as the cases presented in the next section will show.

Some Representative Cases

BHARAT HEAVY ELECTRICALS LIMITED, HARDWAR

This is one of the largest public enterprises in India with six major manufacturing plants and several divisions. The enterprise employs over 60,000 employees in the manufacturing, marketing, R&D, servicing and corporate headquarters units. It also has overseas markets. The corpora-tion has been making spectacular progress since 1972.

The Hardwar unit, located in the north, was mainly concerned with manufacture of heavy electrical equipment such as steam and hydro-turbines, generators and other related equipment. It employed over

10,000 employees and has a self-contained township. Although over 10 years old, the unit was not coming up as well as was expected and productivity was not, by any means, satisfactory. Technical collaboration exists with a large Soviet firm located in Leningrad though gradually the design and manufacturing activities have been taken over by the Indian counterparts as they gathered more and more experience and confidence.

The Executive Director of the unit, having attended a quality of work-life seminar, was keen that some action should be initiated in the plant. The National Labour Institute team consisting of Nitish R. De Subhash Gakkhar, V. Nilakant and Rukmini Rao started dialogues with the managers, the trade union leaders (four identifiable trade unions in operation) and the supervisory staff. The dialogues, held sometimes in camera and sometimes in the open, occasionally in separate groups and at times in joint sessions, gradually moved the groups towards a resolution that a pilot project would be started at a favourable work site.

It may also be mentioned that a comprehensive survey was undertaken in the unit to diagnose the training needs of the middle management level in the plant (Rao, 1976B) and another survey to explore the linkages between the perception of work-life and the life style in the community. The first study indicated that on ten key dimensions significant levels of differences existed in terms of knowledge and information gaps, a summary of which is reproduced in Table 1.1.

This study reveals that in some of the key areas the middle management personnel were lacking in knowledge and there were information gaps. This situation was certainly not conducive to effective performance of their supervisory functions. The other study to establish interlinkage between the quality of family and community life and the quality of life (Rao, 1975), indicates a clear dichotomy between the life of the workers at the workplace and their life around the family.

A section of Block V, newly created with 25 workmen working on fabrication of the upper part of condenser unit was considered to be a favourable site, compact in character, reasonable layout and the positive attitude of the manager and the shop floor trade union leaders. There were other compelling reasons to select the group. The condenser was an expensive piece of equipment. Secondly, for the setting-up of a power station, it was necessary that a condenser unit should be placed at the site before the steam turbine was installed and as such it should be manu-factured and despatched at least two months ahead of the completed steam turbine. Thirdly, the productivity in the shop was not of a high order.

The workers had a series of dialogues with internal and external consultants and they agreed to undertake the work redesign experiment.

Table 1.1
Information/Knowledge Gaps at Different Levels*

Sl. No.	Dimension	Section Leader	Chargeman	Assistant Foreman	Foreman: General Foreman	Non-diploma Holders in Engineering	Diploma Holders in Engineering
1	Company information	$p < 0.05$	—	—	—	$p < 0.05$	—
2	Basic product knowledge	$p < 0.05$	—	—	$p < 0.01$	$p < 0.01$	$p < 0.05$
3	Elementary engineering knowledge	$p < 0.01$	—	$p < 0.05$	$p < 0.01$	$p < 0.01$	—
4	Design and function of product knowledge	$p < 0.01$	—	—	$p < 0.01$	$p < 0.01$	$p < 0.01$
5	Detailed mechanical or electrical engineering knowledge	$p < 0.01$	—	—	—	$p < 0.05$	—
6	Planning process	Everyone did very poorly in this respect and all categories need training					
7	Knowledge of BHEL organisation structures	$p < 0.01$	—	—	—	$p < 0.05$	$p < 0.01$
8	Personnel practices in BHEL	$p < 0.01$	$p < 0.05$	—	—	$p < 0.05$	—
9	Expression in English	—	—	$p < 0.05$	—	—	$p < 0.01$
10	Understanding of communication	All categories need to be improved in this respect					

* Comparisons are with the next higher level.

First, a joint study of the work flow was undertaken which is presented in Fig. 1.1.

The involvement of some of the key workers in the study also provided them with excitement, if not insight, that they were involved in an action-research project. The workforce consisted of the categories shown in Fig. 1.2.

The study of the social system of work imposed by the work organisation indicated that each worker was concerned with his own trade and that none of them identified himself with the product itself. Secondly, there was invariably forced idle time because when a particular worker was working at a spot, another worker who was required to do his job in close proximity, had to wait till the first worker had finished his job. Thirdly, there was uneven demand on the services of the materials supplies group, crane operator and the riggers. Productivity, when the studies were being undertaken in April and May 1975, was certainly low.

Part of the low productivity was on account of the high rate of absenteeism during the summer months.

When all the data, so generated by the workers from their own experiences, were analysed, they decided on two steps:

1. To set up a task force with representatives of each category of workers and the supervisor. The manager, under whom the shop was placed, would also participate in the meeting if the group so wanted and an industrial engineer was also associated with the group as a resource person. The task group had a membership of 8. It was also decided that while two members would continue because of their leadership abilities, the others would rotate except for the supervisor.
2. To devise a new work system which would take care of the workers' motivation as well as overcoming the persisting culture of low productivity.

After deliberations, the task force, with the concurrence of the employees concerned, evolved the work system detailed in Fig. 1.3. According to this design, the direct production groups would each consist of 1 welder, 3 fitters and 1 fettler. Each group would take charge of its totality of the task and would gradually take up one another's skills by undergoing on-the-job training assisted by the supervisor, the industrial engineer and the fellow workers themselves. This would also be the case between the crane operator and the riggers. It was decided that the gas-cutters and helpers on the one hand and materials supplies group on the other would be integrated into the new work system at a later stage. As the system started working in May–June 1975, several positive and

Figure 1.1

Work Flow

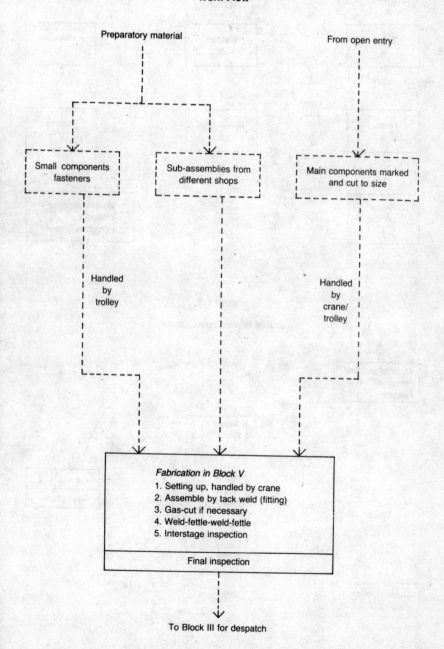

Figure 1.2

Worker Complement

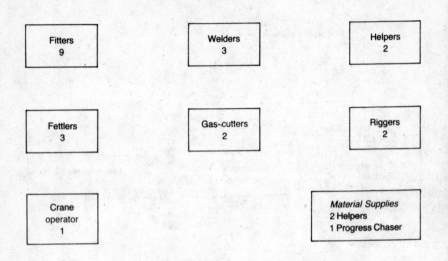

Figure 1.3

Initial Work Organisation

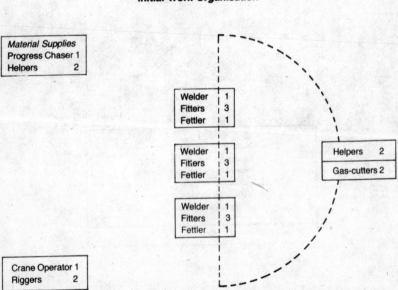

negative phenomena showed up. On the positive side, a welder now started working as a fitter and if he did not know the art of reading elementary drawings, which was a necessity for a fitter's job, arrangements were made by the management to provide for on-the-job training. The same procedure was followed in the case of fitters, fettlers, gas-cutters and others.

With more experience and confidence, the workers working along with the task force brought about a second redesign of their work organisation in the month of September, 1975. It was decided that the workforce would be distributed in two shifts in the following manner.

Shift 1		*Shift 2*	
Fitters	5	Fitters	4
Welders	5	Welders	6
Gas-cutter	1	Gas-cutter	1
Fettler	1	Fettler	1

In addition, there would be crane operators in both the shifts. Each shift group became an integrated group and it was decided that one shift would fabricate the right side of the upper part of the condenser unit and the other shift would do the same with the left side of the condenser unit. As and when several such parts were to be assembled, the two groups would together weld them in order to make a complete upper part of the condenser unit.

While the new system started in Block V in late May 1975, in Block II, the bay which was concerned with the manufacture of the lower part of the condenser unit started in June the same process. The senior supervisor of the shop took the initiative and 39 workmen with similar trade experiences, as mentioned above, were involved. They also designed a similar small work-group module. Here also the task force consisted of eight members with the provision of monthly rotation.

Data indicate that there have been steady increases in productivity although there have been occasional setbacks. Progressively, the old culture of one man—one function was replaced by the acquisition of multiple skills leading to the development of a group system of working with internal monitoring of group norms, internal control of work flow and work allocation, identification with the product and its quality and what, from the management point of view was considered significant, the gradual drop in personal idle time on account of loitering, spending time outside the work-place without any justifiable reasons, etc. The commitment of the workers and along with them that of the supervisor and the manager was distinctly visible. The old culture that higher status work like that of a welder or a fitter would stand in the way of taking up a low status job even for a part of the time could be overcome.

It is worth mentioning that the target of seven condensers for the year 1975–76 was completed by workers of Block V by January 1976, with the result that the management had to give them other items of work from, February 1976. The demand for the year 1976–77 for thermal power units having gone down, the need for condenser fabrication also was much less. Therefore, the workers in Block II and Block V had to take up other product items in the manufacture of which they did not have much experience. Both the groups responded to the challenge with optimism and alacrity. Table 1.2 indicates the product mix for these two groups which were traditionally fabricating condenser units.

Table 1.2 indicates that while in Block II, two major items were being produced during the year 1976–77 and, as such, the two groups working in two shifts had a steady flow of manufactured products, Block V also

Table 1.2
Product Mix

Month		Block	Items
February	1976	II	Lower part of condenser fabrication
		V	Four water boxes – rear and front
March	1976	II	Lower part of condenser fabrication
		V	Tooling items – dies, punches, fixtures, etc.
April	1976	II	Lower part of condenser fabrication
		V	Hydro generator stator frames
May	1976	II	Hydro generator stator frames
		V	Condenser stand for tool room
June	1976	II	Hydro generator stator frames
		V	Lower ring for HT – stainless steel welding
July	1976	II	Hydro generator stator frames
		V	Rotor spiders for HG
August	1976	II	Lower part of condenser fabrication
		V	Hydro generator stator frames
September	1976	II	Condenser fabrication and hydro generator stator frames
		V	Spherical valve body (stainless steel deposits), LPC – rear and front part
October	1976	II	Condenser fabrication and hydro generator stator frames
		V	Water boxes – rear and front, LPC upper part
November	1976	II	Condenser fabrication and hydro generator stator frames
to March	1977	V	Upper part of condenser fabrication (3 in number), 2 LPC – upper part front and rear, and any urgent work

Note: Block V Group also carried out, as and when necessary, fitting and assembly of Heater Section for the upper part of condenser unit.

working in two groups, distributed in two shifts, had taken diverse product lines varying from month to month. This switch-over somewhat adversely affected productivity and caused initial disruption in group working. However, the tension between the management and the workers that would normally arise in such a situation was absent. Both groups worked together on this challenge in November 1976 without conflict.

It appears that despite the new demands on the workers for involvement in new product lines, their urge to maintain multiple skills still continued. The minutes of meetings of the task force indicate a high degree of orientation towards work-interest issues such as delay in repair of crane, repair of welding sets, improving the system of on-the-job training, a joint search mechanism in identifying the forces contributing to lower productivity and a search for ways to reduce job tension as against the usual union-management type of meeting in which interest-related issues assume a divisive bargaining picture. In fact, examining the records of the agenda items and the minutes of meetings of the task forces of Block II and Block V since April 1975 till October 1976, one can discern the distinct qualitative shift towards problem-solving orientation with a view to looking at a problem as a collective one instead of making a scapegoat of the other group.

The work reorganisation experiences led to a new supervisory role in the form of liaison with the input and output departments, service units and involvement with central planning. This became possible because the work groups took substantial control over the production process including routine inspection and maintenance activities in addition to implementing the norms of discipline. All these experiences encouraged the management and the task forces to set up three project teams to deliberate on and submit reports on the three following themes:

1. Multi-skill training, its role in employee satisfaction and higher productivity. Encouraging workers to acquire skills in different trades;
2. Changing role of supervisors particularly in respect of coordination, planning and training;
3. Diffusion of the scheme of work redesign to such white collar areas as personnel, finance and medical departments.

The project teams consisting of managers and the workers from three blocks where the work redesign experiments were on—Blocks II, IV and V—submitted their reports to the management.

The diffusion process had been a matter of active consideration by the workers and the management, but the initiative in starting new projects in shops was left to the employees of the concerned shops. In September 1975 Block IV came forward and, through a series of meetings with the concerned workmen, twenty in number, it was decided to start the project in the Closed Panel Assembly Section. Eighteen workers were involved in the project and the key categories were fitters, electricians and machine operators. Here, too, a task force was set up with five persons including the supervisor and the group confronted the crucial need for in-service training, particularly of the fitters, to pick up the electrician's job. The group did a training need survey and, in the light of its findings, training programmes were introduced along with redesign of the work system. Through a process of dialogue, and trial and error, the group decided that the machine operator's job would be picked up by electricians. Similarly, machine operators themselves would do the fitter's work as well as the electrician's work; otherwise, a fitter and an electrician would become a two-man team to complete the assembly job on a closed panel. While it was comparatively easier for an electrician to do the job of a fitter, it was found that a fitter could not do an electrician's job without committing intolerable errors. In the initial period, this created some degree of tension particularly because it affected the group-bonus earnings adversely, but the workers in the task force gradually came to the conclusion that the only effective way to deal with this problem would be to give top priority to on-the-job training. Accordingly, a revised programme of training was initiated from October 1976. It is to be appreciated that the work in Block IV is considered somewhat more complicated than the fabricating work being carried out in Blocks II and V.

Two particular aspects were highlighted during the experiment in Block IV. Often, after the closed panel assembly work was almost completed, a design change was ordered requiring almost complete re-working. This was considered wasteful as time was being lost, but more than that, this caused a lot of frustration to the workers. When the group system started working, the discontent among the workmen caused by last-minute design-changes came to the forefront and the task force and the management jointly decided that closer liaison with the design group would be maintained to minimise, if not avoid, such an irritating practice. With concerted efforts, improvements started taking place. The management also decided that time spent on re-work on account of certain design changes would not affect the bonus earnings of the workers.

The task force became somewhat confident of the success of the experiment and then, in the month of September 1976 it decided that there would be almost a complete switch-over of jobs between fitters and electricians. This premature enthusiasm brought down the work efficiency to 37.5 per cent and it obviously affected the bonus earnings. The task force, on reflection, decided that the misplaced enthusiasm should be curbed and in October 1976, it decided to concentrate on training programmes which would gradually lead to skill diffusion among electricians and fitters.

From September 1976 the work redesign culture was being introduced in Block I (Turbo-rotor Coil Section and Detailed Assembly Section), Block IV (Panel Fabrication), Block III (Rotor Assembly Production and Blading Section) and in the Personnel Department where a matrix type of organisation had been introduced. In the Personnel Department there were three divisions—one dealing with the plant operation and maintenance, another with the design organisation and the third with the policy matters located in the office of the Executive Director. The Personnel Department attached to the plant consisting of twenty-two persons, organised itself into three operating groups: one dealing with all the problems of supervisory, clerical and ministerial staff, another group with the skilled category of workers and the third with the semi-skilled and unskilled group of workers. Functional division of work was replaced by a total service package but in order to ensure that the three groups functioning simultaneously did not come to contradictory conclusions and policy recommendations, a three-man coordinating team was set up. According to the reports of the office assistants, who belonged to the clerical category, this new system of work was much more satisfying than the fragmented type of work they were traditionally accustomed to (De, 1981A).

BHARAT HEAVY ELECTRICALS LIMITED, TIRUCHIRAPALLI PLANT

Yet another case is that of the heavy boiler plant at Tiruchirapalli which, unlike the Hardwar plant, operated from the beginning with a high degree of efficiency and profitability. The unit was well-known for the quality product, organisational vitality, high degree of innovativeness from top management downwards and sound industrial relations climate. It was singularly lucky in having two highly competent general managers (later on redesignated as executive director), one of whom happened to become the Chairman of the Corporation.

Some shop-floor managers, being encouraged by a seminar given in the unit by Nitish R. De in 1973 on debureaucratisation of the work system, initiated action in two major shops: the drum shop and the header shop. In the drum shop, although productivity was high, it was found that the cycle time of production, could, at times, deviate from the norm to the extent of two months whereas ideally it should not be more than nine months *plus or minus* two weeks. It was felt that steps had to be initiated to overcome the flaw. The steps were identified as involvement of the workers in the planning function, decentralisation of decision-making levels and improvement in the product knowledge at all levels. Accordingly, a plan was prepared in consultation with the workers of the shop, some of the highlights of which are given below:

(a) a comprehensive welding plan for each month, to be prepared in consultation with the supervisors and prominently displayed in the shop, making it available to each work team;

(b) the central lathe machine, the only facility available in the shop, was working only 40/45 standard hours per week. This was considered a bottleneck. In consultation with the work group a number of steps were taken. The shift arrangement was made flexible enough for the workers of the three shifts to decide on the composition of personnel in each shift including provision for switch-over, should occasions demand it. Formerly, workers holding different designations wedded to different trades were concerned with different aspects of the operation of the lathe machine. In the new scheme, such segmented work structure was given up and the whole team started working together considerably reducing the loading and unloading time. Operating time and the lost time for maintenance work was brought down by 10 per cent. The workers also designed some new jigs and fixtures to facilitate the working of the central lathe machine. In addition, a lathe load chart planned for the entire month with a break-down into the weekly schedule was prominently displayed for every worker to see. The shift-wise records of daily performance vis-à-vis the weekly target was also exhibited.

(c) Similarly, in the electrode welding section, the group was faced with the challenge of reducing the rejection rate on account of faulty welding. The group as a whole started diagnosing the problem and improving the method of working. The target set was a qualitative one, namely, that zero level of rejection should be reached. Between November 1975 and May 1976 the group achieved zero level of rejection. The high pressure welding group with fourteen members in each shift was so highly specialised that it could not be integrated with the newly set-up work teams. The members organised themselves into a specialised group and became autonomous in terms of daily allotment of task among members, coordination of activities between the shifts and provision of individual flexibility so that, depending on the pressure of work, some more welders could turn up in one shift compared to another.

(d) In the header shop, the system was introduced in August 1973, more or less at the same time as in the drum shop.

(e) There were five small groups in each of the two shops and one member from each would meet every Saturday morning for a review and planning meeting with the supervisor. The agenda items covered the review of the weekly performance including analysis of shortfall or over-performance, quality improvement programmes, cost reduction and scheduling activity for the next week, the review of safety records and the internal norms of working of the group. The chairman of the review group used to rotate between the supervisor and workmen.

At this stage, one can give the break-up of the manpower details which is detailed in Table 1.3.

It appears from Table 1.3 that productivity, after the new form of work organisation was introduced, had gone up. But more than that, the morale of the workers showed up in many innovative ideas that came from them including the pole-end plate welding technique; high degree of

Table 1.3
Manpower Complement

Manpower Details	Header Shop	Drum Shop
Workmen		
Direct labour	122	152
Indirect labour (semi-skilled and unskilled)	18	22
Total	140	174
Supervisory staff		
Chargehand/Chargeman	6	8
Assistant Foreman	2	—
Foreman	—	1
Total	8	9
Executives		
Production Engineer	1	2
Senior Production Engineer	1	Common with header shop
Total	2	2
All Totals	150	185
Output in terms of standard man-hours man/month		
Before experiment (yearly average)	52	57
After experiment (yearly average)	67	69

(In both the shops a peak of 75 standard hours/man/month was achieved during the experimental period.)

internal control around certain norms evolved in the group released the supervisors for boundary maintenance functions. As already mentioned, the productivity in the shops had always been high but in 1975–76 the group could complete 109 per cent of the production target which, during the year, had been increased by 10 per cent over the original plan target. The performance in the header shop was equally impressive.

In the same plant, encouraged by the result of the two production shops, the work redesign process was introduced in the production engineering department, computer systems section, in August 1974 (Fig. 1.4).

Functions and Results

Prior to August 1974	As at Present
SA was functioning at module level: hence integration at application level was not complete.	All SAs are involved in designing the systems at the application level—integration is complete.
One module was operated by independent programmes.	Entire application is executed by one programme, linking all the relevant modules.
System development was limited to individual SA's limitations.	System development emerges out of group discussions, resulting in efficient system and overall reduction in computer time. (25 hours recurring saving/month achieved—vide data given below.)
Job rescheduling was done independently causing at times under-utilisation.	Participative planning has resulted in effective utilisation of computer time.
	Resulted in good team spirit.
	SA is able to handle more than one application, when required.

Computer Time Utilisation

Application	Time in Hours
Machine shop	30
Comp. code system	55
Valve shop	15
Maintenance of files	35
Reporting system	20
Development (achieved through job redesign)	25
Total	180

Figure 1.4

*Job Redesign in the Production Engineering
Department: Computer Systems Section*

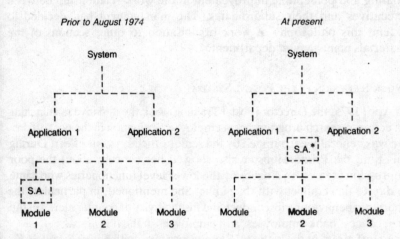

Prior to August 1974

At present

(Note the elevated level of the S.A. in the present position)
*S.A. = System Analyst. Total strength = 8.

An evaluation of the system in May 1976 showed a higher degree of job satisfaction at different levels of employees, better service to the customers and quicker completion of projects allowing more computer time for developmental work.

Similarly, new forms of work organisation were introduced in the sub-delivery section of the purchase department in 1974. This section was responsible for procurement of materials to the tune of Rs. 200 million. Most of the sub-delivery items used to take long lead times for procurement as the specificity of requirements used to create a lot of back and forth correspondence. Nearly 40 to 50 per cent of these items were also imported. A diagnostic study, not unexpectedly, revealed that the executives in this section were continuously under heavy pressure of work, running behind time and suffering from a high level of anxiety. There was a felt need to reduce the strain and lessen the delays. The indigenisation programme created further demands on the group.

The section executive appointed a task force to design an alternative work system. From a bureaucratic assembly-line-type of activity with papers and files moving through a series of processing stations, a desk-oriented system was introduced utilising the job enrichment concept so that a person could integrate different activities in his role.

A review reveals that the control system was decentralised thus reducing the pressure on the supervisors, creating more elbow room for executives dealing with an integrated range of purchase activities. A higher degree of job satisfaction was manifested in lesser tension, bickering and scape-goating and perceptible improvement in the work-relationship between executives and their subordinates. The management had decided to extend this philosophy of work organisation to other sections of the materials management department.

WORK REDESIGN IN THE POSTAL SYSTEM

In April 1975, the Director (Postal Training) took the initiative in launching an action-research programme on employee motivation in the post offices. He was generally encouraged by the senior officials in this effort. During this time the Prime Minister also showed her concern about the poor impression created on citizens by the lower level functionaries who came in day-to-day contact with the public. She mentioned, in particular, the apathetic behaviour, misconduct and insensitivity of counter clerks in the post offices, bank employees, and employees in the hospitals.

A staff group of the National Labour Institute, with Nitish R. De, B.K. Srivastava, Subhash Gakkar and V. Nilakant, had a series of discussions with senior officials in the Postal Directorate and then in more concrete detail with the Postmaster General at Ambala and the Senior Super-intendent of Post Offices at Simla. A series of on-the-spot studies were conducted after which it was decided that Chaura Maidan Post Office at Simla would be an appropriate place to conduct an experiment.

The post office work had been traditionally organised on the bureau-cratic model: one man-one job with hierarchical supervisory chains checking the systems' operation at the end of the day's work and preparing fortnightly minutely detailed records of all transactions to be despatched to the head office. Each public counter was designed on a one job-one counter basis with the result that the same customer depending on the nature of his needs would have to go to different counters, one after another, and, in the process, stand in queues and take his turn for the job to be done. These inordinate delays were a major cause of public irritation with the postal system.

The technical system of work including work-flows and the social system of work interaction were studied along with the employees. The post office had forty-three employees in addition to one part-time employee. There were association (union) leaders located in this post office, two being in the postman category and one a telegraph signaller.

The diagnostic study revealed the following:

(*a*) The work space in the post office was inadequate with a high degree of congestion;

(*b*) Furniture was antiquated and dysfunctional but over-abundant, contributing to the congestion;

(*c*) There was no physical facility at the counters for customers to fill in forms and no seating for old and infirm visitors;

(*d*) Lighting was inadequate and also improperly placed.

The layout, as it was in existence in April 1975, is given in Fig. 1.5.

To give one example, there were fourteen postmen in the post office, while for the purpose of sorting mail there was enough space for six persons only.

A study was also undertaken to find out job satisfaction levels of the employees, particularly of the postmen and clerks. The information, obtained anonymously, showed that in their perception the postal authorities' genuine interest in their welfare and happiness was of only average strength, their receptivity to the needs of the employees was low and there was little consultation before decisions were taken. A majority felt that they had to do this work because there was no alternative and it was just a case of working to earn a living. There was no real happiness with work content or the work climate.

The internal and external consultants decided to initiate a two-level participation mechanism in evolving a new form of work organisation:

(*a*) Participative dialogue between the external consultants and the management, including the sub-postmaster who headed the organisation;

(*b*) Participative dialogue between the management and all the employees of the post office.

The diagnostic phase of the study revealed that the primary tasks of the post office were:

(*i*) Mail delivery activities—collection and delivery of mail, including valued articles, such as money orders, registered mail, insured articles, etc.

(*ii*) Counter service activities which included savings bank functions, booking of money orders, registration of letters, parcels, etc., selling of postage stamps, registration of broadcasting receiver licences, selling of postal orders, etc.;

(*iii*) Receipt and despatch of telegrams, settlement of telephone bills and attending to public call office;

(*iv*) Control functions including Treasury and correspondence activities.

Figure 1.5

Layout of the Chaura Maidan Post Office Simla in April 1975 (Ground Floor: Not to Scale)

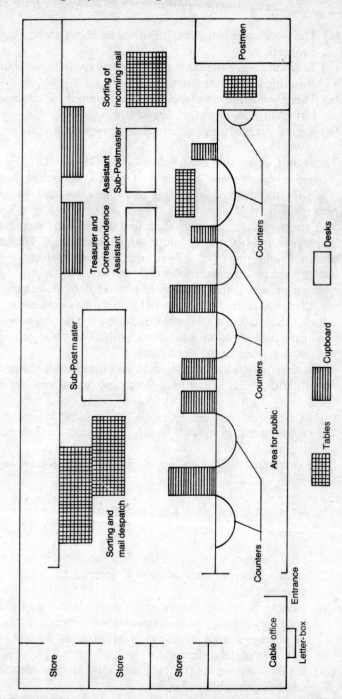

It was felt that before any new form of work organisation was created, the problem of space had to be handled. Accordingly, the management made available the first floor of the building to the post office by converting the residential accommodation occupied by a postal employee into office space. The space thus made available was allotted to the Telegraph/ Public Call office groups, and the entire delivery section, which consisted of 3 delivery clerks, 1 head postman and 14 postmen. Old furniture was replaced by more functional furniture in the first and the ground floors. The revised layout of the two floors are given in Figures 1.6 and 1.7.

Having created these congenial work conditions, the management started a dialogue with the employees and it was decided in a joint meeting that the delivery group would start working as a group instead of on one man-one job basis. The group also decided to have a group leader to be rotated every two weeks, so that every postman could get a chance to be a leader, mainly as a liaison between the group and the sub-postmaster.

Initially there was a leadership struggle within the group which was further complicated by a series of confrontations with the sub-postmaster. The Senior Superintendent of Post Offices decided not to intervene in these disputes, because this might foster dependence on him. Instead, he advised the delivery group to settle all disputed issues in their own forum. The group consisted of 17 members including the assistant sub-postmaster. While most of the issues were dealt with by the group itself, any boundary issue had to be taken up with the sub-postmaster.

Gradually, the group learnt to tackle their conflict situations and by the beginning of 1976, the group started functioning satisfactorily.

Comparative statistics are given in Table 1.4 to indicate some elements of productivity of the group.

The figures in Table 1.4 show a significant improvement in productivity as, before the change, Chaura Maidan had never seemed to post office officials to be in any way unusual. As a matter of fact, because of the rise in productivity, the management had withdrawn one clerk, one signaller and two postmen from this post office and deployed them elsewhere thereby reducing the number of employees from 43 to 39. Nonetheless, productivity was maintained at a high level.

The working of the delivery group indicated more mutual help to achieve the P.O. objective. In the past the *mail collectors* used to bring mail from post boxes located at different beats within the jurisdiction of the post office, stamp letters and articles to deface the postage stamps and seal bags for the railway mail service; *postmen*, including the head postmen, sorted and then distributed the mail along their beats; the *delivery clerks* recorded registered mail and other accountable items. Now the group

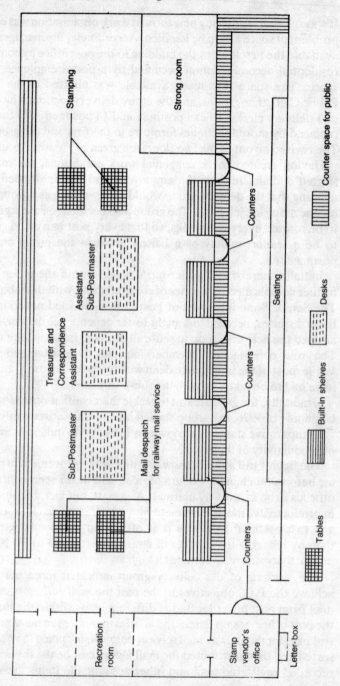

Figure 1.6

*Layout of the Chaura Maidan Post Office Simla
after Work Redesigning (Ground Floor: Not to Scale)*

Figure 1.7

Layout of the Chaura Maidan Post Office Simla after Work Redesigning (First Floor: Not to Scale)

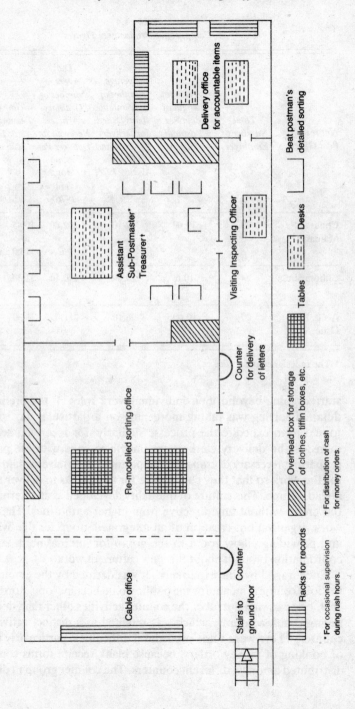

Table 1.4
Comparative Productivity Figures

Name of Post Office	Total Number of Employees	Average Length of Beat Per Postman (Kms)	Average Number of Accountable Items Issued for Delivery Per Postman (6 Months' Average 1976)	Daily Average Number of Ordinary Articles Received for Delivery Per Postman (6 Months' Average 1976)	Time of Postman Leaving for the Beat for Delivery of Mail and Articles		
Chaura Maidan*	39	19.00	42.10	392.80	10.45 to 11.00 a.m.	1.30 p.m.	4.00 p.m.
Chhota Simla	24	10.6	25.00	170.40	11.30 a.m.	2.00 p.m.	4.30 p.m.
A.G., Post Office	29	10.00	26.10	211.00	11.30 a.m.	2.00 p.m.	4.30 p.m.

* The redesigned post office

started going beyond their individual work roles. If the preliminary or detailed sorting was taking more time on a particular day, other staff joined in to expedite the process. Similarly, for recording accountable items, if the delivery clerks were unable to cope with the pressure of preparing necessary documents, the postmen themselves would volunteer for the work so that they could leave for their beats to deliver the letters ahead of time. This culture of mutuality developed as an internal norm in the group without any directive from higher authorities. The layout of work organisation, creation of an integrated group for the 'whole' task and providing elbow room to the group for internal norm setting and coordination brought about this new culture of work.

Encouraged by this experience, it was decided by the employees that the four counters meant for the public would become 'one-stop' counters, each one carrying out all of the counter activities other than dealing with savings bank accounts, which was retained as a distinct activity at one counter. There were some procedural difficulties, particularly in respect of booking of money orders, because blank receipt forms could not be distributed amongst different counters. The counter group in discussions with the Senior Superintendent of Post Offices came up with a solution: by taking the aggregate of money orders booked in the previous year, it was possible to work out average daily money order bookings for this post office. Accordingly, pre-determined number of blank receipt forms could be distributed amongst the four counters and on any day with an unusually heavy rush, the sub-postmaster could authorise additional blanks.

It was decided that the two telegraphists would help with sorting, postmarking or at the counters whenever they were free from their telegraph and related activities. The group also decided that every employee would be able to take the half-an-hour lunch break, as was provided for in the rules but observed more in the breach than otherwise, by closing one counter at a time on the basis of staggered lunch breaks. This would provide the legitimate lunch break to each employee on the one hand, and, on the other, because of the multi-service counters, would not disturb customer service.

Encouraged by the results of this group system of working in an otherwise highly traditional, hierarchical government organisation like a post office, it was decided by the higher authorities to introduce it with the support of the employees in the two other post offices in Simla, namely, Chhota Simla and the Accountant General Post Offices. The authorities also felt convinced that gradually the system could be introduced in the remaining 200 post offices in the state of Himachal Pradesh.

Earlier it was mentioned that there were three union leaders in this post office, about whose role in the experiment some apprehension was expressed. There was initially leadership conflict and some confrontation between the sub-postmaster and these leaders, but gradually the group as a norm-setting and norm-enforcing agency won the union leaders' support in work activities. They were perceived as helpful and constructive, a change that could not have been anticipated in the traditional climate.

STATE BANK OF INDIA

This bank, with over 3,000 branch offices spread all over the country and more than 90,000 employees, was the largest nationalised bank. In response to the rapidly evolving banking policy of the government it was spreading its activities into new and poorer areas and departing from many of the traditional banking concepts. To cope with these environmental demands, the bank in 1969 undertook a major structural reorganisation, but gradually, it became evident that all these structural changes were not enough, certainly not enough to strengthen employee motivation.

It thus became a matter of much concern as to what was to be done to motivate such a large number of white collar employees. There were two sets of contradictory forces that had to be contended with. The culture of the bank reflected in time consuming systems, procedures and detailed supervision was attuned to *security of funds*. On the other hand, there were pressures from the customers for more effective service in terms of promptness as well as accuracy. With the calibre of new recruits in clerical and executive levels continuously improving, with better educational standards and higher aspiration levels in terms of work assignment and career prospects, the traditional work system was becoming more and more incongruous. It was, therefore, felt that a new form of work organisation to deal with both technical problems of banking work and the socio-psychological requirements of the employees, would be a better approach rather than bringing about only structural changes in the system.

To try out this approach, the Mehrauli Road Branch in Gurgaon district near Delhi was selected. The branch was located in an area where agricultural business as well as trading activities were important. It was a medium-sized branch with 71 employees. After a series of discussions with the high authorities in Delhi, officers of the local branch, the union leaders and the clerical employees, a sample survey was undertaken to ascertain as to how the employees evaluated their own jobs on six criteria evolved by Emery and Emery (1974). The data are given in Table 1.5.

The data reveal that, as one goes down the hierarchical level, employees' interest in the work was coming down on most of the socio-psychological job needs and yet another finding was that the clerical employees made a distinction among the clerical desks. Under the one man-one desk formula, as was the traditional work design, some desks were considered as symbolising low status and some others like foreign exchange advances, balancing of accounts and clean cash were considered as more prestigious—jobs which were not plentiful in the branch. Once the data were presented to the employees in January 1976, the employees decided that they would like to experiment with a new form of work organisation in the personal banking branch of activity. A workshop was held in April 1976 with the concerned employees and the officers. This two-day workshop brought about a new concept of deposit call (personal banking), which is briefly presented below:

Task

To plan and organise work relating to personal banking components in such a way as to ensure:

(a) staff involvement;

(b) job satisfaction; and

(c) good customer service.

Table 1.5
Satisfaction with Work

Employee Category Socio-Psychological Needs	Accountant	Passing Officer Grade II	Head Cashier	Counter Clerk	Jotting Book Clerk	Teller	Cashier	Messenger
Learning	10	8	3	5	4	4	2	3
Variety	10	6	3	2	2	3	3	1
Decision-making	8	2	5	0	0	1	0	0
Support and respect	9	7	7	5	5	1	4	3
Meaningful job	10	6	8	1	1	6	5	9
Desirable future	10	7	6	5	5	4	4	2

Note: A low score indicates a low level of satisfaction of a particular need. High score indicates higher level of satisfaction of the particular need.

Service to be Performed
(*a*) savings bank;
(*b*) current accounts;
(*c*) fixed-deposit receipts;
(*d*) recurring deposits; and
(*e*) janta deposits (poor man's accounts).

Activities Involved

(*a*) opening of accounts;
(*b*) operation of accounts;
(*c*) statement writing, completion of pass books;
(*d*) correspondence relating to these accounts;
(*e*) standing instructions;
(*f*) subsidiary day books;
(*g*) balancing of ledger-control; and
(*h*) planning and budgeting (draft form).

Persons to be Involved

(*a*) 3 cashier-cum-clerks;
(*b*) 1 teller;
(*c*) 2 messengers;
(*d*) 3 clerks;
(*e*) 1 officer Grade I; and
(*f*) 1 officer Grade II.

Decision-making

The internal management of the group will be handled by a task force consisting of 1 officer, 2 clerks/clerk-cum-cashiers/tellers and 1 messenger. The task force will handle the following functions:

(*a*) leave (including short leave);
(*b*) allotment of tasks and job rotation within the cell;
(*c*) enforcement of discipline;
(*d*) recommendation to Branch Manager/Accountant in regard to facilities to customers on exchange rates, overdraft, etc.;
(*e*) allotment of day books within the constraints of bank's existing instructions;
(*f*) training of the members of the group;
(*g*) recommend names of persons to be included in the group during leave arrangements;
(*i*) seating in the cell;
(*j*) arrangements for stationery;
(*k*) to keep a record of circulars in the cell;

(*l*) display of publicity material;
(*m*) arrangements of drinking water for customers.

Changes Suggested in Systems, Procedures, Instructions and Practices

(*a*) countersigning of cash vouchers relating to this cell be done by one officer in the cell rather than the head cashier;
(*b*) jotting book entries related to the cell business be written within the cell;
(*c*) security documents be kept in custody of officer Grade II if officer Grade I not posted in the cell;
(*d*) officer Grade II be allowed to exercise powers if officer Grade I not posted in the cell;
(*e*) officer Grade I/officer Grade II to sanction leave;
(*f*) officer Grade I/officer Grade II to hold security charge and sign FDRs.

Possible Criteria of Evaluation

(*a*) number of complaints;
(*b*) extent to which job rotation provided;
(*c*) achievements of budgets;
(*d*) time taken in servicing customers.
(Khandelwal and Nilakant, 1976.)

The major change in the work flow was brought about by the group with two innovations—countersigning of cash vouchers pertaining to this cell by an officer located in the cell instead of the branch accountant who had other activities to perform, and writing of jotting book and transfer scroll was brought within the ambit of the cell.

After a good deal of deliberations within the group, between the group and other employees of the branch and between the branch and the local head office, the scheme was introduced substantially in May 1976. The deposit cell was then manned by two officers Grade II, seven clerks/clerk-cum-cashiers/tellers and one messenger—ten in all. An evaluation of the working of the new form of working which also brought about changes in the layout, seating, in addition to internal work reorganisation, indicates the following:

Work Control

The budgeted levels of deposits in the personal banking segment and performance in achievement thereof at the time of the formation of the cell and at the end of September 1976 showed significant improvements.

Job Variety

Every member of the cell (except the messenger, cashier and teller) had an opportunity to change his desk, which provided elements of variety in day-to-day working, with tangible satisfaction amongst the clerical employees. Efforts were made to integrate the three members left out which did not succeed.

Learning Opportunities

Job rotation had helped learning to the extent that each member of the cell could be better prepared about the procedural aspects of different kinds of work handled in the cell and group working further intensified the need for learning one another's work. In October 1976, the cell took an initiative to form a study circle with the following objectives:

(a) cultivation of knowledge and development of self-confidence in each member through holding of discussion meetings on various aspects of banking operations. Attempts were made to build up study materials, cases and other relevant literature which the members could discuss and deliberate on.

(b) another learning opportunity that had been utilised by the cell was to get involved directly in preparing a draft budget for the next year and in the process acquiring skills in the presentation of budgetary proposals.

Participation in Decision-making

An examination of the meetings of the deposit cell revealed that the members had taken decisions/made recommendations of a concrete nature in respect of the following:

(a) job rotation within the cell;
(b) allotment of day-to-day duties;
(c) taking care of unplanned absenteeism;
(d) recommendations for sanction of leave on a planned basis so as to minimise the disruption of work;
(e) maintenance of discipline within the cell and initiative in counselling activities for erring members whenever such a situation arose;
(f) interest in the upkeep of the premises and keeping the furniture clean and tidy;
(g) periodical review of progress of the new work system;
(h) concrete suggestions for improvement in customer service;
(i) deposit mobilisation.

With the streamlining of layout, simplification of procedures and involvement of staff members, there had been a marked improvement in the customer service for the constituents of the personal banking segment. Time taken for payment of cheques through the ledger-keeper had been cut by half. The teller payments were made immediately. Time taken for opening new accounts was cut by two-thirds. Complaints from the customers had gone down considerably. Fixed deposit receipts were being prepared and handed over to the customer within 15 minutes, a considerable improvement on the past practice.

The group was also more conscious of its problems and was operating on more realistic data. It was still unable to resolve the problem of integration of the cashier into the system. The role of the supervisory officers, as traditionally defined, appeared to be somewhat anachronistic in the context of the new form of work organisation but it was a matter which neither the group nor the branch could resolve: it fell within the competence of the policy-making authorities in the central office of the bank.

It is worth noting that on the basis of the evaluation report presented by the deposit cell to the employees of the entire branch, it was decided in November 1976 to extend the new form of work organisation to other activities of the branch and, to begin with, in the government business segment of activity.

LIFE INSURANCE CORPORATION OF INDIA

The Life Insurance Corporation, a nationalised company, has organised its business in 41 divisional offices all over the country in addition to operations abroad. There are around 50,000 employees in the corporation.

While, over a period, after the private companies were nationalised, uniform terms and conditions of service were gradually introduced; the employees have been receiving generous treatment by way of salaries and other benefits. Employment in the Life Insurance Corporation (abbreviated as LIC) was considered as among the best in the country. However, the expense ratio has been exceeding the limits set by the government and with the socially-oriented investment policy, the margin of surplus was also getting squeezed. At the same time, employee apathy and a relative lack of commitment to work was indicated by customer complaints, deterioration in servicing the policy-holders, sluggish expansion of business in terms of new policies at the end of the first year's premia paid.

The top management of the corporation was growing concerned about the situation, further aggravated by acrimonious industrial relations and legal suits. One particular area of concern was the Salary Savings Scheme (SSS) under which employees in any organisation including the government could authorise deduction from their pay of regular monthly premiums which the employer could send to the LIC as a part of the contract between the policy-holders and LIC. This scheme, therefore, has three parties: (1) the LIC, (2) the employer, and (3) the policy-holder. The direct contact is between the LIC and the employer, even though the ultimate beneficiary is to be the policy-holder.

A study of the operation of the scheme indicated that, by and large, it was not operating satisfactorily, in that the unadjusted premia under SSS were getting accumulated year after year. In the New Delhi Divisional Office, the unadjusted accumulation known as 'deposits' stood at Rs. 58,87,000 in March 1975. There were complaints from policy-holders and employers and protracted correspondence within the different wings of the LIC, between the LIC and the employers and between the LIC and the policy-holders. It was felt that an exploratory discussion could be held in the New Delhi SSS with two objectives in view:

(a) how to reduce the deposit accumulation gradually, thereby, on the one hand, reducing policy-holders' complaints and, on the other, creating a more positive image about the LIC insofar as the SSS is concerned;

(b) consistent with the customer service objective, how to create an internal work system including creating conditions for positive motivation for the clerical employees without whose active cooperation it is not possible to improve upon the operation of the scheme.

The initial discussions held in December 1975 with the management of the divisional office and the concerned employees of the SSS led to the agreement that there would be a collective effort to study the working of the SSS with a view to reorganising the work to achieve these objectives. The joint study undertaken by Nitish R. De and V. Nilakant from the National Labour Institute along with the Assistant Divisional Manager and other employees revealed the following work flow in the SSS department as shown in Figures 1.8 and 1.9.

After this task was over, a task force consisting of 13 members representing employees of the SSS—clerical to officers, was set up. This task force went into the problems that caused deposit accumulation, resulting in customer complaints and consequent harassment to the employees. The diagnosis identified these problems:

(a) Transfer on and transfer off. The record of policy was maintained in pay-authority-wise (P.A.) group ledgers. It had been the experience that whenever there is any transfer of an employee from one office (one P.A.) to another (another P.A.), P.A.s did not generally give

Figure 1.8

Work Flow in the Salary Savings Scheme Department

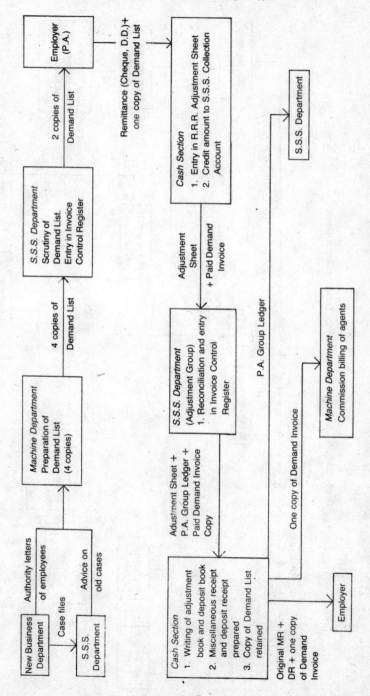

Figure 1.9

Organisation Chart for Salary Saving Scheme Department

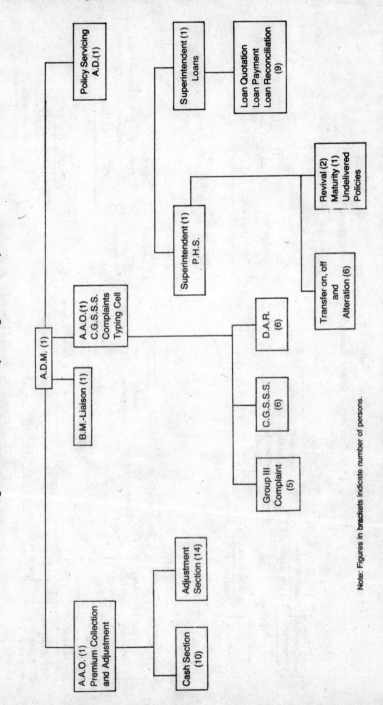

Note: Figures in brackets indicate number of persons.

requisite information in the demand invoice about the latest location of the transferred employee. The same was the case when an employee retired from service, or resigned, or got dismissed. Because the amount demand on the demand invoice did not tally with the amount received every month from the P.A., the amount went into suspense known as deposit accumulation;

(b) Some P.A.s did not return the duplicate copy of the demand invoice but sent their own statement according to their own convenience which caused the problem of reconciliation in the SSS. Sometimes these improvised statements did not contain essential information, the absence of which caused adjustment difficulty;

(c) Some P.A.s did not send prescribed reconciliation statements with the remittance;

(d) In some cases the amount remitted was different from the amount invoiced;

(e) Payment received from P.A.s located outside the jurisdictional limits of the divisional office also created problems, particularly when the records of the policy-holder were not available in the office.

(f) Non-deduction of premium for a few months and then resumption of recovery when the policy had already lapsed is another cause of deposit accumulation;

(g) As opposed to one-unit organisation, the problem becomes serious and complex in multiple-unit organisations where transfer on and off was rather frequent.

The task force working on the diagnostic data, a summary of which has been presented above, started identifying the action parameters. Some of the broad action steps accepted were the following:

(i) Certain improvements were considered necessary within the LIC including better coordination between SSS, the machine section, the cash section and other relevant sections;

(ii) Improvement of certain internal procedures including redesign of certain forms, such as, demand invoices and other returns which had been continuing as a legacy of the past, and found non-functional in the current context;

(iii) Need for a closer coordination with the employers which so far had been only in the shape of impersonal correspondence. In this respect, the group could also identify the employers from whom more problems and complaints were emanating;

(iv) There was hardly any direct contact with the policy-holders who were ultimately the beneficiaries of the scheme and were to be served by the LIC if the corporation was to get more business under SSS.

Having identified the broad parameters, certain actions were initiated by the task force in close collaboration with the employees of the section as well as the management. These are:

1. The existing demand invoice consisting of 11 columns was revised by extending the length of the form from 12.6 inches to 15 inches and certain specific columns were incorporated to obtain such missing information as transfer on and transfer off. It was felt that particular care should be taken to receive the missing information which were the primary sources of deposit accumulation. The machine section did cooperate and a new form was devised;

2. With the revised demand invoice, a simplified reconciliation statement was prepared which was to accompany the demand invoice each month. These would help in clarifying the reasons for the inconsistency between the amount invoiced and the amount received;

3. The group also devised a suitable letter that would accompany the demand invoice every month highlighting the importance of the changes brought about in the demand invoice and the introduction of a new type of reconciliation statement so that the employer was reminded of the new system introduced to serve the policy-holders more effectively. The group also prepared a letter giving the basic instructions to the SSS policy-holders so that they could themselves know about the basic rules and regulations that would govern their policies. The objective was to fill up the communication gap that was existing among the policy-holders;

4. Another letter was devised which would be sent to each policy-holder if premia for 4 successive months were not received from him through his employer. This would act as a reminder to him so that he could pursue the matter.

The management started implementing these decisions with favourable response from the employers. By the end of October 1976, with the introduction of the new system, four hundred letters were received from the employers/policy holders in response to letters sent to them with the result that the SSS group could start attending to the problems raised by the policy-holders. In this divisional office, there were, as on 1 April 1976, 1,10,000 policy-holders. With the introduction of the new system, deposit accumulation was coming down at the rate of Rs. 50,000 per month which gave a lot of satisfaction to the clerical and supervisory employees as an immediate feedback to the new system that they had devised.

Thereafter, the group paid attention to their internal work structure.

A large number of task force meetings held between June and September 1976, with the process interventions of the external consultants, came to the following conclusion:

1. In addition to each P.A., having a code number, the primary reasons for each deposit accumulation would also be put in codes so that it would be easier to take action once the causes were known through the code number;

2. The group decided that instead of an integration of the total task system of SSS, initially, six integrated work groups would be created, each with 4 to 5 persons, to handle a specific number of P.A.s with roughly about 20,000 policies. This integrated team would handle the correspondence work, transfer on and transfer off work and maturity work. All matters relating to the concerned P.A. or a policy-holder under that P.A. would be dealt with by this group. Within the group, the members would develop their own work norms including a rotational system of work;

3. It was felt that issues of revival, alteration and some other activities could also be incorporated in the group's activity; however, the group felt that in the first stage it would begin with a limited number of inter-connected tasks as mentioned above. Each group would be sitting in an identifiable place with necessary readjustment of furniture and layout with easy access to the essential registers and documents;

4. A review meeting held in November 1976 with all the 25 persons involved in the redesign of the new work system, indicated their commitment to the system that they had designed and they expressed their conviction that it would work better than what had been achieved in the past.

In this connection, it may also be mentioned that before the experiment was undertaken, apprehensions were expressed that the unionised employees would not cooperate with this programme. In reality, however, with the introduction of a participative design from the diagnostic stage to the implementation stage, some of the union leaders took a keen and active interest in the participative design process. In a sense, therefore, the experiences of the Bharat Heavy Electricals units and Chaura Maidan Post Office in Simla have been further confirmed in the LIC Divisional Office, New Delhi.

INCOME-TAX DEPARTMENT

In early 1975, in a meeting of the Direct Taxes Advisory Committee, Nitish R. De, a member, raised the question of the low work motivation level of a large number of white collar employees, running into thousands, located in hundreds of work centres in India. It was considered desirable to change the reality not only for the purpose of improvement in work efficiency in the system of revenue assessment and collection but also in view of the large number of assessees involved, who often expressed their dissatisfaction with the delays caused by assessment formalities and consequential harassment. The meeting discussed the issue briefly and felt that some action on a pilot project basis could be undertaken, preferably in the capital city of India.

Subsequently, a number of meetings were held with the Directorate of Organisation and Management Services and the Income-Tax Department by Nitish R. De and V. Nilakant of the National Labour Institute. In the meantime, the Director of the Management Services Wing attended a quality of work-life seminar in the Institute and he felt that it might be a good idea to explore the possibility of a pilot project in the office of the Commissioner of Income-Tax, New Delhi. Accordingly, a meeting was held in which the basic ideas of work redesign were explored with the illustrative examples cited from white collar organisations from Europe. In this meeting it was decided that work would begin in Range II-A which was working under an Assistant Income-Tax Commissioner, supervising the work of eight income-tax officers with a substantial number of clerical employees.

The external consultants initiated the study in a typical record room where all the records of the assessees were maintained in the form of files. One typical record room consisting of six record-keepers and one supervisor was subjected to detailed diagnostic study. A picture of the record room is presented in Fig. 1.10.

The record room served six income-tax officers, each record-keeper being attached to one officer. The physical environment of the record room revealed that the room was congested, dingy, poorly lit and was not regularly dusted with the result that the files stacked almost everywhere in the room—shelves, tables, floor—were full of dust. There was hardly any space for the record-keepers to walk round. The work environment surely was not congenial.

The technical system of work was also studied, along with the record-keepers and the supervisor. A record-keeper maintained records of various decisions, notices issued, dates fixed for meetings, etc., and he was concerned with the movement of files in addition to bringing out old files whenever a dispute arose on decisions made. In addition to maintaining the files, the record-keepers had to maintain several registers. In addition, there were two junior clerks attached to the same officer working in a separate room. Their work was to look after the actual task

Figure 1.10

Layout of a Record Room in the Income-Tax Department

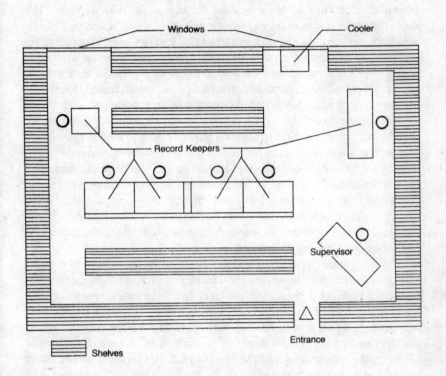

Note: The dimensions of the room were approximately 25 ft. × 15 ft.
        There were 32 shelves in the room, each shelf 8ft. × 3 ft. with 5 racks.
        There were 4 lights (100 watts); 2 fans and 1 cooler. No heaters in the room.

of decisions on assessment and recovery of assessed amount. The supervisor had two types of jobs. He was to maintain discipline in the record room where six record-keepers were seated ensuring that unauthorised persons did not enter the room and that the records were taken out with proper authorisation. The other part of his responsibility was to supervise the work of 4 clerks attached to two officers. As pointed out, these two groups were physically located in different places and as such the act of supervision could not be effective.

As regards the social system of work, it was found that there was very little inter-dependence in the working of the total task. Each record-keeper had been working independently even though there was close physical proximity in their seating arrangement. Theoretically, if a record-keeper is absent on any working day, then another record-keeper was expected to look after his work but this had not been happening. So, with those segmented aspects of work reality, the technical system, in terms of physical layout and the systems of work was out of tune with the social system of work. Secondly, the two junior clerks seated close to the officer were physically separated from the record room and, as such, the inter-dependence of the work system was not socially facilitated for the record-keeper in relation to the two junior clerks. Thirdly, the officers themselves were not taking any direct interest in the record room particularly to the system of record maintenance and the persons responsible for the upkeep of the same. In fact, some of the record-keepers expressed the view that a substantial number of officers were promoted from clerical ranks and it was, therefore, baffling that having become officers they had turned apathetic to the working conditions of the clerks to which rank they once belonged.

In view of sudden pressure of work in the office on account of the new policy decisions that the government came out with, it was not possible to feed back the data to the Commissioner, the Assistant Commissioner and other officers after the diagnostic study was over. However, a short note was prepared and sent to the department with the hope that this would provide minimum information which could form a basis for dialogue between the consultants and the department. In this note, among other issues, the following points were made:

1. The possibility of integrating the job of the record-keeper with the jobs of the two junior clerks making it a team of three working along with the officer so that it could become an integrated, self-sufficient work team;
2. The possible role of the supervisor in case the integrated team work concept was accepted;
3. The question of layout in terms of the decentralisation of the record room and the team of three keeping the records with themselves in a self-contained room/cubicle.

In September 1976, the senior consultant was contacted by the Commissioner which resulted in two visits to the office—one in October and another in November 1976.

These visits revealed the following changes:

1. The original record room that was studied and reported on, was reorganised by changing the physical layout with vastly improved working conditions. Some of the record-keepers were removed from the room and the congestion of records had gone. The room was made more airy. The steel racks, desks and chairs looked clean, tidy and more functional.

2. Several small work centres were created placing the record-keeper and the two junior clerks together, wherever possible, with the records kept by their side. In the process, this three-men servicing unit became an integrated one for the purpose of the officer.

3. The other record rooms were also similarly reorganised with the congestion considerably removed.

A review meeting was held with 8 officers, the Assistant Commissioner and the Commissioner. In addition, the senior consultant had informal meetings with the clerical employees. What transpired in these meetings is recorded below:

(a) The decentralised record room system and the small work-team set-up had perceptively brought about a closer work inter-dependence between the record-keeper and the clerks and between the team and the officer resulting in files moving more expeditiously and a smoother coordination of activities. While it was too early to judge whether the assessment cases were being disposed of more quickly, the feeling of the officers was that this would happen in the course of the coming months;

(b) The minimum facilities of a functional kind, i.e., steel racks and removal of old wooden furniture provided a distinct incentive in work motivation to the clerks, who, based on their long, past experience, did not expect that such desirable changes could take place in this traditional, bureaucratic system;

(c) The Commissioner's personal initiative in reorganising the system acted as a high motivating factor to the clerical employees whose commitment was found to be positive in sharp contrast to what was observed during the diagnostic study in 1975;

(d) Proceeding a step further, the department organised a series of decentralised reception centres for the assessees with provision of comfortable furniture and reception clerks with intercom-telephone facilities so that the flow of assessee traffic could be regulated in an orderly fashion. This system, on the one hand, earned the gratitude of the assessees and, on the other, reduced irritation of the junior clerks who were, in the past, subjected to queries and unexpected interruption in their work by the assessees. The present system protected them against such interruption;

(e) There were, in the past, a large number of attendants whose skill level was not only very low but whose work had no meaning. Under the new system, a few attendants were provided at the reception halls and the rest were being retrained for higher skilled jobs like record-binding, electrical repair jobs and repair of furniture. This effort also acted as a motivating factor to the employees in the department.

All in all, it has been found that even in a highly traditional department like the income-tax, work system design innovation could become possible and employee responsiveness could be constructively evoked so long as the persons with high status and visibility within the organisation could see the meaning of the new work system design and took the initiative in this matter. The group had proposed that the experiment in Range II-A would be extended to Ranges II-B and II-C, two other ranges reporting to the Commissioner.

It is true that no deliberate attempt has been made yet to foster a closer work-related team spirit with plan for semi-autonomous group working involving job rotation, but, at the same time, the initial steps taken and stabilised might lead the department to this direction, perhaps by a step-by-step approach.

A Tentative Evaluation of Indian Experiences

The cases presented, inevitably in a capsule form, offer a number of insights and concurrently do pose a number of problems and dilemmas.

In the first place, the cases are, by no means, a complete picture. There are other cases indicating success as well as failure, some of which will be mentioned to illustrate or supplement some relevant issues. Secondly, it will be interesting to note that all available information on the Indian experiences, barring the very first one in Ahmedabad, are from public enterprises and government system. There is no on-going project in the private sector. It may be noted that some of the transnational corporations like Imperial Chemical Industries, Dutch Royal Shell Group and so on, who have had experiences with new forms of work organisation in their home bases, have not taken any meaningful initiative in this regard in India. It is a matter of speculation whether in the third world countries, the transnational corporations have taken steps towards action research in debureaucratising work culture. Indian experiences indicate that the transnationals are glued to the Weberian-cum-Taylorism culture in their work organisation with concomitant values of 'economic men' as the primary force in the work motivation programme, the appropriate instrumentality being the union-management bargaining culture.

With these preliminary comments, one may come to grips with some specific aspects of Indian experience.

A. DIFFUSION STRATEGY

P.G. Herbst (1976A) has insightfully conceptualised diffusion strategies in a number of ways. In one formulation, he has examined the bottom-up approach, the top-down approach with the concept of downward cascading strategy, the centre-down approach, the horizontal project approach, the vertical-slice approach, and the centre-out approach, with a review of the significance of each model. In particular, he has discussed the likely consequence of the one step transformation model. His review of the literature indicates that till 1975, taking the European experience into account, the bottom-up approach, the step-by-step approach and the centre-out approach, have had more acceptability compared to others. One may, however, mention that if one takes the Australian experiences into account, then, the vertical-slice approach of the Emerys has gained currency in that part of the world. Yet another module in work system redesign started in Japan in June 1962. By September 1970, the diffusion effect was quite remarkable. The module known as quality control circles (QCC) started with 3 and in 1970 there were 4,00,000 circles operating in the Japanese industry. According to Davis and Trist (1974), the QCC are 'groups of workers and foremen who voluntarily meet together to solve shop-oriented production quality problems.'

According to the authors, the basic objective of the movement is to facilitate the continuing education process of the first line supervisors, particularly in the area of leadership and supervisory skills; to raise the morale of the employees in the shop through involvement in quality control activities by identifying the problems and working towards their resolution and, in the process, gradually reducing social distance and status problems based on age and position; and, thirdly, to provide an opportunity for the circle members to identify themselves with the products by being quality conscious. One survey report covering 1,566 companies showed that 91 per cent of them were involved in the movement. Apart from the fact that the QCC movement is quite unique in many ways as a new form of debureaucratising work culture, the phenomenal growth of the movement in Japan is equally impressive if one compares the comparatively slower growth of the quality of work-life movement on both sides of the Atlantic.

While discussing the process of diffusion, Herbst has also paid attention to the problem of encapsulation of field sites as reflected in the experience of Norway in the 1960s and early 1970s (i.e., local encapsulation; the sites have been overrun by foreign managers and unionists); the problem of incremental modification of work technology, particularly in the mechanical manufacturing industry as opposed to the breakthrough in such assembly-line production system as the automobile industry (the Volvo experience); and the problem of over-commitment to a particular approach both by the researcher involved in the project and the actors themselves in their failure to develop an appropriate strategy for a wider diffusion effect. He has drawn a sharp distinction between the demonstration project and the approaches oriented towards a purposeful concept of the quality of work-life that in turn can lead to a continuous search for newer forms of work organisation. From this Herbst has concluded that we still have an inadequate picture of the total gestalt of supportive conditions essential for an effective diffusion process. He has also explored the potential of the network concept in the diffusion strategy and he finds that there have been hopeful developments in recent years. While it took, to provide an example, almost twenty years to put demonstration projects in the manufacturing industry on to a diffusion track as reflected in early British efforts to the stabilisation of those efforts in Sweden, the shipping and the education projects in Norway did not take more than five years for a diffusion effect. Herbst has also speculated on the directions of diffusion including the concept of the role of the 'leading part' as developed by Emery. It has been his considered view, from the lessons of Sweden and Norway, that the diffusion process has interesting dynamics. The dynamics lie in a sense of inevitability in looking for almost entirely new types of technical solutions, whether that be in the manufacturing sector or the shipping sector or the education sector.

The Arden House Conference in 1972 set up a task force on international and national diffusion processes in the quality of work-life movement with Kenneth Walker as Chairman and Einar Thorsrud as one of the members. The task force, while dealing with the question of diffusion, raised five issues: (1) what is diffusion? (2) who is to diffuse? (3) what is to be diffused? (4) to whom to diffuse? and, finally, (5) how to diffuse? The significant points emanating from the report are that the diffusion process would mean four aspects:

(a) bringing about changes which would not otherwise occur;
(b) accelerating some changes which were going to occur anyway but which the diffusers would like to see happening more rapidly;
(c) preventing changes which are coming by doing something about them; and

(*d*) guiding changes which are coming anyway but which one would like
to influence in direction and outcome.

It was also felt that the central objective of diffusion would be to sharpen
the consciousness level about the possibility and the desirability of bringing
about a qualitative change in the work-life of employees along with the
point that the seeding process as a way of diffusion should take into
account 'key individuals', a more effective formulation of which is perhaps
the concept of 'leading parts'. One more point that the task force made
and that stands as valid even now is that in the task of diffusion, resources
should not be monopolised by any particular institution or any interest
group. Although the word 'resource' was not defined, it is presumed that
it meant both human as well as other facilities (Davis and Cherns, 1975).

In the context of these insights and experiences, the Indian data present
certain features which call for attention.

The diffusion process is to be conceived in two ways which are also
interconnected: diffusion of the idea, knowledge and skill about new
forms of work organisation amongst an increasing number of persons—
managers, administrators, trade union leaders and action researchers,
and diffusion of a demonstration project from one site to another within a
corporation, among corporations and over a whole sector of organised
activity. The first aspect is related to the issue of development of an
organic network of resource persons and the second aspect leads to
creating potential conditions for social transformation utilising work
activity as an instrument of change. The mythification of bureaucratic
work structure is sought to be resolved by the concept of liberation
through the process of what Herbst has happily termed as 'alternatives to
hierarchies'. Some of the Indian cases, for example, that of the State
Bank of India Branch at Gurgaon and the Life Insurance Corporation
Unit in New Delhi, are still at a stage of slow stabilisation at the demonstration stage. The Hardwar demonstration projects in Blocks V and II
are getting diffused to other work sites including the personnel department.
The Bhopal unit and the Hyderabad unit of the same corporation opted
for shop-floor work system redesign in 1980–81. At the Tiruchirapalli unit
the successful stabilisation of demonstration projects in two production
shops were brought into production planning and materials management
departments. The postal case, unlike the income-tax case, is already
leading towards a process of planned demonstration to other post office
sites territorially located in the same and other regions with the possibility
that in the coming years it may spread over to more post offices in the
country. As a matter of fact, so far the most fruitful diffusion has taken
place in the postal system: Kalkaji and Swami Ram Tirth Nagar post offices
in Delhi, Kotagiri in Tamil Nadu and Vaikom in Kerala (De, 1978, Sharma,

et al, 1978; Madala, 1982; Doraiswamy, 1982; Srinivasan, 1982). The experiences gained from the Simla post offices helped considerably in an improved redesign—process and product-wise—of the Kalkaji Post Office. Employee participation was visibly high and several structural innovations could be incorporated.

The differential results so far visible in the matter of diffusion, time-wise and spread-wise, can be accounted for in terms of organisation culture, leadership role, consultant commitment, process of initiation and the strategy of planning, the issues that will be dealt with in this chapter.

In the meantime, it will be worthwhile also to look at the diffusion process in terms of human resources. The initial projects in the early 1950s at Ahmedabad started with A.K. Rice. Some of his Tavistock colleagues were also involved in the project along with the Indian social scientists, Kamla Chowdhry and B.R. Deolalikar. There was no purposeful plan, however, of the diffusion process in the project with the result that with the departure of Ken Rice, the network of human resource to carry forward the lessons from the Ahmedabad experiment to other sites did not materialise. Another lesson from the evaluation study of Miller, referred to earlier, is that the management were not sensitive to the need for effective boundary management and protection with the consequence that the demonstration project has survived over the past twenty years only in one of the four project sites.

These lessons, understandably, played some role in the efforts initiated by the group working in the National Labour Institute. From the beginning, an objective was kept in view that among the cadres involved in each demonstration project, persons would be identified, belonging to trade union and management groups, who would, not only carry the effort within their own systems, but would be available to help other systems. The Hardwar unit has, for example, a cadre of a dozen employees including a couple of trade union leaders who have acquired a commendable degree of knowledge and skills in the diffusion process. The State Bank has developed two identifiable persons; eight in the postal system; and half-a-dozen at the Tiruchirapalli unit. There is a continuous effort to augment the number. Another observation that deserves mention, is that the response amongst social scientists oriented towards action research continues to be poor (as in Norway). There appear to be two reasons for this:

1. Positively motivated academicians are oriented towards classroom activity and scholarly research and, as such, the dynamics of action research which would invariably mean acceptance of the concept of praxis (action-reflection dialectics) is still not well accepted or appreciated;

2. All the demonstration projects presented in the report have been taken as research projects and not as what is traditionally known as consultancy projects. The expenses for the projects were either met by the concerned organisations such as Bharat Heavy Electricals Limited or met by the Research Organisation itself as by the National Labour Institute in respect of the LIC case, the income-tax case and the postal case. In neither set of cases, however, is there any payment of a consultancy fee to the researchers. Action researchers who are working in the field of human relations, particularly utilising the insights of organisation development strategy, do essentially work as paid consultants and, perhaps, for them to accept an honorary role in socio-technical system work is still a new culture. In the Norad-ILO-NPC project in India (1977–79) the fund was provided by NORAD through the ILO.

Essentially, the initiation process as well as the diffusion process of an industrial democracy programme is a motivational issue. This does not, however, mean that the way some psychologists have dealt with the concept of motivation is altogether appropriate. Most of the theories backed by experimental research do not go into the societal issues such as socio-economic variables and cultural variables (De, 1976).

We would, therefore, use motivation in a wider context with diffusion dynamics over time. The various sectors of human activity will be conceived in socio-cultural motivational parameters of which a tentative picture is presented in Fig. 1.11.

One aspect of the diagram in Fig. 1.11 is worth mentioning. The last linkage between the quality of work-life and the quality of life with the comprehensive socio-economic-political system is important in the social transformation process. If this linkage is kept in view, then, the Indian experiences have not yet been able to make any tangible impact on the macro-change process in the industrial sphere. We shall revert to this issue later.

B. INITIATION PROCESS

No doubt, the diffusion process, in sequential steps, comes after the initiation process; yet the way demonstration project on a work system redesign begins, has some relationship with the strategy of diffusion. The insights that we have generated from the Indian cases will be mentioned here in order to get a clearer perspective on the dynamics of diffusion.

We will not refer to Ken Rice's work as to how the project got started since it has already been documented by him. But it would be interesting

Figure 1.11

Motivational Base for Industrial Democracy

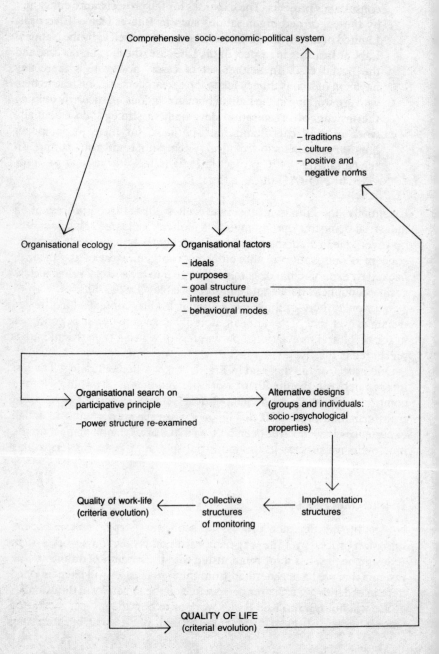

to note that a number of projects did start in India in the 1960s and later on, on internal initiatives. While the role of preparatory and consultative planning is inevitable in the redesign of work system, managerial initiative arising out of day-to-day work experience and its continuing irritation have acted as a strong motivation to self-initiated action. One such project was started in the centralised cash collection centre (abbreviated as CCCC) in 1969 by R.H. Umadikar, a young manager of the Life Insurance Corporation of India. This centre was dealing with 50,000 policies in July 1967, when the computer system was introduced. The CCCC became a part of the EDP system. Computerisation of the scheme created the usual problems of resistance to change. Employee resistance with strong union support was a major problem that Umadikar faced as a manager.

On his own initiative, he started performing some of the essential tasks required by the new system though they were, strictly speaking, not his responsibility. The sincerity with which he carried out the additional responsibility acted as the first break-through in an otherwise strained relationship between him and his clerical employees. A dialogue developed and steadily a group system of work evolved as employees got involved in meeting the new technological demands. Umadikar and the clerical employees worked together and ultimately a new work system was designed and successfully implemented. A report was prepared in 1969 which was commended by the then Chairman of the company. Having looked into the report we got the impression that effort on the part of Umadikar created a new form of work organisation that could simultaneously take care of technological demands and employee requirements (Umadikar, 1969).

Yet another similar spontaneous effort is reported from Neyveli Lignite Corporation, located near Madras, a public sector undertaking with 17,500 employees. The corporation is concerned with the mining of lignite, operating a large thermal power generating station, manufacturing fertiliser, briquetting and carbonisation activities. This corporation has had a long history of disturbed operation and a chequered industrial relations background. At one point of time, there were more than two dozen registered trade unions of which six are still active.

Under a dynamic central minister, the late S.M. Kumaramangalam, this undertaking, like other public sector undertakings, was also subjected to change of leadership in 1971 with infusion of new blood at the top. While the situation was gradually improving, in late 1974, a young administrator was inducted as director of personnel. In early 1975 he decided, on the basis of his diagnosis of the problems of productivity and worker motivation, to break away from the work system based on compartmentalisation. Since then, S. Srinivasan has been able to introduce in the central workshop, the foundry, the thermal power station and at the open-cast mining site, a multi-skilled system with a view to giving a sense of totality to each worker in his operation. In the machine shop, for example, almost every worker has two skills to his credit, if not in three. In the foundry shop, a core-maker also does the work of a moulder and a worker involved in the cupola operation is equally involved in the tilting furnace operation and, if occasion so demands, in furnace lining. Similarly, fitters, welders, riggers, blacksmiths, turners and machine operators involved in various shops have become poly-skilled. This effort at job enrichment carried out over a period of 18 months matched by a commensurate group incentive scheme has brought about some semblance of group functioning without achieving the level of sophistication of either the Tiruchirapalli unit or the Hardwar unit of Bharat Heavy Electricals. Nonetheless, employees' involvement in the work system is visibly greater. An evaluation done by us in October 1976, reveals that workers are more satisfied now compared to what it was before, because they feel that they have some control over the work process which was absent before.

One can provide other similar cases, but, we believe that the essential point of such spontaneous efforts is a reflection of the sensitivity of some internal change agents, usually some perceptive managers, who realised that the dialectics of traditional work organisation and the social system of work are incongruent. Based on their practical experiences, they do try to innovate in their own way new forms of work organisation. External consultants have not played any role in this kind of project.

The second mode of the start-up process is the impact created by work redesign and quality of work-life seminars organised by the National Labour Institute since 1974. Some of the managerial personnel attending some of these seminars/workshops, on return to their workplaces, have taken initiatives in examining the task system with a view to reorganising it using the participative design method. One such case already reported is that of the Tiruchirapalli unit of Bharat Heavy Electricals. A second case is that of the Hindustan Machine Tools factory at Pinjore. This factory which specialises in the production of machine tools, sent its production manager, D.K. Chakravorty, to one of the workshops. On his return, he studied the work system of the accessories shop where some key accessories are manufactured for the main machine tool unit. There are two major operations involved—buffing and assembling. At the time of his investigation these two operations were being done by two sets of workers, assuming, on the usual bureaucratic rationale, that this kind of division of labour would bring about efficiency in operation. However, his experience was that absenteeism was a major problem with problems of redeployment of workforce and, secondly, with the younger generation of workforce the fact of monotony was getting reflected in work efficiency. So, he generated a series of problem-solving dialogues with 21 workers and gradually the idea emerged that the same worker, with a little bit of training, would be able to deal with both operations. The group also felt that as there were accessories of different dimensions, the products could be grouped in a suitable manner and small groups of workers could handle different types of products on a planned rotational basis.

Productivity improved gradually with the introduction of the system both in terms of quantity and quality and, after a period of 18 months, seven workers could be deployed elsewhere in the factory as fourteen were found adequate for the job. The only help that Chakravorty asked for from the National Labour Institute was relevant literature in the form of case analyses on work system redesign which was supplied to him. Similarly, trained internal change agents carried out experiments on the postal system in Delhi, Tamil Nadu and Kerala.

The third form of initiation process was the more obvious one. External consultants (as action-researchers) were involved in a project from the beginning, interacting with concerned managers, trade union leaders and workers, helping them to gradually evolve a participative system of laying the foundation for new forms of work organisation. This is how the Hardwar project started as well as the projects in the State Bank and the Life Insurance Corporation. In monitoring the progress of a demonstration project, however, different systems have been followed at different sites. In the State Bank, for example, the progress was being continuously monitored by an internal change-agent, an engineer-cum-behavioural scientist, G.K. Khandelwal, employed by the bank in a social science research position. A researcher from the National Labour Institute, V. Nilakant, was called in for occasional advice.

The case of the Life Insurance Corporation is somewhat different. Here the external consultants acting as researchers were involved at each stage of the demonstration project and there used to be monthly review meetings with the task force to review the progress as well as to evolve further steps. Even after a year's experience the initiating role of the external consultants continued. The particular reason why this continuing relationship existed in the Life Insurance Corporation will be explained in the next section. In the case of the Hardwar unit the external consultants as researchers were also involved, on a month-to-month basis, not so much for review of what the group was doing but for the purpose of diffusion to other shops. However, there are definite signs of an internal change agent gradually taking over this role.

In the ILO–NORAD–NPC projects the initiation process failed to evoke a response in three of the six projects. In one case, the union leaders failed to convince the members—not an unusual situation in India. In two other cases, the management lacked the necessary enthusiasm. What is evident in these three cases is that there was no felt need to experiment with alternative forms of work organisation. The bureaucratic forms of work logic remained the enduring value. The cases from India unerringly indicate that top management commitment, even if guarded, is essential for creating the minimum opportunity for consultants—internal and external—to launch a project, however small. In the cases that were non-starters, the management remained convinced that technological considerations with appropriate inputs of modern management techniques were of paramount consideration. The recurring problems emanating from the social system, though recognised, were sought to be resolved through traditional personnel policies and practices.

Of the three projects where some progress was achieved, one was a post office. The postal system was already a convinced client. In two other cases, the management showed initial interest. Through the processes of interaction and trial and error, the initial plan underwent changes and this was accepted by the consultants (Singh, 1979).

C. CONSULTANT ROLE

The consultant role in the participation scheme of things should become rationally obvious, namely, an involvement which is not so much as wearing the hat of an expert in a product-consultant role but more to help the dynamics of democratic operation from diagnosis to planning, to implementation, to stabilisation, and to diffusion. However, in reality, there were several nuances to this general proposition. In the first place, one can draw a broad distinction between an external consultant and an internal consultant. An internal consultant is often assisted by external consultants to acquire the skills and confidence required in initiating work redesign projects. The relationship, therefore, is one of mutual esteem and trust and a role which is often complementary. This is the case with respect to the State Bank, the BHEL Hardwar unit, the LIC and the Chaura Maidan Post Office. However, depending on their culture, some organisations like the State Bank, BHEL, and the post offices, allowed adequate elbow room to internal consultants to function effectively. In some others, like the LIC, the internal consultants, pegged to their managerial responsibilities, did not find the time or the autonomy for the project—though this was essential at the initial stage. Secondly, a correlation can be made between the status of the consultant as seen by the higher management, and the degree of dependence on him: the higher the status, the greater the dependence.

Yet another case is provided by the HMT component centre experiment. M.S.S. Varadan (1976) and his group as internal consultants were allowed to do an evaluation study but the enterprise was somewhat hesitant in allowing him and his colleagues to get involved in a work redesign demonstration project. It became eventually clear that the diagnostic data emanating from their research did not permit them to be more actively involved in an action-research role.

The Indian cases show that while the role of an external consultant is gradually becoming redundant after the initiation phase with some degree of stabilisation having taken place, they are still considered relevant for the diffusion process. The Hardwar unit of Bharat Heavy Electricals and the post office case—two comparatively successful cases—are examples of this dependence.

It may be mentioned that practically all the external consultants and most of the internal consultants involved in the Indian cases have had an organisation development focus in their earlier work experiences. Some of them were active in the organisation development movement with a high degree of process orientation. However, OD work, that is, dealing with the people system somewhat divorced from the task system, did not provide them with adequate satisfaction in their role and they steadily moved towards the socio-technical systems approach.

Another observation is in order. In the more successful cases, the consultant's role was one of a dedicated missionary. In the Tiruchirapalli cases the sustained, patient and active interest shown by the internal change agents were essential to make the Saturday morning production review and planning meetings genuinely participative contributing to the enhanced learning experiences of the workmen and supervisors. Persistent and positive interest showing genuine involvement in the technical and human problems of the participants by the consultants were also evident at Hardwar, LIC and the postal cases, particularly at Kalkaji. A time-bound, 'limited' consultancy role, it appears, did not work in any of these cases.

D. Organisation Culture

Organisation culture, as reflected in the overall leadership style of the managers/administrators and the trade union leaders, on the one hand, and the dynamics of their relationship, on the other, is an important factor in generating interest about the relevance of work redesign as an alternative to the bureaucratic form of organisation. It is also relevant to the diffusion process. If one takes the income-tax case, one will find that a note prepared by the external consultant appealed to the Commissioner.

A series of actions were initiated by him along with his colleagues resulting in a modular system of work organisation as described earlier. In a traditional hierarchical organisation, this strategy was effective, particularly where there was no strong trade union movement. On the other hand, in the Hardwar factory, the top leadership of the unit played a supportive rather than a directly involved role. The General Manager (Production) and his counterpart in the administration, the two key men next to the Executive Director, were also indirectly involved and their interaction was more with the external consultants than with the day-to-day functioning of the project. The shop managers and supervisors were thus able to operate autonomously in the demonstration sites as members of the task forces. With a more open system culture and comparatively more democratic functioning of the managerial system, this strategy was conceivable at Hardwar but not in the income-tax office. Yet, it would be rather premature to conclude that one approach works in a bureaucracy, while a different approach would be relevant to an industrial culture. The post office, for example, is part of the bureaucracy; yet, in the Chaura Maidan Post Office, the Senior Superintendent of Post Offices and the Director (Postal Training) who are considerably senior to the sub-postmaster and his subordinates, played a more indirectly supportive role in the change process, unlike the direct involvement by the Commissioner of Income-tax.

On the whole, therefore, it is difficult to identify any aspect of predominant organisation culture prevailing in India that can be upheld as critical for the success of a project. In negative terms, opposition or total apathy at the top level will harm any effort at change. In positive terms, management at one or two levels above the committed parties, if definitely supportive, is of significant help.

Associated with success were factors like a minimum continuity of the top management cadre and the availability of change agents. Frequent changes of committed personalities often acted as causes for delays. At the Tannery and Footwear Corporation, the haltingly slow progress is partially explained by the frequent change of guards. Continuity apart, one major value discerned among the action researchers was their positive and stable self-concept. Realistically oriented, they shared a belief that they could contribute to improving the quality of work-life by their intervention and that the participants could also make matching contributions.

Yet another identifiable aspect of the culture was the comparative economic viability of the organisation. In the more enduring cases, there was no major financial crisis. The top management and the trade unions were not pre-occupied with 'survival' problems. The organisations in financial terms, were doing reasonably well. This factor has contributed to their taking 'risks', despite many reservations.

E. ROLE OF THE TRADE UNIONS

The role of organised trade unions is as significant a factor in India as it is in the UK, Sweden, the USA, France and Italy.

In the USA and UK, the union-management relationship has been built on a distributive collective bargaining culture. As such, there is a confrontative culture, a culture which has made a significant difference to the work system redesign movement in these two countries, compared to the Scandinavian countries. In the USA, for example, many of the success stories as in Proctor and Gamble, have taken place in non-unionised organisations. One major exception, however, is the Bolivar case (Maccoby, 1975). Except for the leadership of the United Automobile workers, no other major unions have come out in support of work redesign as a way of workers' control over the work process. Interest-related issues continue to dominate the trade union movement in the USA. In the UK, the culture has been the same more or less, except that in some organisations like the Shell Refinery at Teesport, trade unions at local levels have cooperated with the management in the initiation and stabilisation of work system redesign experiments. When adverse economic conditions set in, as in the mid-1970s, the trade union movement, wherever it had given initial support to the projects, withdraws its support in order to minimise the tragedy of unemployment. On the whole, however, trade union support has been highly selective in the UK.

Selectivity has also been a major criterion for the very powerful communist trade unions in France and Italy. The interviews we had in 1975 with the Marxist trade union leadership in both countries indicate that while, on the whole, it looks upon work redesign experiments with suspicion, the reputation of the management vis-à-vis its relationship with the working class as reflected in the companies' policies and practices would make a difference to the trade union movement extending its support to the project. Therefore, Olivetti, Delamine and other large organisations in Italy were successful in their work redesign projects and their diffusion; while in France, BSN and other companies were similarly successful in their autonomous group working experience. However, neither in France nor in Italy has the trade union movement been a partner in the experiments even while it allowed the workers to participate.

The experience in Sweden and Norway is quite distinct. Not only has the trade union movement on the whole supported the experiments but it has also facilitated the diffusion process, particularly in Sweden. In both countries the trade union movement is strong and is built on a collective bargaining culture; but the tradition, as distinct from that of the USA and the UK, is more oriented towards an integrative bargaining system. The democratisation of societal structure in Scandinavia has surely contributed considerably in making a strong trade union movement responsive to the quality of work-life efforts.

In India, the cases reported in the study fall into two categories:

1. At the Hardwar and Tiruchirapalli units of Bharat Heavy Electricals, for example, the trade union movement is quite strong, although both units have multiple unions organised on political lines. Here again there is a difference: at the Tiruchirapalli unit, there is a tradition of harmonious union-management relations and, as such, the unions were not opposed to the work redesign scheme in the drum shop and the header shop, although the recognised trade union has not been actively involved in the project. At the Hardwar unit, on the other hand, the relationship in the past had been strained and inter-union rivalry persisted. On account of this reality, the external consultants had to spend, in the initial period, a considerable amount of time with the trade union leadership of rival groups explaining the objectives of the experiment vis-à-vis the new role of and opportunities for the workers. Occasionally, joint meetings with the unions and management were also necessary.

2. The other category is where the trade union movement is either weak or, even if not weak, apathetic to the demonstration projects, partly because of the low-key beginning of the project and partly because of the lack of interest of the union leadership in work-related issues and apathy towards work and work-life.

It has been mentioned in describing the cases that in the Chaura Maidan Post Office, three union leaders had initial difficulties in adjusting to the group-based working system but, gradually, they saw the 'elbow room' aspect of an otherwise unchallenging job and became committed to the project. On the whole, the Indian data, so far, indicate that the grassroots trade union leaders who have been involved in demonstration projects have not only responded positively, but, as in the Hardwar unit, they have taken an active part in the diffusion process. The national level trade union leadership, however, is still not involved in the process of overcoming work alienation and its orientation continues to be towards bargainable issues.

It may, however, be hypothesised that the local trade unions have either cooperated or desisted from offering opposition to localised work system redesign because the public enterprises and the public services operate on the principle of multiple goals tending towards a purpose-oriented system. The creation of employment potential with the prospect of employment generation is one such objective. Expansion projects and product diversification schemes can take care of this objective.

F. REWARD STRUCTURE

Recognising the distinct contribution of Miller and Rice (1967) to which further insights have been added by Colman (1976), it may be pointed out that with the concepts of sentience and adaptation of the positive aspects of operant conditioning, it is possible to conceive of a reward structure as an overall norm for fostering and stabilising the values enshrined in the new debureaucratised forms of work organisation. Miller and Rice, in their search for developing an integrated system, recognised the differential boundary conditions of task systems and sentient systems. Sentience, as they have defined it, signifies a system or a group that demands and receives loyalty from its members. Then, again, they have also talked of plant design as distinct from organisation design, according to which, one deals with the physical resources and the other with the provision of human resources in the form of people prepared for certain roles. The significance, therefore, of the reward system lies, on the one hand, in developing relevant reward structures to help acquiring appropriate work-system-related-behaviour which will include skills and knowledge and, on the other, fostering certain positive norms in order that group sentience assumes a totality of culture enshrined in the concept of participative design and participative functioning. The operant conditioning approach figures here. The objective would be to evolve a form of appropriate technology for groups rather than for individuals. This observation is significant because, in a major way, work system redesign distinguishes itself from job enrichment in that the former is essentially group-based and the latter is essentially individual-based.

In the Indian context, the HMT component centre dramatically presents one side of the positive aspects of achievement, productivity rise and creation of increased elbow room for the supervisory cadre. The other side reveals the consequent dissonance of not creating an appropriate group system to utilise the technology. Here is a case which shows that the plant design in the form of the component centre dictated the organisation design essentially based on an individual operator. The dissonance between the two systems created problems which Varadan and his colleague identified in their evaluation report.

As a matter of reality, the designing of appropriate reward structures continues to remain an unresolved problem in the Indian situation. It remains unresolved because there are too many variables which complicate the picture. At the Hardwar unit, there is a group reward scheme, which, by itself, would have been satisfactory to the groups working on work redesign demonstration sites, but, unfortunately, the continuing culture of overtime payments for extra work done in the other shop is tangibly so rewarding that at times the workers who have volunteered for the participative system are puzzled about the inequity of the reward structure. The vicious circle of production shortfalls, partly if not substantially, caused by the segmented traditional work system, fosters a culture of overtime payment and, as such, vested interests develop of which both the management and the workers become unwilling prisoners. At the same time, at the Tiruchirapalli unit of Bharat Heavy Electricals this dilemma does not exist. From the beginning, the financial reward structure was based on an equitable payment system with no hidden attempt at bringing in the vicious circle of overtime payment. On the positive side, various forms of tangible and intangible reward structures directly related to effort and performance were installed. The element of sentience received, from the very beginning, due acknowledgement in the plant with the result that the totality of the reward structure has been perceived as fair and equitable and, as such, the experimental sites did not suffer from the problem that haunted the Hardwar unit.

In the government system, such as the post office and the income-tax, the scope for financial rewards for being multi-skilled or for accepting the socio-technical system of work organisation is limited, if not absent. There are some reward schemes in the income-tax department but hardly any in the postal service. In a situation like this, the other form of reward that is conceivable is to appreciate the dynamics of sentience that operates in a group and then to develop a reward structure accordingly. In the income-tax department, the change of physical layout and bringing the work-related group around the concerned income-tax officer are two factors that have strengthened the sentient system. Similarly, a drastic change in the physical layout at the Chaura Maidan Post Office with sufficient interest taken in the project through participation by the senior officers, has been perceived by the postman and the counter-clerks as a significant symbolic expression of the care and concern that the authority figures have taken in them. These factors have contributed, in no mean measure, to make the delivery group an organic one and, later on, the counter-clerks.

The reward structure raises a bigger issue in the context of designing an appropriate system. Even where the management of an enterprise and the concerned workers are rationally committed to developing a reward system for the employees involved in experimental sites they often hesitate to act because those sections of an enterprise where such an experiment was not or could not be started might react adversely to such steps. In case the diffusion process could be hastened throughout an enterprise, the dilemma posed in respect of developing an appropriate reward structure could perhaps be resolved. Yet another issue being debated at the Hardwar plant deserves mention. In case the reward scheme is found acceptable for workers becoming multi-skilled because of the new opportunities offered to them, the point at issue is whether one should reward them for acquiring additional skills or whether such reward should be linked with the creation of opportunities to utilise the skills. When the utilisation of skills becomes the objective, an enterprise would face a new challenge, namely, a greater sophistication of work system redesign which would involve higher levels of supervisory and managerial structures so that the human potential activated under the new scheme of things could be utilised in real-life work situations, distinct from the novelty of experimental sites.

G. The Problem of Criteria

The issue of measurement is vital indeed. The efficacy of new forms of work organisation cannot be assessed without developing appropriate criteria for measurement. Measurement would no doubt depend upon the larger issue of goals leading to purpose which would then be linked to the more fundamental issue of ideals.

As in other countries, in India too, there is a tussle, explicit or implicit, between productivity criteria and human criteria. By and large, there is also a convergence here that workers and managers seek to perceive the experiment in productivity terms because this would help them in the matter of dealing with the problem of financial rewards. Industrial culture being what it is, even social scientists are essentially concerned with before/after productivity measurement.

The cases presented indicate, though data were not adduced, that on traditional criteria of productivity, the experiments with new forms of work organisation have proved their worth. One aspect of productivity, however, deserves mention. With participative design, certain neglected areas received attention. In the case of the post offices, for example, when the working of the system was being diagnosed, it became obvious that precious space was being occupied by old records which, under the regulations, could have been disposed of long ago. It would be interesting to note that the organisation and method study group, which operates on the premise of the Tayloristic principle, suggested a complement of 44 employees for the Chaura Maidan Post Office. With the work system redesign on participative principle the number could come down to 39. So, even if one uses the traditional productivity criteria one lesson that emerges is that the O&M approach or the industrial engineering orientation would be 'suspect' when one seeks to find relevant productivity criteria to measure the effectiveness of new forms of work organisation.

Similarly, at the Hardwar plant, while productivity measurements were being discussed, it became evident that the traditional concept of the primacy of direct labour was questionable because in a fabrication shop where movement of heavy materials was essentially regulated by overhead electrical cranes, the crane operator and his colleagues, the slingers, could not be considered as indirect labour or less significant contributors to productivity. Thus, an integrated concept of measurement developed where direct and indirect labour became equally relevant.

However, one danger of using productivity criteria rather exclusively to evaluate the quality of work-life is what might happen to the income-tax department. Looking at the work system redesign from the layout reorganisation point of view, it was possible to create decentralised work centres around the income-tax officers. This has resulted in a productivity rise in terms of a quicker rate of assessment and disposal of files and these are certainly impressive indicators. Should the senior officers view these achievements as the fulfilment of their objective, then, the demonstration project would suffer a one-dimensional assessment. That is why it is important to look at other dimensions. The sentience criteria are relevant in this context.

Lammers (1974/1975), while discussing self-management and partici-pation as a democratisation concept, has mentioned two aspects which may be recalled here. He has quoted a politician in Holland who said that 'participation does not form an aim in itself and by itself. It is a means for an apparatus to function more adequately … indeed democratisation is a matter of efficiency not of ideological necessity.' It is important to be aware of such a limited concept of democratisation of the work process because this concept can be a new label for the traditional reality, a reality represented by the Taylorian approach to work organisation. The second item that Lammers mentions is the concept of functional and structural democratisation. The functional concept is the representative system in the form of shop councils, plant council and so on and the structural concept, according to him, is the concept where power equalisation figures. One insight from the Indian experiences is that the power issue is certainly a vital one but sharing of power by itself would not be a sufficiently motivating factor for launching demonstration projects unless additional criteria for the quality of work-life are conceived. (Negative control over organisation power or veto power cannot be a valid criterion.)

However, one significant distinction which emerges from the Indian cases is the awareness that new forms of work organisation are quite distinct from the spirit of Taylorism because productivity criteria are not the sole motivators behind the movement. That the quality of work-life will be shorn of any meaning unless the regulatory concept of management is replaced by a genuinely participative concept, that the tyranny of technology should be tamed by the flexibility of technology in its working form, that the concept of hierarchical control should give away to appropriate forms of self-regulation and control through autonomous or semi-autonomous group working and that, in the end, working men and women should be measured as creators of meaningful work rather than as instruments of production, is gaining slow acceptance as the rationale for new forms of work organisation. That the alternatives to bureaucracy cannot but be conceived of in terms of work as a therapy for mental health, efficacious family and meaningful community existence are gaining acceptance very slowly indeed by the actors involved in the demonstration projects as well as in the diffusion dynamics. One internal change agent at Hardwar put his version of industrial democracy in these words:

> If the parameters of productivity remain unchanged in the new system of work, but working life becomes meaningful resulting in commitment to new work challenges and I can see overflow of this feeling of self-responsibility to the family and the community life of an employee, I would consider that the quality of work-life movement has succeeded.

It will be a tall order to claim that all those who have either sanctioned or participated in the new experience would subscribe to this point of view but they would not hesitate to admit that, from the limited experience of success, they are convinced that the traditional conflict between productivity and employee satisfaction with work-life may become a non-issue. The new system can provide meaning to both.

Essentially, the basic concept of the quality of work-life will have to emanate from the ideal of liberation from the entrapment of technology because it is the onerous, sovereign role of technology that has so far determined the form of organisation resulting in not only a segmented work system but much more than that, a jaundiced view of the objective reality of work and life. This is reflected in Argyris' (1972) critique of organisational sociologists like John Goldthorpe and David Lockwood who have made the point that the working class itself is not interested in participation. They are interested, as is often suggested by industrial managers and administrators, in financial largesse and that is all that they are concerned with. Quantitatively oriented social scientists would be able to utilise a sophisticated questionnaire to substantiate such findings from India and abroad. Such findings, however, should neither be a surprise nor a shock because these reflect the tragedy of jaundiced reality where the alternative of liberation does not figure in the consciousness of the workers. Incidentally, such an attitude whether it is in the USA, or in India, almost reflects the Hindu concept of fatalism. This appreciation of the distinction between falsified reality and objective reality, we believe, is the *sine qua non* for committing oneself to the quality of work-life movement. Accordingly, therefore, certain qualitative criteria should be evolved to measure the quality aspect of work-life, by no means, neglecting the productivity hardware. This realisation is gaining ground in research literature (Hopwood, 1979).

H. Supervisory Role

The role of supervisory personnel in any organisational innovation including training and developmental needs has been discussed and written on at length. Even though Human Relations Training began with the spirit generated by the Hawthorne experiment, it has often been debated that human relations training for the supervisors put them on the horns of a dilemma in that they are misunderstood both by their subordinates and by their superiors. It is also the experience that workers' autonomy in an institutionalised form of participative relation has caused supervisory personnel anxiety in their fear that their authority would be eroded. In many cases, this did happen in India and abroad.

Confronted with this reality, the new forms of work organisation would be committing the same folly unless a good deal of care is taken to work on the emergent role of supervisory personnel. Emery and Thorsrud (1976), from their experiences with industrial democracy programmes in Norway, have discussed the fears and apprehensions of the supervisory personnel at Hunfos and Norak Hydro and they have documented how supervisors gradually saw their future roles which are listed below:

1. One possibility is that the supervisor will concern himself primarily with coordination between his own department and adjacent departments. In other words, he would become a source of information and a planner. From time to time, he could act as the department's joint leader in the handling of important and unforeseen issues which arise suddenly and which other individuals or groups are not prepared to deal with;
2. Another possibility is that the supervisor will primarily take charge

of training and personnel administration questions on the departmental level;

3. A third possibility is that the supervisor will become mainly a technical assistant, perhaps with special responsibility for local maintenance or local quality control;

4. A fourth possibility is for the supervisor to continue to combine most of the tasks mentioned above, but this means that he will be continuing in a traditional organisational pattern. In view of the other changes which will inevitably be taking place in modern industry, his position in this case would be increasingly weak and unclear;

5. A fifth alternative is for the supervisor to become absorbed into the operator group and participate in both manufacturing and supervision.

They believe that the middle management would not only require development education in their new roles, but almost certainly would emerge as the first level of management.

Given this developmental scenario in Norway, we can see the roles that are emerging for middle managers in the Indian experimental sites. Some of the common features that are visible are as follows:

(a) The intensity and quality of interaction between the supervisory personnel of the experimental groups and their counterparts in other departments have invariably increased. Practically in all the cases it has improved positively except perhaps in the case of HMT component centres plagued by competitive relationships;

(b) The supervisory personnel have been involved in a somewhat longer-term planning process—one week and more—which has provided a stamp of distinction to their position. In units like the Tiruchirapalli and Hardwar plants of Bharat Heavy Electricals, supervisory personnel have found themselves more and more involved in production planning programmes and scheduling for a period of two to four weeks;

(c) The control function of the supervisors has undergone a change, although not in equal measure in all cases. This is partly conditioned by the supervisor's leadership style and partly by the ability of the experimental group to develop internal norms of work including handling of the problem of discipline. At the Tiruchirapalli plant, the supervisory role in the matter of control is perceptibly diminished whereas this is not so in the case of the HMT component centre, with Hardwar, Chaura Maidan Post Office and State Bank lying in-between;

(*d*) Supervisors' interests in their own development have gone up perceptibly in practically all cases. They now see their own training and developmental needs in a better perspective than they were able to before. At the Hardwar unit of Bharat Heavy Electricals, for example, there have been specific requests from the supervisory personnel from experimental sites for training on planning and coordination functions as well as for developing the ability to undertake technical and social analysis of the work system.

It would, however, be pertinent to mention that there are cases of individual supervisors who have not been able to adjust themselves positively to the experimental site. One representative case is provided by an old supervisor in one of the production centres of the Hardwar unit. With his long experience of tight-fisted supervisory style, he just could not adjust himself even though the management was responsive to his dilemma and sought to help him during the painful process of readjustment to the new role. These efforts did not succeed and ultimately it was necessary to transfer him to a job where he would not be faced with such a dilemma.

Supervisors who depended greatly on their superiors and, simultaneously, expected their subordinates to depend on them, did, initially, find themselves in a predicament. This problem could be tackled the participative way—an essential prerequisite for the success of the industrial democracy programmes.

I. Cultural Relevance

In an earlier section, we have had occasion to mention certain aspects of the cultural elements in the Indian situation. It has been pointed out that it would be over-simplistic to conclude that Indian history primarily provided an other-worldly approach to life thereby debunking work as a meaningful activity. There are traditions of the this-worldly aspect of work culture as well.

At the same time, it would indeed be difficult, if not impossible, to come to definitive findings to the effect that there are specific identifiable characteristics in the Indian work culture which would either support a traditional form of work organisation or its modern alternatives as are gaining ground in many countries of the world. In Norway, for example (Jenkins, 1974), it was found in a survey in 1964, that 56 per cent of the blue collar workers were more oriented towards democratisation of work culture in that they wanted more control over their work and working conditions. In Sweden, the culture of public debate about industrial democracy was a very significant issue in public life. Not only the trade unions, news media and political forums, but the common men and women have also been showing immense interest in the matter of day-to-day running of work organisations. A public opinion poll in 1969 showed that 72 per cent of all Swedes believed that there was a great need for increased employee influence in decision-making in industrial organisations. Even the younger generation, teenagers, for example, were interested in the issue. In more recent years, the dropouts from the school system in Norway joining the operating ships have further focused attention on the quality of work-life indicating that it was not just a problem of industrial or commercial organisation but also of the school system; in fact, all learning/working systems.

The Indian experience, however limited in number, does indicate that it is possible to establish a culture of industrial democracy even in a large pluralistic society. This is evident from the case of the postman or that of the unskilled worker located in a place surrounded by the tradition of the holy Hindu pilgrimage. Even in a traditional Hindu pilgrimage centre like Hardwar, responsive behaviour was generated as a sequel to a nurturing organisational milieu and not because of transfer of technology. This points to an inner urge the workers had, to get some meaning out of their own day-to-day work experience. Some of the spontaneous projects on new forms of work organisation further support this contention.

It is necessary, however, to mention certain distinguishing features of Indian experiences which could act as a pointer to the pervasive character of Indian culture.

(a) The vital role of interpersonal competence of the external consultant while working with the 'leading parts' of the experimental sites is common experience. Trade union leaders would not, for example, be as much influenced by the researcher's scholastic ability as by his ability to establish a relationship with them. It is the same case with the managerial system;

(b) Interpersonal competence, however, can get compromised by the dependence culture. There is a tendency to depend increasingly on the external consultant, even in the initiation and the stabilisation phases and certainly in the diffusion phase. Two major exceptions, of course, are the Tiruchirapalli case and the Central Foundry Forge of Bharat Heavy Electricals;

(c) There are cases where the external consultant has not been required to play a crucial role because of the interpersonal trust generated by the internal consultants. Trust apart, this also reflects the hierarchy-based dependence on authority figures. A typical example is that of the income-tax department;

(*d*) In the matter of developing autonomy for group functioning, most of the groups have found it necessary to depend on an authority figure for ideas and direction. To a certain extent, however, this is on account of the traditionally passive role played by the rank and file workers in the work system, further complicated by the lack of requisite flow of information to them. Developing collective norms on the premise of superordinate goals is a long struggling process. The organisation culture strongly supported by the culture of the larger social system is undoubtedly oriented towards dependence on superordinate persons or force.

These elements can be a reflection of the cultural heritage, or a product of the hierarchical, bureaucratic organisational ethos. Stabilisation of the process initiated by new forms of work organisation and its diffusion, whether it is in Scandinavia or in countries like France, Holland and Italy, do not necessarily throw up any findings to the effect that the tradition of Indian culture is a significantly hindering force.

We have had occasion to discuss Indian cases with some of the internal change agents in early December 1976, and these interactions have brought out certain elements, somewhat common amongst the cases reported. These are presented in a tabular form (Table 1.6).

Table 1.6
Dynamics of Development of New Forms of Work Organisation

Phase Stage	Essential Characteristics	Remarks
I Hostility	This is a stage where despite preliminary explorations, discussions and clarifications sought and offered, when the experiment begins, there is a feeling amongst employees irrespective of their positions and roles, that the experiment is a motivated one, conditioned by the management's desire to gain and the researcher's desire to conduct the research in order to publish. Internal consultants are seen as motivated by career considerations.	
	High degree of selective perception of failure cases not necessarily related to new forms of work organisation experiments but other past efforts to bring about any change—technological or otherwise—in the system. Success cases are not remembered or mentioned.	
	Depending on the dynamics of the situation in most Indian cases, this phase has been operating covertly. Overt expression of hostility has often come from isolated individuals.	
	There is hardly any sign of inquisitiveness to know more about the experiments to establish non-hierarchical organisational values.	

II	Reluctance	During this stage some degree of curiosity develops amongst the members but no visible symbol of commitment. Some cues are available that a few persons involved in the experiment feel that something is possible and some changes for the better can be established.	

Positive leaders among the experimental groups do play an important role in this phase as well as in the earlier phase.

III	Guarded commitment and indifference	During this stage, a substantial number show interest in what is happening, seeking data, taking initiative in group discussion, offering suggestions while the majority still remain indifferent. Indifference is more passive compared to the two earlier stages of hostility and as a feeling of ambivalence in not being sure whether they are getting into a better work situation than before.

IV	Inter-group dynamics	During this stage, an interesting dynamic develops between the experimental group and other non-experimental groups in the organisation. Something of a Hawthorne effect in terms of attention received provides, on the one hand, an in-group feeling to the experimental site and, on the other, a feeling of jealousy and some amount of hostility often expressed by way of jokes and caustic comments by the other groups.

During this phase as well as during phase V, it was found in the post offices that the functional conflict developed between the post man and clerks combined and the sub-postmaster, the authority figure.

V	Positive interest	This is a stage where, on the one hand, in-group feeling has brought some degree of stability to the experimental group and, on the other, some internal dynamics go on in terms of a power struggle regarding the experimental scheme at times aggravated by caste and regional considerations, factional in-fighting between sub-groups with negative attitudes and those with positive attitudes and others who are in-between.

The positive groups, however, acquire more visibility because they now take more active interest and gradually take the control functions in the autonomous groups.

VI	Isolation of negative elements	During this stage, the majority are already committed to the experiment having experienced some positive gains, if not on all the six criteria spelled out by the Emerys, but at least on some of the key criteria such as variety of job, meaningfulness, social support, challenge, autonomy, and evolving norms for the group.

The isolates are the negative elements who, depending on how the majority treat them, either indicate withdrawal of a passive kind or personal hostility. By and large, however, the group settles down to work out the operational details of the scheme at this stage.

VII   Interaction and interlinkage with other experimental groups and organisations

This is a stage when an experimental group takes initiative in looking outwards, seeks to compare notes and experiences with similar other groups. This phase becomes a potential force for the diffusion process.

While the phases outlined in Table 1.6 could be overlapping and were by no means the logical sequence in all the cases reported, these phases appear to highlight the dynamics as perceived by the internal consultants, which sometimes the external consultants could not identify.

Three aspects, however, appear from the Indian cases to be vital. If the employees of an organisation are highly frustrated and the organisation itself has a strong negative image, creating new forms of work organisation is somewhat more complicated. Inputs of planned, multi-dimensional but specific reward structures would be an important requirement here. Secondly, should the jobs in an organisation provide opportunities for resorting to corrupt practices, the resistance to developing new forms of work organisation would be stronger. This is often not perceived by external or internal consultants because the reality of corruption cannot be openly explored. Thirdly, the visibility of sequential stages of success is an important factor in gathering momentum. The Hardwar case, the Chaura Maidan Post Office case and the Tiruchirapalli case indicate that the feedback mechanism on some key performance criteria as an ongoing process has been of considerable help in stabilising the projects. Yet another factor is the size of the group. The optimum number depending on the task system could be important. The Engineers India case (not reported in this chapter) indicates that the totality of the group consisting of all employees of the corporate personnel planning group had a tendency to become a sensitivity training group rather than a socio-technical task group with task orientation matched by a corresponding degree of sentience.

As an overall picture, we provide a table (Table 1.7) which will give a visual presentation of some of the key elements in some of the Indian cases.

Concluding Comments

We shall conclude the chapter by paying attention to some selective aspects of our experience in India with new forms of work organisation. These aspects are, by no means, the only ones that matter nor are they necessarily the most critical. However, in the context of the experiences in other countries and the lack of clarity that persists about the search for institutions and new forms of work organisation, these items are relevant. We shall touch upon select macro issues as well.

1. Campbell (1976), while discussing the measurement of the quantum of happiness of people in a society, made a distinction based on research experiences, between objective indicators and subjective indicators. He stipulated that one could make a distinction between 'happiness' and 'well-being' and his preference is for the term 'well-being'. He surveyed the psychological researches in the work of Cantril, who developed a 'self-anchoring scale to get an overall picture of the reality worlds in which people live'; the affective balance approach of Bradburn where subjective experiences of daily life are studied; and the psychological and emotional stress studies by Gurin and others. Based on this survey Campbell, along with his colleagues, developed criteria for identifying the major dimensions of the experience of well-being.

   These studies present a complex picture and there are findings to show that

   > people living in different life circumstances express different patterns of well-being and that these patterns reflect the peculiar quality of the situation they live in. It is not surprising to find, for example, that positive affect is lacking in the lives of the widows and that stress characterises the lives of mothers of young children.

   Campbell has also referred to Rensis Likert's observation that statistical enquiries are capable of producing information about the *nature of a system* as well as the *state of a system*. For the purpose of developing criteria for the measurement of well-being and the objectives of purposeful institutions, it is necessary to generate adequate valid information about both.

   Researches, reflecting on what Campbell has done, do not, however, measure up to the gestalt that represents the third world countries. Productivity criteria, although somewhat undermined by the criticisms of gross national product strategy and trickle-down effect strategy, are still predominant. The concept of surplus has a magic halo around it. The productivity orientation of an enterprise is, perhaps, the single largest factor in undertaking experiments with new forms of work organisation. The objective and subjective criteria of efficacy, well-being and the quality of life are still somewhat romantic concepts. The element of romance is not irrelevant in that the software variables are not looked upon with hostility nor are they perceived as unnecessary. At the technical level there may be some difficulty in clarifying what the concept of 'well-being' implies but, more importantly, experimental organisations have so far not succeeded in establishing a meaningful linkage between the productivity criteria and the human criteria of well-being. That the productivity concept could become a viable instrumental value with quality of life criteria as measuring terminal values, provided that a genuinely participative design mechanism was adopted, is still wide off the mark. Goals have not yet projected themselves to purposes and to ideals and the practice of freedom has not yet been conceived of as the development of critical consciousness, free from the bondage of repressive myths and the culture of silence.

A perception of themselves as a part of what Trist (1976) described as organisational ecology—an active environment conceived of in terms of inter-active organisation systems—and a meaningful interlinkage with them is still lacking in the experimental organisations. In the organisational ecology sense, therefore, there is the dysfunctional reality of encapsulated existence and as such the productivity criteria continue to dominate the scene.

Poverty and other problems that affect a typical third world country need not prevent organisation designers from seeking a meaningful interlinkage of one problem with another, thereby recreating in their minds the not-so-visible objective reality of man at work in a social context.

Only in the Hardwar case has the movement taken some steps to seek information about the state of the system by measuring the quality of work-life, the quality of family life and the quality of community life and the dynamics of their interaction.

2. Yet another aspect of the Indian reality seems to be the inability to utilise, to the best advantage, the range of search mechanisms. The experiments that have been carried out in the offices or in production shops are still somewhat hamstrung by structural limitations, as a hangover of the hierarchical system. The Hardwar experiment started with what Kahn (1974) calls the 'work module'. The modular approach, as adopted at Hardwar, seems to have conditioned several

other experimental sites and there is a lurking feeling that this may be on account of the reluctance to search for other alternatives. No doubt, there are cases reported where individual job enrichment has been highlighted more than autonomous group functioning, but that too, is a transfer of technology from the copybook of Herzberg. While it may be unfair to expect that Volvo-type innovation in work organisation should have emerged in the Indian reality, one could expect that the spirit of innovation in designing a work system in a children's school, *Shishu Vihar* (Rao, 1976A) could be more productively explored in different situations.

3. The third element about the Indian experiences is what Herbst (1976A) has called the Scenario Concept of Diffusion. Using the ideas generated by Herbst, Thorsrud (1976) has examined the likely impact of the new laws on work environment adopted in the Scandinavian countries. He believes that while the technocratic scenario and a sociocratic scenario do not have much chance of success, the bureaucratic scenario, despite the industrial democracy spirit that exists in these countries, may assert itself in preference to the local community scenario. While one should take Thorsrud's apprehension seriously, the Indian reality appears to lie between the technocratic scenario and the bureaucratic scenario or perhaps an admixture of both. The local community scenario, the best that new forms of work organisation movement can so far offer, is still in an embryonic stage in India.

Many progressive legislative and executive measures, even in developing a new interface between civil servants and the public, are conceived of in bureaucratic terms. Administrative reform measures, which have assumed particular significance and urgency in India's accelerated developmental strategy still see the above-discussed innovations in work organisation as marginal. In that context, whether the Chaura Maidan Post Office experiment or that at Kalkaji will be a strong contender as an alternative is still in question.

4. By and large the Scandinavian countries and Australia have adopted, in recent years, a network strategy for diffusion of organisation innovation even though this has not been easy. Despite the ups and downs, the new concepts stress a lessening dependence on external consultants or researchers and an increasing interaction among the experimental units; each learning from the other. This pattern of mutual help will not necessarily completely replace the external consultants but will certainly change their role drastically.

Looking at the Indian reality, this option seems promising. The researchers who have been active since 1973, are steadily re-examining and evaluating their roles vis-à-vis the internal consultants and the active participants in projects are gradually making it possible for them to take charge of the projects by way of diagnosing, designing, implementing, evaluating and then taking charge of the process of recycling.

There is, however, an emerging danger. The quality of work-life movement is fast acquiring the value of a new fashion, almost like what happened to organisation development in the 1960s and still happening to the transactional analysis movement. In the process, consultants' motivation, capability and values might stand in the way of the organic evolution of a network strategy.

5. In India, where the macro policies are almost exclusively in the hands of Government, the policy relevance of new forms of work organisation is still not clear. The more perceptive among the policy-makers are concerned about the social transformation process. But in their gestalt, the transformation process is primarily a structural problem; the configuration of the structure does not always figure in their strategy. To give an example, these perceptive policy-makers do relate the dynamics of agricultural development to production relations in the rural community, which is linked to the reality of land holdings, dynamics of exchange between services rendered and rewards received, the credit structure and socio-cultural disabilities. However, even though they recognise this cascading interlinkage of various realities, when it comes to action steps, most of them succumb to the bureaucratic model of legislative reforms and creation of executive agencies to be monitored by certain hierarchical control agencies. They do honestly believe that this process can succeed, a major assumption being that this bureaucratic structure could generate a meaningful *interactive process* as opposed to a dialectic of *reactive processes*. Ackoff (1974) has shown with empirical evidence that the interactive process is a matter of designing alternatives in a participative form rather than the creation of a legislative measure or executive fiat.

It is not evident yet whether India will draw appropriate lessons from the new movement that has started with experiments on alternative forms of work organisation. This challenge, however, is not peculiar to India. The challenge is equally real for all countries including the affluent ones, but the cost of negligence in deriving appropriate lessons from history, is likely to be more tragic for the third world countries than for others, even though in terms of human suffering one would not seek to make a distinction between a suffering man in a hamlet in Georgia or in a village in Palamau in India.

In the end, one submission may be made. The question of quality of life is as ancient as recorded history. In the Greek city states, for example, the concept of quality of life was deliberated upon by philosophers but it was based on the foundation of the institution of slavery. Slavery is indeed an object of universal condemnation today and its existence is perhaps a rare phenomenon. Nonetheless, the issue of the quality of life as a super-structure is premised on the quality of work-life as a major structural property of work organisation. This dialectic of structure-superstructure retains its character all the while although the rhetoric of polemics may have changed over the years.

In the early 1930s, Antonio Gramsci (1973) while deliberating on the consequences of Taylorism, observed that 'quality should be attributed to men, not to things; and human quality is raised and refined to the extent that man can satisfy a greater number of needs and thus make himself independent of them.' The concern for the 'human content' of work led him to the far-sighted vision of the 'collective worker' and the factory council. In a similar vein, almost after half-a-century, Herbst (1974) has declared that 'the product of work is people'. His other observation, verbally conveyed to us that 'the learning system should be work-oriented and the work system should be learning-oriented', dramatically sums up the on-going quest for new systems of work-design that can energise men and women to strive for higher ideals, without which human beings will remain mere instruments of production.

We wish to mention here some basic challenges that confront the action researchers in the movement of the quality of work-life. The logic of the hierarchical, bureaucratic forms of work organisations and their inability to jointly optimise the technical system and the social system of work have been well documented by the western researchers engaged in the movement (Cherns, 1979; Emery, 1977; Emery, *et al*, 1978; Klein, 1976A, 1976B; Herbst, 1974, 1976A, etc.). Some of them have also offered the ways out of the bind (Emery, 1970, 1976C; O'Toole, 1974; Emery and Thorsrud, 1976; Duncan, *et al*, 1980; I.L.O., 1979, 1980; Coates, *et al*, 1972; Unit for Industrial Democracy, 1978; Foster, *et al*, 1970; Jenkins, 1981; Trist, 1981, etc.).

We may draw a broad distinction here. Some students of the theme have rooted their alternatives in the micro context of an organisation system. The larger politico-economic and socio-cultural environmental forces have been taken as given by them. The ideas contained in Duncan, *et al* (1980), Jenkins (1981), Cherns (1977) and the East European projects (I.L.O., 1979, 1980) reflect this mode of thought. Some others (e.g., Emery, 1977; Trist, 1981; Unit for Industrial Democracy, 1978; Parts Two, Nine and Ten; and Coates, *et al*, 1972) have touched upon the larger though not-so-comfortable issues. One need not undervalue the contributions of the first group. Democratic functioning of an organisation may lead to sensitising the employees to the societal problems. One may, however, add that with few exceptions, even the members of the second group have failed to grasp the stark realities of the politico-economic dimensions of the organisational society of the first and the second worlds. The social scientists from the second world countries are keen observers of the structural flaws of the capitalist system. At the same time, they maintain an assiduous silence about the rigid bureaucratised caste structure that their societies have devised in managing human organisations. A similar myopic vision is manifested among the action researchers in the first world. In the contemporary world, many social system designers have failed to comprehend the import of Reaganomics and Thatcherism in presenting their organisational alternatives.

The basic issue of managing the labour process in the management of an enterprise and an economy as voiced by Braverman (1974) is as relevant to the capitalist economy as the centrally planned economies, although the dimensions of the problem do differ in details. It is observed that similar social insensitivity is present in India among those who are engaged in the QWL movement. The political-economy of systems operation has so far remained beyond their range of interests.

2

Organising and Mobilising: Some Building Blocks of Rural Work Organisations

Common sense and historical experience combine to suggest a simple but compelling view of the roots of power in any society. Crudely but clearly stated, those who control the means of producing wealth, have power over those who do not. This much is true whether the means of coercion consists in the primitive force of warrier caste or the technological force of a modern army. And it is true whether the control of production consists in control by priests of the mysteries of the calendar on which agriculture depends, or control by financiers of the large-scale capital on which industrial production depends. Since coercive force can be used to gain control of the means of producing wealth, and since control of wealth can be used to gain coercive force, these two sources of power tend over time to be drawn together within one ruling class.

Piven and Cloward (1979)

The previous chapter described the organisation design changes which were initiated by social scientists as action-researchers. Study and change were co-determined through the mediation of active participation of organisational actors. This chapter deals with organisations which were designed by the actors themselves reminding us that social scientists can learn from purposeful doers.

Our insights into systems of human organisations and theories so built have largely arisen from military, industrial, commercial, service, governmental and supranational entities.

While the process of building theories is going on and empirically based refinements are taking shape, certain other changes are simultaneously taking place acquiring significance for improving people's life and their organisations. In the third world, in the wake of political independence, the usual developmental strategies had been adopted, the basic limitations and contradictions of which started surfacing in the 1960s. Since then, there is a visible emergence of alternative forms of organisations based on different premises of future-oriented, socially desirable models of change. In the richer countries of the world, too, there is evidence of a growing counter-culture in search of alternative models of organisation system (Kanter, 1973; Trist, 1979). In all parts of the world, thus, the search for alternatives is on to interconnect two premises: one relates to *forms* of organisations, and, the other to the *ideals orientation* propelling these organisations. The experiences accumulated in this process can provide further insights leading to identification of new elements for developing a corpus of organisation theories.

In our search for identification of these new elements, we intend to introduce an element of distinction. Ideally, we would like to isolate the establishment-sponsored organisations which somehow or other are thought to be influenced by the interests of the powers-that-be. Such isolation, however, for the purpose of our analysis may not be an *easy task*. A polity may be dedicated to a radical alternative redesign of core human sub-systems. In such a situation the twin objectives of new forms and the desire to realise socially desirable ideals through organisational experiments, though officially sponsored and/or encouraged, will not be irrelevant for our purpose. An example is provided by Guinea Bissau (Freire, 1978). The post-revolutionary character of the officialdom of this country is somewhat distinct from the bureaucratic ethos of many other countries which gained independence *through negotiations or struggle*. However, there are other evidences that such an optimistic promise may not be substantiated in many cases. Even though the picture is somewhat unclear, the recent developments in the People's Republic of China provide a *lurking* apprehension that the development-oriented state-sponsored organisations may be resorting to the beaten track *type* of organisation design (M.R., 1978, 1979; *Asia Year Book*, 1982).

Our attention will, therefore, be focused on voluntary and non-governmental *type* organisations even though an all-comprehensive concept of voluntary organisations may not be *useful*. There are voluntary organisations which have sprung up in support of the *status-quo-ante* and, as such, are not future oriented or else are purported to reverse the march of history by weakening the already established institutionally valid social purposes (some obvious examples are the Ku Klux Klan in parts of the USA and some obscurantist organisations in India seeking to shake the secular base of the politico-social fabric). Therefore, we shall be selective in pursuing our objective while using voluntary organisations from rural settings for study.

Organising, Mobilising and Movement

One feature of voluntary organisations that deserves attention is the source of their origin and sponsorship. We shall examine the issues that motivate them to undertake such a project and the underlying interests, goals and ideals.

In other words, we conceive that the *organising process* is the first step in the formation of a voluntary organisation depending on the awareness of the issues at stake calling for such an effort. Awareness is just not an ingredient of the personality variable of the founding actors. It is the awareness of reality, subjective and objective, as well as the reflective and tentative conclusions emanating from it. Awareness affects the leaders' behaviour in the form of positive tactical moves or counter-moves. Awareness or consciousness of the reality can either be theme-based but inadequately related to the socio-political nexus, or adequately related to it. In a development-type organisation it is easy to take up a theme such as mitigation of poverty at the grassroots level without taking into account the forces which generate, foster and stabilise poverty. The leadership orientation will be one-dimensional if consciousness operates in a narrow focus. On the other hand, if consciousness is a *becoming process* then it can extend the appreciative capacity which will get reflected in a change of tactics as well as strategy.

The organising process encompasses members as well. A primary issue is how the leaders look upon their constituents. If members of a voluntary organisation are taken as followers, then the leadership style will tend towards a directive organisation. If, on the other hand, they are perceived as colleagues, then it is likely to emerge as something of an egalitarian organisation. This distinction is important because a developmental organisation's viability and efficacy will depend upon the emergence of societal consciousness which Etzioni (1968) defines as an aggregation of the member's individual consciousness. This is particularly so if the organisation's task is to alter the political framework of the societal structure. It is the collective consciousness that can locate the chinks in the armour of power configuration and make an assessment of favourable and unfavourable elements. This has an implication for our second building block, namely, the mobilising process which we shall deal with later on.

The organising process, however, involves at least in the initial phase another dimension, namely, identification of the 'leading parts' among the extended organisers. Initially, leadership may remain confined to a few, or it may include those who are otherwise peripheral in the existing power hierarchy but are nonetheless significant in their own sub-set or reference group. In a typical Indian village, members of outcaste groups and tribals, though physically isolated and distinctly economically backward, have, nonetheless, their own horizontal homogeneity with their accepted leaders. Whether these leaders, at the formative stage, are treated as leading actors in the organising process or not will determine the form that the leadership will take—i.e., an elitist form or an egalitarian one. In short, a degree of consciousness with unique properties exists at the periphery.

On the basis of this analysis, our next contention is that consciousness need not precede collective action. Some form of collective action can contribute to a further sharpening of consciousness. Consciousness and concrete action have a circular flow adding quality to each. This aspect is important because, during the organising process, what is sought are alternative courses for action—and the search for alternatives can become more effective if the founding actors are composed of the leading parts. This is a crucial test for a rural voluntary organisation.

Mobilisation is what is embedded in the organising process. Mobilisation is just not an attempt to redistribute the existing assets and liabilities but also to generate fresh opportunities (creating new assets) as well as to achieve more clarity about the ideals guiding action in the operational sense. Mobilisation, as Etzioni points out, is one way of overcoming the dangers of organisational entropy. As such, mobilisation is a continuing process which leads to a dynamic concept of the organising process as well. We conceive mobilisation in a concrete form in the concept of *movement*. A movement may be transitory in the sense of embarking upon specific action to rectify a wrong or to establish a new configuration of base to attain a specific goal. If that is the objective, then a movement can peter out in the logic of entropy law as often happens in an insensitive societal system with various types of *protest* movements. At best it can achieve a symbolic gain. On the other hand, achievement of a proximate objective can fortify an organisation to extend its horizon of objectives and keep a movement alive. It is also possible that, from the initial stage, a movement can aim at larger objectives and from the beginning its strategy may be the attainment of successive goals which are conceivable in the context of an ascending order of interests, goals and ideals. An approach, such as this, will again be reflected in the organising process itself. The initial process of organising will need to undergo a structural change in the style of working and change of tactics and strategy. There is thus a recycling of mobilising and organising at higher reaches of achievement.

The impact of a movement on the organising process will be determined by the characteristics of the movement itself. The kind of mix that a movement displays in its utilitarian component, coercive component and collective component (Etzioni, 1968) is pertinent. There cannot be any fixed ratio among the three variables, but one point is evident that the more the coercive component within an organisation and the less the normative component, the more it is likely to cause a movement to degenerate and the organising efforts to weaken.

Let us now revert to the dynamics of the organising process. Weick (1969) sought to understand this process in terms of internal and external dynamics. Internally, he believes that the purpose of an organising process consists in resolving elements of uncertainty and unpredictability in an environment by means of what he calls 'inter-locked behaviour'. Inter-locked behaviour refers to the inter-dependence of actors involved whereby consistency of reciprocity, repetitiveness and adaptability in order to deal with non-programmed challenges can be established. We submit that this aspect is indeed important because a 'collective' will emerge from a state of diffusiveness among members, to a state flexible in structure which understands and complements one another and leads to a consistent and yet dynamic pattern of behavioural responses. We also suggest that for this to happen the perception of interests, goals and ideals of each actor should be the starting point for mobilising psychic energy for the immediate task. The immediate task should be seen to be based as much on ideals as on the characteristics of the environment. Weick's definition of an 'enacted environment' does not adequately describe what we are looking for in a voluntary organisation which has the twin objectives of new forms and socially-oriented purposes for a target group which is as much the initiator as also the potential beneficiary of that action.

It is relevant to recall that we have drawn a distinction between the organising and mobilisation processes as reflected in a movement. The mobilising process will offer a more comprehensive base for the realisation of goals and sharpen the consciousness about emerging ideals. The organising process, on the other hand, is essentially directed towards the actors who are the core of the movement. With this distinction in mind, we believe that the environment for the type of organisations we have in view can be described as *experienced environment*. Experience is subjective but when the organising process leads to a collective reflection of experiences, it cannot go further unless it also acquires an objective reality. Exploration and experimentation are the two among various interventions through which the world of experienced environment can acquire greater salience. In our view, *experienced environment* takes into account the politico-legal structures in the totality of their favourable and unfavourable components.

To make it more explicit, in an under-developed country like India the powers-that-be are not actually a comprehensive, monolithic, homo-geneous entity. There are internal contradictions within them. It is possible to take advantage of these diversities and contradictions. As our cases will show, it is possible to use governmental intervention selectively in favour of a movement rather than dogmatically rejecting all the forces which are 'identified' with a hostile power structure. There are allies, at least potentially. Certain rules, regulations and procedures can well be converted into favourable forces provided the reflection on *experienced environment* operates effectively (De, 1979A).

This leads to yet another dimension. Organisers have the option of setting their eyes on a fixed goal or if unguarded, as the process goes on evolving, they may be led to the other extreme of the diffusion of goals resulting in peripheral action. We suggest that much will depend upon the internal process of inter-dependence to avoid both extremes and instead the organisers can persistently explore the prospect of goal extension. Goal extension is a non-linear concept and yet, not to lose the potency of coherence, it is to operate within a network of ideals.

Internal consistency is conceivable provided there is flexibility of operation within the organisation structure. There is an option between 'absorption of protest' and the 'domestication of dissent' (Thomas and Bennis, 1972:19). The diversity of views articulated vigorously or otherwise has to be dealt with in a manner that does not discourage members or cause disaffection among them. There is a danger that one seeks to hear a counter-view in order to ignore it. That approach will gradually weaken the decision base. The other way will be to incorporate the protest in a manner that internal cliques do not get formed to the extent that they can lead to goal diffusion or goal fixation. For the type of organisation that we have in mind, this is particularly relevant because there is a major challenge to organisation redesign to prevent the assertion of authority-based hierarchy and bureaucratic impersonalisation of roles and norms. Indeed, there is a need for norms and consensus but the difference that we suggest lies in the quality and nuances of the consensus building process. The ultimate touchstone of building such a decision-making structure is allocation of priority to goals which are consistent with the ideals rather than the domination of preferences of interests of the engaged personalities.

Let us now summarise this section in a schematic form. Table 2.1 is an illustrative approach to what we visualise as the emergence of socially relevant voluntary organisations. In this context, let us now turn to the cases.

Table 2.1

Interaction between the Organising Process and the Mobilising Process

Organising Process ⟵⟶	Mobilising Process
*leadership motivation, values and styles of operation	*t*
*clarifying goals and ideals	*h*
*consciousness-raising while exploring goals and ideals	*r* *o* *u* *g* *h*
*tactics and strategy to determine target groups and approach to them	*Movement*
*assessment of experienced environment (scanning and reflecting)	*emerging objectives
*membership characteristics	*time perspective for specific action/ actions
*participation mechanisms	*flexibility and adaptability in assessing the adverse environment
*matching interests, goals and ideals of members	*handling of external actors (potential allies)
*dealing with differences and dissent	*evaluation of incipient norms and controls
	*developing sensitivity to the organisers' internal style of operation

Next Phase

*ensuring revitalisation of the organisation process (awareness of entropy law)	*dealing with emerging opposing/ supporting forces and resource creation
*mobility of leadership	*relating accumulated experience to strategic objectives
*charisma and organisation metaphors	*extension of target base
*expanding consciousness about internal and external reality	*stabilisation and consolidation of gains
*movement towards goal extension	
*experimentation with organisation forms and designs	

Next Phase

*qualitative changes in the forms and content of organising process on dimensions listed above	*the process moves forward instead of repeating itself

The Cases

We shall confine ourselves to five cases, four from India and one from Bangladesh with a passing reference to one from Pakistan. It is not our intent to go into details but to focus on the characteristics of the organising and mobilising processes in order to clarify our understanding of the alternative forms of work organisation.

A. CHIPKO MOVEMENT
(Mishra and Tripathi, 1978; Mishra, 1979)

The locale of the Chipko movement is the Himalayan forest area of Uttar Pradesh around the region of Uttar Kashi. The movement of the forest people had its beginning in the 1960s. These hill people are simple, straightforward and most of them unexposed to modern education. They are poor and traditionally dependent on forest products.

The process of indiscriminate felling of trees had been going on for a long time to secure timber for construction and furniture making, and for such purposes as preparation of herbal medicines and toiletries. The deforestation process accelerated considerably in the wake of the China–India war in 1962. Development of an all-weather road became a strategic necessity in this difficult terrain. Felling of trees became easier. Contractors came in a big way and while skilled labour was being brought from outside, a local youth was employed at a pittance of Rs. 1.50 to 2.00 per day for unskilled work including the movement of heavy logs of wood. Not everybody got employment.

At this juncture, some young men of the newly-created Chamoli district got together with the initial objective of providing jobs to the local youth. They were led by C.P. Bhatt, a local man, who gave up his job in a transport company in order to concentrate on the organising process. The first effort was to persuade the local contractors and the public works department of the government to give labour contract jobs to their cooperative. The Malla Nagpur Cooperative Labour Society with thirty permanent and 700 temporary members came into existence. Initially there was some response and those who were employed could be paid double the wages earlier earned by them. Pretty soon they realised that without official patronage it was not easy for them to get contracts even though their tenders were lower. Secondly, the income would be more if they could develop skills. So another organisation, the Dashauli Gram Swarajya Sangh was set up to establish small workshops for making wooden and iron implements to meet the local demand. Some young men were sent by the Sangh to the nearby trades training school to acquire the necessary skills. Business started trickling in. However, while involved in these two organisations, they realised that another source of exploitation is the monopoly business of some traders in collecting wild herbs used for making drugs for diabetes, heart ailments, local cosmetics and tooth powder. They conducted a survey in 1969 and the findings were that the traders could make large profits from metropolitan markets. They turned their attention to this problem by setting up a small rural factory for making resin and turpentine from pine sap known as lisa. They organised marketing channels in some of the trading centres. At this point, the

Khadi and Village Industries Commission (KVIC), a central government enterprise, came to the help of these enterprising groups and assisted them with grants, loan and working capital.

These planned activities, coordinated by Bhatt and a few committed colleagues started the process of horizontal mobilisation among the local people for whom all these are not only money-earning propositions but also a way of coming closer to one another.

A natural calamity took place in 1970. An unprecedented Himalayan flood swept over the area. The bridges were washed away, at least 55 persons lost their lives and 142 heads of cattle were drowned. The groups started reflecting on this calamity instead of blaming destiny for the event. Reflection led to the conviction that the destruction of soil was caused by sapping the forest wealth and that the forest had to be preserved in a planned manner. They wanted the felling of trees to operate under a forest policy controlling and guiding the contractors and the forest officials motivated by narrow interests. This is where the major obstruction came from—the forest department and the organised contractors.

The Chamoli block was the first target. Simon and Company won the auction bid for the villages around Gopeswar and came in to fell the trees. The local organised labour decided on 'non-cooperation' with the company. A series of meetings were held where the concrete facts of miseries of the local people were brought home linking these to the need for preserving the forest wealth. The resolution was that if the contractor wanted to fell the ash trees, their axes would have to fall first on the local people who would cling to the trees marked for felling to protect them. Thus the Chipko movement was born in 1973. The collective resistance of the entire population of the area forced the contractor to withdraw, thus creating a confrontative situation with the lower as well as higher authorities of the forest department.

The authorities went in for a contingency plan by allocating, to the same company, another forest at Phata, 80 kms away from Gopeswar. News travelled fast and thus the Chipko movement was carried to the Phata area. The same organising process—a series of consciousness-raising meetings and demonstrations—was used and it attracted the attention of the local leftist political leaders. The Chipko group did not join any political party but welcomed cooperation on the 'save the forest' campaign of all political parties interested in the movement. Even in the Phata area, the contractor failed to get the trees cut. The next move was at Reni near the Tibet border. Although news of the success of the movement in other areas had travelled to Reni as well, but that was not enough. Bhatt and another friend who joined the movement, Bahuguna, started organising the people at Reni as 2,451 trees were branded for felling by the forest authorities. Response from the local people was favourable.

The movement had already drawn the attention of the state headquarters at Lucknow. Some saw it somewhat sympathetically while others saw it as a potential political threat in the sensitive hilly areas. Bhatt, Bahuguna and other leaders were called in, persuasive discussions went on and committees were set up to examine the problem and submit reports to the government. The Chipko leaders presented their case this way. They were not against the felling of trees. For various development purposes it was a necessity. However, in the name of development of this backward region with inputs of roads, schools, primary health centres and so on, they did not want to barter away the forest wealth. They wanted development to take shape around the forest as the centre-piece. For that to happen, they required schemes which would break the stranglehold of irresponsible contractors under the patronage of various governmental agencies. They conceded that, for highly technical projects, specialised contract firms were indeed needed. However, they gave primary importance to the renovation of destroyed forests and preservation of soil. In principle, the higher authorities accepted these suggestions but, in effect, the practice was quite to the contrary. The Chipko activists gradually grew disillusioned with the Committee report and recommendations and abandoned collaboration in a mood of disgust.

As it is now referred to, 'the finest hour of the Reni women' came when one day all the men of the area were called away to the nearest town for certain payments due to them for an earlier acquisition of their land. That was the day when the contractor decided to launch the assault on the forest. A little girl saw a group of outside contract labourers with their axes stealthily moving in the village. She ran to Gaura Devi, a matronly woman of the village. She knew about the Chipko movement and its tactics to protect trees through having attended some of the meetings. She raised a hue and cry and, initially, twenty-one women and seven little girls came and confronted these contract labourers. They tried to persuade the labourers to understand their problem in its totality, but these people refused to take the women seriously and dismissed the rationale of the Chipko movement. They were determined to carry out their assignment. The women then turned to the marked trees and simultaneously sent a message to the village for other women to join. The hired labourers were dumb-founded when they found the women clinging to the trees. They did not know what they should do—specially when the women asserted that, short of killing them and the little girls, no single tree could be cut. Now the contract labour could understand the intensity of feelings as reflected in the determination and unfaltered collective expression of the women. The labourers turned tail and they came, pursued by the women, to a point where there was a stone connecting the two sides of a stream. The women collectively dislodged the stone thereby snapping the link with the targeted part of the forest. Thus the labourers were isolated from the area concerned. Meanwhile, someone took a bus to the town to inform the men as to what was happening. The latter rushed back to find that the women had performed a 'miracle'.

This time the government took the movement more seriously and an expert committee with some outsiders was asked to look into the forest policy for the area. The Chipko movement representatives were associated with this project. In the meanwhile, the voice of Chipko reached Almora district. Young students started taking more and more interest in the movement and they offered to help in eradicating the age-old exploitative practice of felling precious pine trees and illegal lisa tapping. In Almora, the interest of a big paper mill which held the forest lease had to be abandoned because of strong collective resistance. The anniversary of the Chipko movement continues to be celebrated throughout the region so as to keep the spirit alive and to spread the message among more and more people including boys and girls. In a way they were fortunate in several critical stages of the movement when ugly confrontative situations were saved by sympathetic and tactful handling by the heads of the district administration.

The movement started a new phase in 1975 with a mass afforestation drive in the area. The cooperatives first paid for and planted 9,000 trees on the vulnerable hill slopes with voluntary labour. At another place, in Almora district, another 6,000 trees were planted. Around Gauna lake, 35 kms away from Gopeswar, which was the scene of devastating floods in 1970, 4,000 willow cuttings were planted. As per the Expert Committee Report, 1,200 sq. kms around Reni forest was declared as protected. Thus the movement that started at Gopeswar in the early 1960s reached a stage where protection of forest in a limited way became a reality.

The future is, however, unpredictable because one cannot be sure of the State government forest policy as the revenue from felled trees is an attractive proposition to the forest authorities. The modernised version of development as conceived in physical targets of roads, buildings and multiplicity of government agencies may indeed get preference over the preservation of the forest. On the other hand, the concerted Chipko movement has raised the level of consciousness of the people in protecting forests in their collective interest. It is interesting to observe that the organising process in the form of productive cooperatives did not take a monolithic organisation design but a series of them came up for different purposes and in different areas. At the time, the resistance was organised in the form of a movement not confining it to one area but spreading it out into the region. Women were never directly involved but their participation in the meetings even as passive listeners seemed to have raised their consciousness in a constructive and effective manner. The Reni resistence of the women became an eye-opener to the organisers. Even the children became active members of the movement, benefiting from this experience. Here is a case from which one can observe a number of features:

(a) Immediate economic goals led to an extension of goals proliferating into various activities;

(b) Ascending order of consciousness leading to a conclusion that economic viability, life-style and harmony with nature—practically all aspects of life for the present and future generations—depended on the preservation of soil which was possible by planned effort in cutting the minimum required trees and at the same time, by adopting a planned strategy of afforestation in vulnerable areas;

(c) Deprived of modern mass media, meetings of the people were organised using each hamlet and village as an operation base. Direct contact was made and maintained with the local people. Nobody was ignored. Meetings and demonstrations were not a one-shot operation but a continuing one. The local leaders could be supported in all these full-time activities from the surplus generated by productive co-operatives. There was no need for them to beg for money or to swindle the local people in the name of the movement;

(d) The confrontative model was maintained all through but violence could be avioded. Active violence was replaced by passive 'violence' premised on collective resistance rather than individual acts of heroism;

(e) Only after the movement became a force to reckon with, was selective cooperation extended to different agencies of the government;

(f) Preservation of the forest as an ideal in the collective interest helped them to take support from politically active groups and, as such, the Sarvodaya group could work with the activists of the left-wing political parties. A steadfast faith in the ideal itself could thus bring diverse political interest groups together giving it a pluralistic pattern. This is an indicator of an open systems approach to a protest movement. Dogmatic exclusiveness was eschewed.

B. MAHARASHTRA VILLAGE DEVELOPMENT PROGRAMME
   (I.C.A., 1976, nd; M.V.D.P., 1978)

The Institute of Cultural Affairs is an international voluntary association initially established in the ghetto areas of Chicago. From that beginning it has spread over to different countries in the Americas, Europe, Africa, Asia and Australia. Membership is from different nationalities. The volunteers are, subject to certain national restrictions, able to move from one project to another, from one country to another. The funding sources of this international network are private business, private donations, government, developmental agencies, and mobilised local resources.

Its unit in India is headquartered in Bombay. In 1975, it decided to start integrated rural development programmes in India. There were discussions with the government authorities. Interest was shown by the state of Maharashtra and, at the initiative of the then Chief Minister, the village Maliwada was selected as the first integrated rural development project. Maliwada is located 15 kms away from the town of Aurangabad which over the past decade has been emerging as an industrial centre, apart from being a major tourist attraction because of the historic Ajanta and Ellora caves.

The objective of this integrated rural development scheme is to develop the village through the intervention of training, demonstration and experience generated in improving economic and social conditions of the villagers with the intention of helping them to acquire self-sufficiency and self-reliance. Funds have been mobilised from private business, local and outside, foreign sources and banking institutions, rural development resources earmarked by the state and local people's contributions. The scheme covers all villagers irrespective of their economic and social standing and, as such, it is a case of development within the politico-legal structure and close to the government establishment. It operates on a collaborative model.

The area is located in a semi-arid belt. Soil is usable subject to availability of water resources which are indeed in short supply. On the economic front, attempts have been made to improve the status of agriculture by introducing a high yielding variety of jowar (millet) and provision of water for growing vegetables, wheat and pulses. 40 acres were allotted to sugarcane, yielding 26 tons per acre; 450 acres to hybrid jowar with a yield of 14 quintals per acre. Recently 10 acres have been given to tobacco cultivation. After a house-to-house survey to ascertain the needs of the people, a plan of economic development on appropriate local resource-based technologies was evolved. A series of meetings were held with the local villagers assisted by external change-agents coming from Bombay but living with them for an extended period. Productivity has gone up. Fertilisers, tractors, pump-sets and other inputs have been invested upon.

The village has an association with 11 representatives. Two of them belong to the scheduled castes. Of the population, which has increased from 1,699 in 1976 to 1,898 in 1978, 70 per cent consist of caste Hindus, 30 per cent scheduled castes including 3 Muslim families. 37 per cent of the population are daily labourers, 48 per cent farmers, 14 per cent in private trade and business and the rest in the service and professional sector. A bank branch has been opened with 160 accounts out of about 350 potential accounts. Thus, most of the potential is still unrealised. Before the project, 104 persons were engaged in different types of activities which in 1978 has gone up to 343. The average family income has gone up from Rs. 2,080 to Rs. 4,270 annually since the project was launched.

The village council meets once a week and it has been operating on the basis of developing a scenario of practical vision identifying the steps that can be implemented to use the potential facilities and to overcome the various constraints. To help the local people, a Human Development Training Institute was set up after the programme in the village was launched. The objective of the training programme which is now the central training forum is essentially built around skill development in economic activities, community integration and social improvements in terms of a health care system, education and community welfare. In the matter of economic development there has been no deliberate effort to raise the level of consciousness of the villagers in understanding the forces behind the socio-economic reality of a stagnant rural economy. Consciousness-raising is confined to improvement of knowledge, skills and techniques with a view to raising productivity. There is no exposure to the overall socio-political structure of a typical village in relation to its context (environment).

There have been extension activities in small industries as well. One enterprise is a food processing and packaging unit to manufacture 'sukhdi' biscuits which have a protein content of 13 per cent and are made out of local resources. Each 100 gms packet contains 40 calories and is sold at 27 paise per packet. It has an investment of Rs. 65,000, has 40 employees but the factory was owned by 9 partners. So, in effect, it is a partnership firm and not a cooperative. Production was 11,000 packets per day for 24 days a month for a period of 10 months in a year. There was a stable market for about 2 years because the factory got a contract with the school system under the District Development Council. However, recently the contract has lapsed and not been renewed. As a consequence the factory is now closed. Attempts are being made to find alternative employment for these 40 unemployed. On the one hand, it shows dependence on government developmental agencies and, on the other, a state of comparative weakness in establishing a marketing network for such rural based agro-industries.

There are other problems as well. While irrigation facilities have been made available to some extent resulting in raising farm productivity, not much headway could be made in developing a cooperative movement. Emphasis has been on self-employment and entrepreneurial development rather than a collective approach to the socio-economic upliftment of the people. Discussions with the villagers indicate that despite the thrust towards village integration, the deeper roots of caste feelings persist. The different forums of the village association are still dominated by those who own land and who are otherwise occupied in farming and trading activities. The landless families of the scheduled castes reside in quarters subsidised by the government development schemes but investigations reveal that many of these quarters do not have any roofs. It was expected that the local branch of a nationalised bank would extend loan facilities to these Harijans to purchase corrugated sheets to construct roofs. For this the Harijans were advised to deposit Rs. 5 a month in the bank. The economics of rope-making from local grass, leaves a Harijan family with an income of Rs. 2 per piece of long rope not including the cost of labour. As such there is no question of saving to the tune of Rs. 5 per month. Those are some of the contradictions in the development of a unified village culture where the socio-economic scales are weighted against the poor.

Drinking water is a classic example. It has to be brought from a distance of about 3 kms on a trailer driven by a tractor. 18 litres of drinking water cost 10 paise and many of the families have to spend up to Re 1 per day for drinking water. This is again an issue which the model village organisers have not been able to resolve. Voluntary labour has certainly improved the conditions of village roads and local sanitation. But it would necessarily imply that the landless labour is confronted with the choice of either going out in search of a living or else to render voluntary service for development of the village infrastructure. This is not the case with those who are better off. Thus the superstructure of the harmony model has yet to come to grips with some of the mundane but basic contradictions showing up in the village. There is a lot of importance given to the improvement of health. Whereas some infrastructure of medical care has been created, local medical practitioners still thrive. For the landless labourers, the problem of a daily wage is such a burning issue that each young boy and girl is a unit of labour in which context education is as much a luxury as health care. Apart from anything else, because of the recurrence of malnutrition-caused diseases, the infrastructure of socio-cultural benefits can hardly bring succour to the economically poorer groups. Be that as it may, this model village development has received outside attention including the World Bank because of the fairly effective publicity media in India and abroad. The 'show-piece' example provided by Maliwada is now attempted to be replicated in 24 districts of the state with 232 village projects. Schemes have been prepared and some favourable responses are expected from the World Bank.

This particular case highlights the following issues:

(a) The Institute of Cultural Affairs is operating within the premises of the politico-legal structure. It is seeking to avail of opportunities offered by the state agencies, and technical and financial assistance from external sources including foreign funds;

(b) Objectives are limited to the improvements of the economy as well as the socio-cultural development of the village. Internal contradictions are not confronted in the process;

(c) The organising process has not led to a movement in terms of focusing on some of the strategic issues such as non-availability of drinking water and poor housing conditions for the landless Harijans. That challenge would mean resorting to the mobilisation process and some amount of confrontation. This has been avoided.

(d) At the same time the external change-agents are trying to develop an autonomously functioning administrative system in the village by withdrawing themselves from direct continuing involvement and their role is now getting confined to monitoring the project progress and offering help and guidance as and when necessary. From Bombay, which is the headquarters, these external change-agents visit the village twice a month and stay there for a period of two to three days. However, the peripheral population's active involvement is still to be attained.

(e) Some degree of bureaucratisation is evident in the village association as well as in the national coordinating agency. By using certain traditional criteria of economic progress, the village has certainly made some headway. To some extent this has been possible because the land distribution pattern is not as skewed as in many areas of rural India. There is no definite identifiable landholding interest operating as a power bloc in the village. However, the differences between the farmers and the landless labourers in the social sense still exist.

(f) The target population is premised on a pluralistic concept. The village has been taken as a homogeneous entity which it is not. Leadership is still not shared and the decision-making actors are still those who have more economic power and social status.

(g) This case is significant because this is a somewhat revised model of usual rural development strategy adopted in India for under-developed regions, with the initiation of community development projects since mid-1950s. One major difference is that a voluntary organisation with origins in a foreign country has taken the initiative and not the state bureaucracy;

(*h*) The training strategy is skill, technique and knowledge-based. It is consciousness-raising in a technical sense but not in coming to grips with socio-economic realities. On the whole, in terms of ideals, it is operating within the politico-legal framework in order to improve matters on the gradualism scale and not on the scale of qualitative change. This voluntary association is apolitical which, operating within a framework of conflicting interest groups in India's rural society, is but a support to the existing politico-legal structure.

C. JHARKHAND MUKTI MORCHA

A brief account of the movement and its achievements including some of the unique organising properties have been reported elsewhere (De, 1979A). That was the story up to 1976. A recent visit to the area extended over three districts provides fresh insights which are relevant to this study. Shibu Soren, the guru of the movement, had the harrowing experience of his active tribal father being murdered by a money-lender in 1957 in Hazaribagh district when he was 12 years old. His mother persuaded him not to avenge his death but to finish his school education. He did that but his active mind was working all the while, reflecting on the dynamics of the money-lending business. He could link up, in his analysis, the subjective and objective elements to conclude that money-lenders and traders (usually called *dikus*, meaning the outsiders) are the disrupters of tribal livelihood and culture. This became possible apart from their money power and support base in the lower echelons of the administrative machinery, on account of the tribals' acquired habits of drunkenness and infructuous expenditure on marriages and indulgence in other superstitious rituals and cermonies.

So, he aimed at mounting an attack on the totality of the problem on two fronts. Mobilising the tribals is an essential task. Mobilisation requires a core group of organisers, however small in number, who are dedicated to the cause emotionally as well as rationally. While their dependence on the leader as well as the influential supporters from outside is initially necessary, they should also learn to work autonomously in the organising process so as to mobilise the tribals effectively. A favourable force was the basic core of tribal communal culture which could not be totally disrupted although it had been considerably weakened. In 1966–67, he moved to Dhanbad as many tribals from Hazaribagh migrated to this area because of the rapid industrialisation process, in particular hastened by the establishment of one of the largest steel plants of the country. The migrant tribals invited him to be among them.

However, industrial labour did not attract him as much as the tribals in the rural belt of Dhanbad. He initially concentrated on the Tundi Block. An attack on the social evil customs, which is really socio-cultural re-orientation, would have been meaningless unless he could link it up with the economic issues of the exploited tribals who, through the machinations of various hostile agencies, were alienated from their land against the provisions of law. Restoration of lost land, implementation of government laws, rules and regulations in a fair manner, and the practices of the *diku* traders became the targets of attack in the mass meetings of the tribals. While this gathered momentum over the years and land was being restored to the tribals, three main centres were established called *ashram* to spread the spirit of cooperation among the tribals: one at Pokharia village, another at Palma and the third at Pirtanar. These are small communes where the core organisers lived on the principle of self-sufficiency and inter-dependence. Cooperative farming on the land available to get necessary food items, animal farm with goats, indigenous chickens and pigs so as to make the *ashram* self-sufficient and for selling the surplus at a subsidised price to the non-resident members were organised. These three centres began spreading the message of horizontal mobilisation of the tribals in different clusters of villages.

There was confrontation on different fronts. Distillation of liquor in tribal homes was banned and social sanctions were invoked under collective pressure, particularly with the assistance from women. However, there are traders in practically every area who are non-tribals and engaged in liquor distillation and surreptitious sale. This practice still continues but has considerably abated. The success no doubt is tangible. That brings the larger question of the role of local administration. Illicit distillation of liquor is banned. Under the Excise Act, raids should be carried out in villages to identify the guilty parties and bring them before the Court of Law. When some local excise officials are serious about their responsibility, the provisions of law are effective, but this is not always the case. The same is true about other government agencies. With development-minded local bureaucrats, the movement gets a boost and suffers setbacks when the local officials with enormous power of formal and non-formal discretion behave differently. The major conflict comes with the basic orientation of the administration in the matter of development. The development orientation is to provide inputs and services to individuals in order to pinpoint accountability whereas the movement's aim is to foster and sustain collective effort. This is where collective efforts go unrewarded. Even in individual cases, the bureaucratic procedures and rigid inter-pretation of rules ultimately act as a hindrance apart from costly delays.

A case in point is what happened in a village. One tribal was sanctioned

Rs. 9,000 for digging a drinking well, which, it was informally understood, would be used by the fellow villagers as well. The actual cost was Rs. 16,000. Labour was contributed by the villagers but the rules provided that the well should be brick-built, and in the locality only stones were available although at a price. So, stones were used and the well is as good as any other. The official interpretation was that since stones were locally available, it should be taken as a cheaper material and, the sanctioned grant of Rs. 9,000 was brought down to Rs. 6,000. The villagers had to find the balance amount of Rs. 10,000. This is only one of many such instances.

The forest is yet another problem. The situation here is the same as in the Uttar Kashi area in U.P. There are forest contractors working in league with the forest department and mahua trees are auctioned for collecting flowers which have multiple uses including distillation of liquor. The movement organised several concerted efforts to obstruct the forest contractors from intruding in the area, more so on account of their misbehaviour with tribal girls. In many cases they succeeded but where the contractor could make a 'law and order' issue out of it, the local police would intervene in favour of the privileged party.

In effect, the movement in Dhanbad district gives one the impression that the progress made earlier, till 1976 when the local leaders were active and attending to the needs of the members, has stabilised. In fact, there has been some improvement. The local cooperative in one village, won a tender for Bandhih Minor Irrigation Project at an estimated cost of Rs. 52,000. It was completed in June 1979 and the actual expenses were Rs. 38,000. Despite many alarms and impediments created by the local government technicians, the project was adjudged satisfactory.

On the other hand, there have been distinct setbacks. The village bank, in the form of grain collection from each household in order to help the community at the time of distress, has become moribund. In some villages they are surviving at a low level of effectiveness. In some others they are no longer operating. The night schools for removal of illiteracy have become practically defunct. Because of two successive bad crop seasons in the area, which is in any case not fertile, enough grain could not be collected to support the teachers.

The support that was available from district administration in 1974–75 was withdrawn during the period of national emergency and, in fact, a reversal of policies affecting developmental projects started. To give an example, the tribals prefer Sal trees and Kendu leaves in the area. Although they are not direct beneficiaries of the trees, as such, there are fringe benefits as Sal leaves and Sal seeds can be used by them which has been a customary right for a long time. Similarly, Kendu leaves have commercial value and, therefore, when the leaves are plucked the daily labourers, many of them tribals, get jobs. But the government policy is to have, instead, acacia trees which provide quick returns but hardly any benefit to the villagers. One sympathetic administrator came in early 1979 but, because of his straightforward policy of dispensing justice fairly and squarely, he was found inconvenient by local vested interests. In July 1979 he was transferred.

The movement has now come to the conviction that, with these ups and downs in the style of functioning of the administration, it cannot depend on the administrative system for the development of the poor tribals. It has to rely on its own strength.

Partly motivated by this objective, and partly encouraged by the image that he has acquired among the tribals in the Jharkhand belt which spans a number of districts, Shibu Soren has practically left Dhanbad as an activist. He has moved to Santhal Parganas and Giridih districts. The strategy is the same as it was in the Tundi Block but with a difference. The movement is spreading in the form of demonstrations and protests in order to raise the consciousness of the tribals, but there is commensurately lesser emphasis on building up local organisations around tangible economic activities. Indeed, there are night schools and grain golas but many of these have yet to take roots as entrenched and sustained leadership has not developed village by village. Territorially the movement has spread without taking deeper roots. The second tier leaders also move along with Shibu Soren rather than concentrating on particular areas.

The movement has acquired a political dimension in the form of a demand for a Jharkhand State or at least an autonomous region consisting of the contiguous districts of Bihar, West Bengal, Orissa and M.P., where tribals form a sizeable section of the population. In a sense, this movement to establish tribal identity on a political platform is seen by many as a separatist movement. On the other hand, in mass meetings it is projected as a collective movement for the oppressed people whether they are tribals or not. In a way, Shibu Soren has become a mobile political hero addressing mass meetings and holding small group discussions instead of following the original strategy of using his organising ability, insights and charismatic personality upon a series of inter-related tasks to strengthen the grassroots. This is in contrast with another supporter of the movement, A.K. Roy, who, although became a Member of Parliament while still in jail, continued to concentrate on mobilising the coal-miners and steel workers in the Ranigunj–Jharia belt. His extended role as a parliamentarian has not diffused his activities, as his primary task continues to be to lend active support to building up the grassroot base of action-oriented workers groups in the Dhanbad–Ranigunj belt (Pradeep and Das, 1979).

On the other hand, Shibu Soren, compelled by subjective as well as objective imperatives, may have been propelled towards the new role that he has adopted for himself. Let us take the case of land alienation laws that exist in Bihar. In some districts of Jharkhand, alienation of the tribals from their land, by whatever means, is illegal and restoration proceedings can become retrospective up to 30 years. This is not so in Dhanbad, Giridih and Santhal Parganas. In order to rectify this anomalous position, which is an important issue for the tribals, political action is desirable and mass mobilisation to influence the legislature is one of the effective means. Secondly, money-lenders, traders and contractors are a strong collective force throughout the Jharkhand belt with a long tradition of continued exploitation of the poor tribals and non-tribals. This phenomenon also requires a movement across the frontier. Thirdly, Shibu Soren has acquired a mythical image in the eyes of the tribals many of whom have not actually seen him. According to one senior district official, who is an objective analyst of the situation, he has seen the picture of Shibu Soren in many tribal homes in the farthest corner of the district, even in the kitchen, so that the women can establish their tribal identity by looking at it. That it why the image of Shibu Soren has acquired a halo. He has also shown a subjective desire to project himself as a liberator. Then again as in the Chipko movement, it is necessary here to fight against the anti-developmental policies and practices of the government which cut across the boundary of any area. These are some of the factors which have catapulted him into a position of a symbol-registering regional leader.

At the same time, there is a potential danger that the movement, having been deprived of his active involvement in the grassroot organising process, can suffer from goal diffusion rather than goal extension. This movement thus runs the risk of what overtook the Sind-Hari movement in the Sind province of Pakistan where an organisation was established in 1930 to protect the interests of landless sharecroppers, or tenants-at-will, both on the economic and social dimensions. The objective was to mobilise them to get their rights established on land and its produce. The fight was directed against the rich landlords and their close allies and there were successive collective mobilising activities under the inspiring leadership of a well respected person who was known in the region as a litterateur and was dedicated to the cause. However, the movement took various turns and twist, including involvement in the politically-oriented *khilafat andolan*. Later on, after Pakistan emerged as a nation and a strong centralised control was established, a 'Sind for Sindhis' movement sprang up and the leader of the Sind-Hari movement Hayder Bux Jatoi got involved in it. He became politically visible but his grassroot connections were weakened. The interests of the Haris suffered partly because the movement was dependent on him for providing direction and leadership for too long a time. With his death in 1970, and the rise of the Pakistan People's Party, which took up land reforms as one of the key pronounced programme components, it came to a halt.

As Khan (1979) suggests, the Sind-Hari movement did, through the process of mobilisation and localised decentralised units, achieve a good deal for the sharecroppers, some within the framework of the legal system and some by getting a number of wrongs rectified by bringing about pressure to change the legal provisions. The movement ultimately lost its potency on account of goal diffusion and inability to strengthen the grassroot organisation against the onslaught of landlords, obscurantist religious leaders and hostile or otherwise alienated bureaucracies.

We see some parallel between this movement and Jharkhand Mukti Morcha, particularly because the halo effect of Shibu Soren may insulate him, from not only his own people but also because an objective assessment of the realities around could become clouded by being fed with information from the 'yes' men clinging to him. The recent developments in the grassroot units in Dhanbad indicate a gradual weakening of the Morcha and perceptible lack of enthusiasm compared to what was seen in 1974–75.

We can identify some of the characteristics of this organising process:

(*a*) From the very beginning a target group was clearly identified. The rural tribals who had lost their economic wherewithal, were also getting lost in their social identity. The opposing forces were also demarcated. The combined muscle power of the money-lenders, traders and contractors was too obvious to be ignored. So, the twin strategy of mobilising the target group around economic interests and eradication of social evils was a part of it. The other part of the task was to confront the opposing forces by enlisting the external facilitating forces among the local administrators. In a situation like this, the confrontation model may be a desirable option: confront the target group with its socio-economic realities to arouse its consciousness for mobilisation which harnesses its collective strength and external confrontation with the help of the mobilised internal resources. And this was successful at the time of forcible occupation of land, illegally possessed by the powerful landlord group, or at the time of harvesting, when with the sheer strength of numbers, in hundreds, the muscle power of the vested interests could be kept at bay. The lesson is obvious. Use of coercive force by the powers-that-be can be blunted by the collective power of the people which is always the strength of the powerless provided they can organise themselves and in the process overcome powerlessness.

As such, it is distinct from the Maliwada case because of the naked nature of exploitation. Similarly, the non-violent methods could not work as effectively as they did in the case of Chipko.

(*b*) The legal system, the case shows, is a two-edged weapon. The collective will of the people can utilise progressive components of various statutes to their advantage. Unless the mobilisation process is effective along with the solid foundation of a grassroots organisation, the same progressive measures would remain confined to the statute book itself and would not be reflected in practice. In the process of utilising the legal system appropriately, the movement also proved that the negative components could restrain the local administration, as on an overall assessment, it would not like to implement the punitive provisions of law leading to an escalation of conflict. This is an extra-legal way of counteracting an unjust and unfair legal system. The movement is an example of how the relations of production and property could be modified and it is one way of acquiring power against the powerful.

(*c*) As distinct from the Maliwada case, a collective socio-cultural superstructure was built on the foundation of collective economic mobilisation. The grain bank, setting a limit to infructuous marriage expenditure by resorting to a convention of several marriages being celebrated at the same place and on the same day in order to save on expenses, are tangible economic gains. The Maliwada experiment has sought to strengthen the rural people selectively, as self-employed individual entrepreneurs, though on a small scale.

(*d*) Given the political scenario of the Jharkhand belt in the context of the caste complex of Bihar, it is but natural that the mobilising process sought to acquire political overtones, which is what the current emphasis of the movement is. Whether it will follow the entropic logic of the Sind-Hari movement or not is anybody's guess. Should, however, the grassroot base weaken, this is likely to happen. For example, in Santhal Parganas, there is the government developmental scheme known as MESO (an area development programme between the mega and micro levels). In four sub-divisions of the district, there are several tribal blocks covered under the scheme. Although there is a project manager for each project, the project fund is allocated to different departments of the government which deal with minor irrigation, road construction, forest development, house building, animal husbandry and so on. The project manager without any authority to allocate funds cannot exercise effective control. Funds are handled by the regular government departments. The movement has yet to turn its attention to this problem in the interest of the tribals by generating collective support for an integrated budget in the hands of the project manager so that money can be spent more effectively. This may well turn out to be a missed opportunity.

(e) The overall ideals of the movement appear to be somewhat blurred. The Jharkhand movement is indeed political in nature. One of its components is to establish the collective identity of the tribals. On the other hand, another objective also seeks to mobilise the poorer sections of the area irrespective of whether they are tribals or non-tribals. These conflicting pulls may result in a contradiction in the movement itself. If the movement is aware of this potential danger, it has not shown it by taking any action to overcome it.

D. Operation Barga

This venture was initiated by the leftist government in West Bengal which came to power in 1977 with an unquestioned majority in the legislature and took up the task of unfinished land reforms which it started under severe constraints in 1967 and carried on later for a short duration in 1969. Although in our original framework we planned not to include a government-sponsored organisational movement in our study, this project has, however, certain features which qualify it for inclusion.

West Bengal is one of the most populous states in India, aided by the three decades of inflow of people across the border from East Pakistan (now Bangladesh) and from the populous adjoining states of Bihar, U.P. and parts of Orissa. Land tenure has been skewed as in many other states of India. However, the peasant movement in undivided Bengal and later in West Bengal has a well-known history. There have been three distinct movements to protest against the land distribution system as well as the relations of production—the Tebhaga movement, the Kakdwip movement and, later on, the Naxalite movement in 1967. Originally, there was one undivided 'Kishan Sabha' mainly under the control of the Communist party which, after the division of the party into two distinct parties, also underwent vivisection. However, the Kishan Sabha exists in all districts with varying degree of effectiveness. The structure of the Sabha is loose, somewhat hierarchical. The more basic feature is that the membership pattern is varied, in the sense that in many areas middle and small peasants are in the membership list along with sharecroppers and rural landless labour. This has resulted on many occasions in compromises within the Sabha and, by and large, the interests of the lowest strata of the members could not be protected. Much, however, depended on the quality of local leadership. In some districts some of the political leaders with progressive orientation were active on the agrarian front while most others concentrated on the industrial workforce in and around Calcutta and other industrial centres.

After Independence, successive state governments enacted a number of land reform measures under various names. One of the first measures was to enforce the Land Ceiling Act, but its implementation was tardy because of manipulative tactics of the landlords and partially because of lack of enthusiasm in the implementing agency. Between 1955 and 1966, approximately 400,000 acres of surplus agricultural land came under the state's possession through voluntary surrender by big landlords. However, when two short-lived United Front governments were in power between 1967 and 1970, 500,000 acres of land were acquired through active involvement of the poor peasants, spurts of mobilising activities by the Kishan Sabha and some amount of initiative by the local bureaucracy, but it was considered still an incomplete task in the matter of land acquisition.

The story, however, is quite different when it comes to redistribution of land among the most needy. In 1979, the Bikram Sarkar Committee (an official body) examined the pattern of working of land distribution. It deliberately selected Coochbehar district for study, as it had remained comparatively stable practically throughout the post-independence era in terms of the rural law and order situation, thereby making it potentially favourable to implement the laws effectively. In the district 51,715 acres of vested land were available in as early as 1955. Concentrating the study on what happened to 1,000 acres of such land in a particular area, it was found that for agricultural purposes 913 acres were distributable. However, the official formalities and red tape on an average took 18 months to distribute the land to the needy. Even then only 370 acres could be distributed over a period of 15 years. Ultimately, there were 432 beneficiaries, thus each having less than one acre of land (*The Hindu*, 1979).

In the context of these realities it was decided that the following measures should constitute a strategy for land reform measures to change the structure of property relations in rural West Bengal:

1. Explicit political will at the top in support of making land reforms effective. This was done by policy decisions and issuing unambiguous directives to the appropriate agencies and wide dissemination of these among the rural poor;
2. Need to activate the otherwise rule-bound government agencies, which are the instruments of the government in giving effect to

various policy directives. In a hierarchical system, it has been experienced that if the key top men are carefully selected on the strength of their dedication to the purposes of development backed by competence and integrity, they will be able to motivate the lower echelons sooner or later.

Accordingly, two key persons were entrusted with the task of gingering up the land reforms machinery along with that segment of district administration which was responsible for district development programmes;

3. As a tactic it was felt desirable that the bureaucracy makes a direct approach to the lower strata of rural poor, instead of its going directly to the politically-oriented Kishan Sabha which might expose it to the allegation of political 'hobnobbing', a danger which is potent in a parliamentary form of democracy;

4. It was premised that once this direct approach was made to this vulnerable section of the rural areas, the Kishan Sabhas which developed high expectations from the leftist government would accept the challenge to assist the rural poor in asserting their rights instead of making visits with the political 'bigwigs' in the state capital. It will provide them with an incentive to mobilise the rural poor.

Based on the limited experiences generated in the National Labour Institute, New Delhi, it was decided to organise a series of reorientation camps with selected potential grassroots level leaders who represented the poorest section, to expose them to understanding the rights and facilities they could enjoy under various laws and regulations, and, at the same time, to raise their level of consciousness to the politico-economic dimensions of rural West Bengal. Members of the Kishan Sabhas were informed about these camps held in villages, district by district. Although their initial response was negative, as the rural labour camps gained in popularity, these local leaders gave up their opposition and joined in.

For a variety of reasons, the target group was selected from among those who were sharecroppers. These were persons with either no land or a meagre piece of land, cultivating land for others and being unorganised, deprived of their share of the produce as provided for under the law. More than that, they had no official record available in which their names were registered to indicate as to how long or for how many generations they were cultivating the same plots of land or additional plots for the owners. This age-old evil was sought to be rectified by launching Operation Barga (sharecropper's rights recording movement). There was another purpose. The sharecroppers are in a favourable position to report on the real owners of land. These data would then be collated to find out the ownership pattern, as also whether the owners were cultivators or engaged in other activities getting their land attended to by sharecroppers or wage labour. An additional component was to find out as to how many exceeded the provisions of the Land Ceiling Act.

The survey also collected data on the subsidiary occupations of share-croppers and the extent of their economic vulnerability. So, the objectives of Operation Barga were multiple. The first camp was held at a place called Halushahi in Hooghly district in May 1978 and since then it has been extended to different districts. The rural labour camps were only the beginning. The main challenge was how to get the sharecroppers to talk frankly to the recording officers and provide all the necessary data, keeping in view that the land owners and money-lenders had a strong grip over them because of their continuing vulnerability and dependence. It was not easy to overcome their fear psychosis which made them victims of the exploitative system.

Instead of requesting people to come to a local revenue office for the purpose, the officials after due publicity went out to open areas where the plots of land were situated with all their books, files and records so that the people at work could come in broad daylight while involved in the process of work to give their depositions. Care was taken that the owners of land were also informed and adequate opportunities were given to them to make their own presentations.

The results of Operation Barga from September 1978, till January 1979, of which two months were lost because of unprecedented floods in West Bengal in late 1978, are given below:

1. No. of revenue villages covered   4,835
2. Total number of plots covered   42,219
3. No. of sharecroppers put on record   1,62,544
4. Total number of sharecroppers recorded so far
    in West Bengal after Independence   6,01,360
5. Size of plots cultivated by each sharecropper
    (average), in acres
       1955   0.91
       1978   0.78

The last figure indicates that, despite the right to record earned by him, the economic vulnerability of a sharecropper has increased over the years, which raises a host of other questions.

The following lessons can be derived from Operation Barga:

(a) Unless the basic legal structure which is but a reflection of the dominating politico-economic framework is sought to be altered, such progressive measures can only be implemented haltingly. A recent report indicates that hundreds of court injunctions have stalled the work involving at least 162,000 acres of vested agricultural land in West Bengal. This figure does not include the pending litigation about the claims of sharecroppers (Bandyopadhyay, 1979).

(b) Undoubtedly, the government implementing agency has been revitalised, but there are instances where, in the absence of supervisory officers' vigilance, some cases of malpractice have occurred. During the author's field trips to two districts, some sharecroppers covertly told him that some of the officials of the Kishan Sabhas would not hesitate to collect some money to expedite procuring the record of right certificate from the Land Reforms Office.

(c) This phenomenon, though rare, brings to the fore some of the contradictions in the Kishan Sabha leadership. As earlier mentioned, the active membership of the Kishan Sabha is pluralistic, composed of disparate interest groups. There are middle farmers as well as small farmers. They resort to the sharecropping system as well. Many of them being influential in the Kishan Sabha, would not hesitate to protect their interests by persuading their own sharecroppers by subtle or other means not to have their names recorded. Others also see this as an opportunity to earn a fast buck. If anything, this is a basic weakness in the existing active membership pattern of local Kishan Sabhas, which is further complicated by the elected representatives to the local institutions at the district, block and village levels which provide an opportunity for uncommitted but influential local persons to secure 'tickets' from the leftist parties to win the elections. Our study indicates that their number is not considerable. Nonetheless, if a progressive political party does not have a strong sustained grassroots cadre of dedicated workers, this type of infiltration is unavoidable.

(d) The initial prognosis that activation of the government machinery in the matter of land reforms might act as a challenge to somewhat complacent local Kishan Sabhas, turned out to be true. In most of the places these Kishan Sabhas have shown signs of increased activity, particularly when records of rights movement has been launched in a district. One can, however, only speculate about how this initial enthusiasm will sustain itself.

One tentative conclusion that can be drawn from this movement is that redistribution of land is fast reaching a state of saturation, and that even the beneficiaries, namely, the sharecroppers, will continue to remain vulnerable unless a number of concrete measures are adopted to make them at least partially self-sufficient. The government has adopted a scheme of a zero interest rate whereby sharecroppers and assignees of vested land would get loans from banks or cooperatives but would not be required to pay any interest till the investments start showing results. The government would absorb the interest component. That measure alone is not enough. Fragmentation of land on account of population pressure has reached a stage in West Bengal where two types of alternative technologies of production and organisation of productive work might be considered. One is to move away from the economic viability of a single family unit to some form of cooperatives of agriculture-related activities. Economies of scale are thus possible and even the World Bank strategy of rural development could be utilised under certain safeguards to make these sharecroppers improve their lot. This is possible because of the 'umbrella' protection that can be expected from a progressive government. Secondly, other supplemental activities, particularly highly decentralised rural industries and agro-based activities, can be conceived. Considering the fact that West Bengal alone has a large potential market, in quantity as well as variety of essential consumer items, sophistication of products is secondary to meeting the essential needs.

Unless the economic rehabilitation of sharecroppers and landless labour are linked with these extended activities, no legislative measures will go far. In this the Kishan Sabhas will have to take the lead. To give an example, the minimum wage rate for agricultural operation is Rs. 8.10 per working day. Our limited field investigations indicate that the most it reaches, even during the harvesting season, is Rs. 6, but on most occasions it does not exceed Rs. 4 per day.

On the whole, this experiment is unique in that a state government has, for the first time, experimented with an otherwise expensive bureaucratic machinery to harness its potential capability to raise the consciousness of the rural masses thereby generating a potential for an induction effect on the Kishan Sabhas which were otherwise geared to demonstrations, protest meetings, or at the extreme, individual acts of violence leading to no concrete results.

There is another lead from this case. Within a given framework of a constitution gradually tending to centralised power, a state government is required to plan for a transition strategy for transformation. Voluntary agencies and activated bureaucracy can become potential agents in this venture.

E. Gonoshasthaya Kendra
   (Chowdhury, 1978A, B; Das, 1979; G.K., 1977; etc.)

This voluntary organisation of Bangladesh is unique in many ways. Its beginning itself is unusual. When the liberation struggle started in Bangladesh in 1971, the liberation forces operating inside Bangladesh and at the Indian border needed medical care. Zafrullah Chowdhury, giving up a medical career in England, returned and joined with several volunteers to essentially provide health care to the liberation forces including emergency operations. That continued till the country earned its freedom.

Thereafter, instead of accepting an assured position in the new government, which surely required the services of such a dedicated person, Zafrullah with a band of colleagues set up Gonoshasthaya Kendra (G.K.) in a rural area of Savar, away from the city of Dhaka. It is a voluntary agency. The objective of the Kendra has been expressed in many documents. One statement summarises the approach:

> The health problem in our rural areas is a consequence of under-development, and, at the same time, a cause for its perpetuation. Malnutrition, for example, is basically a problem not for a physician but for the agronomist, the teacher and the community organiser. Strictly, medical approach cannot produce community health. Without the involvement of the community anything that is produced will have a questionable value (Chowdhury 1978A).

Impediments were many, since such an objective was sought to be achieved. The teaching of modern western medicine and its practice are expensive, essentially curative, and at best can serve the needs of those who are reasonably well off, well cared for and protected. It is estimated, to give an example from India, that most of the life-saving drugs as well as such items as vitamins can, at most, reach 20 per cent of India's population (Medawar, 1979). The situation in Bangladesh may be more severe. Secondly, an under-developed society, Bangladesh, as well as others, is essentially a politico-economic system with those who have power and those who are powerless. An agency such as this could not but decide that health care should be an intervention strategy for development. As can be easily predicted, there were hurdles and obstructions to overcome. No less important were the accumulated prejudices and superstitions of the potential clientele because of their blind reliance on current medical tradition which, however, is beyond their reach. The demonstration effect of what the leaders of the community do and show is indeed considerable. So, even the target group, to begin with, was sceptical if not hostile. The other challenge was to create a spearhead of volunteers who could only be offered the bare necessities of life by an organisation such as this. It called for sacrifices of all kinds.

The Savar centre, which is still the main base, started with over 100 part-time volunteers, many of them from the student community whose initial assignment was to carry out a vaccination drive and be educated in health care programmes based on certain values of work and inculcation of participative orientation.

The centre itself developed many dimensions as time went by. One of its first tasks was to create village paramedics, boys and girls. Girls were likely to be more effective as barefoot doctors in the villages where women were also to be reached. It was not easy to get Muslim girls to come out of their seclusion for such training and work. Secondly, in order to be autonomous and self-sufficient, they would be required to become multi-purpose in their activities. For this a minimum level of education was necessary. Most of the girls in the village have, at best, an exposure to five years of schooling and, as such, are deprived of the basic qualifications for the job. Initially, some educated girls came from towns but, over a period, even the semi-literate girls were put under intensive training varying from six months to one year.

An assessment of rural Bangladesh and its requirements convinced the organisers that it was just not a matter of providing health care services to the rural poor but also, in the process, actively contribute to, slowly and steadily, the liberation of women from their conservative upbringing. To pursue the subject, the trained paramedics are expected to cover at least 3,000 people spread over a number of villages, coverage of which on foot would be time-consuming as well as physically strenuous. That apart, they might be subjected to indignities by the conservative elements in the villages. They were taught to cycle but this was not easily acceptable to the community. For Muslim girls it was not a 'done' thing. With patience and adequate explanation even to the orthodox leaders of the village community, it was possible to overcome the resistance partially. In the second centre, established at Shapmari in Jamalpur area, over 100 kms away from the Savar centre, even towards the end of 1977, paramedics were unable to move on bicycles as this was not socially sanctioned.

As regards health care, it was necessary to identify the health needs in terms of priority. Diarrhoea, scabies, a high mortality rate, infection of eyes and ears and immunisation against small-pox and cholera were some of the main challenges to be attended to. It was not possible, apart from the curative services, to respond to these challenges in the centre at Savar. To begin with, mobile paramedics were deployed but gradually four sub-centres were created with the main centre acting as a referral base. Doctors would also be mobile in order to help complicated cases in the sub-centres. Similarly, once a week the sub-centre based staff, at least some of them, would report to the Savar centre about various problems and share their experiences. They would also carry along with them the essential medicines. The variety of activities undertaken by the organisation can briefly be reported.

1. *Primary Health Care*

The number of fully-trained paramedics came down to 22 by the end of 1977 as some of them were offered better jobs by hospitals and government departments. The paramedics' duties included:

(*a*) Registration of births and deaths;

(*b*) Identification of pregnant women and establishing at-risk cases;

(*c*) Identification of at-risk children, defined as those suffering from severe malnutrition, diarrhoea/chronic diarrhoea and night blindness;

(*d*) Immunisation, BCG for children under 15, DPT for children under 5, tetanus toxoid for women during pregnancy and primary small-pox for all;

(*e*) Nutrition and health education;

(*f*) Treatment of diarrhoea and dysentery;

(*g*) Preparation and use of rehydration fluid; treatment of scabies;

(*h*) Motivation, delivery system and follow-up of the family planning package.

There were sceptics for whom this was a tall order. What really brought success to this bold, unorthodox experiment was a basic faith in human capability and an imaginatively planned training programme, in addition to the examples set by the doctors themselves.

It is enough to mention, without quoting statistics, that the scheme which covered, till the end of 1977, a target population of 100,000 has succeeded most favourably compared to the organised health delivery system under official and other agencies.

2. *Education*

The data indicate that 46 per cent of school-age children do not attend schools. Among those who complete five years of schooling, only 14 per cent are girls.

The Kendra started a school with 50 children drawn from five villages near the Savar centre. They came from landless or quasi-landless families. Curriculum design and programme implementation were imaginatively planned in order to overcome parents' resistance. The object of traditional school education is to provide knowledge and its negative consequence is a lessening of regard for manual labour. Literacy is a felt need because poor illiterates are subjected to fraud by various interests through obtaining of thumb impressions on papers.

Formal dress was not a requirement because that would involve additional expenses for the parents. Children were provided with inexpensive slates and pencils. Working hours were flexible so that children, over 6 or 7 years of age, could attend to the services required by their parents. This was particularly so during the agriculturally busy seasons. At least one full meal was provided free to them so that the burden on poor parents could be somewhat relieved. Even with all these measures, it was expected that most of them would not stay in the school for more than five years.

First thing in the morning, children would attend to the vegetable plots and chicken farm so that they could retain respect for manual labour in the midst of the mental work that was carried out in the classroom. Lessons were also devoted to understanding the village life, the roots of poverty and causes for disease and malnutrition. Group work was more predominant than the lecture system. Thus education was aimed at raising consciousness in addition to removing illiteracy.

It is not as if all problems of pedagogy have been satisfactorily resolved. For example, the centre is still not sure whether it should go in for the rural language of the common man or standard Bengali which is the preserve of the educated gentry.

3. *Vocational Training*

Starting with two, the women's centres now cater to over 450 women at the main centre and the sub-centres. Despite initial difficulties, women started taking interest in learning such trades as carpentry, shoe-making, plumbing, blacksmithy and electrical work apart from sewing and baking cakes and biscuits. These are also the trades which are in short supply in the rural areas as many skilled artisans have been going to the Middle East.

The technical workshop employs 12 full-time workers, 6 men and 6 women. Apart from acquiring practical training, they produce simple agricultural implements, window frames, hospital cots, operation tables and so on. Some of these are purchased by the centre and others sold outside. This is another way of helping the cause of women's liberation.

4. *Agriculture*

This is the most important economic activity in Bangladesh. The centre could not neglect this reality. The project staff include four full-time agricultural workers and a French volunteer specialised in biological farming. That apart, other members of the staff devote some time every day to food production activities. The centre is self-sufficient in rice and vegetables. Surplus produce is sold in the local market. There is a tank for rearing fish. Soyabean experiments, though successful in the experimental farm, did not work out well with the local farmers.

The problem of financial resources for agricultural purposes is well-known and the government agencies, for reasons fairly known and common to practically all under-developed countries, reach only those who have land and property. The centre started giving loans on very easy terms to the extremely poor sharecroppers in two villages. After initial resistance, it took root. Out of 43 cultivators only 2 defaulted. One was a well-off farmer whose financial status could not be established earlier. The other one lost his entire harvest because of his landlord's high-handedness and illegal seizure of his produce. This scheme has been most difficult to launch in the absence of appropriate land reform measures. Nonetheless, efforts are on and various funding agencies are being tapped to funnel their resources through the centre so that funds can reach the most needy.

5. *Family Planning*

The centre exercised a good deal of caution to avoid repetition of the mistakes that are still being committed in the name of family planning. The centre's approach was different. It was understood that, unless the family planning efforts are meaningfully linked with economic revival of the poor, no amount of technical sophistication and persuasive skills would work. That is one reason why the centre undertook other associated activities some of which have been listed above.

In 1974, this approach of the centre started receiving favourable responses from women of the Savar area. Many were disillusioned with the pill and other preventive measures because of side-effects and inability to follow the strict routine. They wanted a simpler method. It was possible to persuade them to accept tubectomy. This was also extended to sub-centres and then to the second main centre located near Jamalpur. At Savar, as the system gained popularity, the charges were fixed at taka 6 per case whereas in the Jamalpur area, it was provided free against a subsidy from Government funds. The established medical practitioners and the local family planning officer were indeed unhappy because these efforts resulted in depriving them of their lucrative income. However, corrupt practices still continue in many areas of Bangladesh supported by many expensive programmes emanating from US AID, Family Planning International Assistance and the International Projects of the Association for Voluntary Sterilisation, although it could be presumed that these agencies did not intend the funds to be used for coercively implementing the sterilisation programme.

The centre has always maintained an attitude that pregnancy and babies are not to be treated as an epidemic. The issue has to be judged on the merit of each case. As a result of such a discriminating and ethical approach, there are more and more demands on the centre's staff to terminate pregnancies. While, initially, women at an advanced stage of pregnancy would turn up, the paramedics' efforts to educate them and other women resulted in their turning up at an earlier stage of pregnancy making surgical operations easier.

The most significant achievement of the scheme has been to train and use, effectively, the paramedics for tubectomy operations and for termination of pregnancies. There was strong initial opposition and scepticism. But it has worked well. However, in complicated cases, the paramedics did always turn to the doctors for assistance. Post-operational complications are not rare. Tetanus infections are most serious and even result in deaths in some cases. The number of such cases has fallen considerably. Statistics show that the birth rate among the target population is significantly lower compared to the national average and is an indication of its success.

The second main centre at Shapmari is working effectively under the guidance of a trained paramedic who joined Zafrullah Chowdhury as a nurse in 1971. She is an effective administrator and commands the respect of those who work with her (incidentally a Bengali Hindu girl) because she has not turned out to be a paper-pushing administrator. She works with her own hands. Of course, trained doctors from the main centre maintain close liaison with this centre despite communication difficulties. Running this centre is more difficult than running the one at Savar. It is necessary, for example, to get to Sherpur town everyday to buy a bagful of ice to keep vaccines cool as the village does not have electricity.

Yet another development project that has been successfully launched is Gonoshasthaya Pharmaceuticals Ltd. (GPL), which is owned by GK as a trust. It aims at producing 15 to 20 per cent of essential drugs for Bangladesh under generic names. The list includes 31 drugs, such as, antibiotics, antacids, analgesics, anti-diarrhoeics, ENT preparations and hypnotics. The aim is to bring down the market prices by 30 to 50 per cent which, with the first few production items, has started happening. Eight transnationals produce taka 850 million (71 per cent) of drugs consumed in the country, many of which are not essential, and yet sold at high prices. Half-a-dozen indigenous companies control 15.6 per cent of the market by value and imports account for the balance 13.4 per cent. With per capita income at current prices (1981) at $120, with well over 50 per cent of the population eking out an existence below the poverty line, the bulk of the expenses go to medicines arising out of malnutrition caused diseases after food, clothing and shelter. Prices of drugs are high and many drugs, thanks to media-influence and the medical practitioners' preference, are elevated from an irrelevant status to an essential status.

GPL aimed at weakening the stranglehold of the multinationals on the one hand and, on the other, to demystify the intricacies and expertise of the medical profession and the drug industry. It was decided that the overall profits (with some essential drugs sold at cost or at a loss) will not be allowed to exceed 10 to 15 per cent, of which 50 per cent will be reinvested and the balance 50 per cent spent on research and charitable activities (Chowdhury, *et al*, 1982).

These elements of purposeful objectives have been underpinned by the recruitment of a female workforce with a poor, rural background. Out of 31 unskilled workers, 27 are women of which 13 were exposed to elementary literacy training. There are 10 skilled workmen drawn from GK and retrained for new responsibilities. Against heavy odds (lucrative offers from multinationals and the Middle East) the GPL employees, even with the inevitable turnover rate, have adapted themselves to the democratically-run organisation with a strong accent on internal norms of discipline, an extension of GK ideals.

Comments on this case can be confined to the following:

(*a*) It is a unique and practical case as to how such a technical service as health care can be conceived of as a part of a total package in a country which is among the poorest in the world with a conservative outlook of many people in respect of what is 'done' and 'not done'.

(*b*) It is also unique that an egalitarian culture has been sustained by maintaining no distinction between manual labour and mental labour. Professional knowledge and skills differentiation have not created a hierarchical work system in the Kendra.

(*c*) Leadership is shared and as events have turned out now, Zafrullah Chowdhury, the moving spirit behind the movement has switched over to other activities without snapping his link with the Kendra. His latest effort is to develop an indigenous drug industry in Bangladesh which is at present dependent, essentially, on foreign supplies and multinational companies. He is still a part of the centre and this withdrawal has not created any void or crisis in transfer of leadership which, in any event, continues to be a shared responsibility.

(*d*) This case is an example of goal extension in inter-related activities, linked with an alternative approach to development. Considering the enormous dimensions of problems in Bangladesh, this alternative model of development is pregnant with challenging replication in other under-developed countries.

It is yet another example where confrontative tactics have been skilfully deployed and yet selective cooperation from different agencies have not been dogmatically rejected. It may be mentioned that even the foreign agencies, such as the UNICEF, Kaufman Footwear in Canada, Oxfam, voluntary groups in France, Terre des Hommes of Holland and Switzerland, Inter Pares of Canada, have provided financial assistance without any strings attached. The Bangladesh Government too, although initially not involved in this experimental venture, has started utilising the services of the Kendra for the training of medicos and paramedics having thus recognised the utility of the Kendra.

(e) The extent of hostility to the Kendra cannot be under-estimated. In the not too distant past, an active paramedic of Shimulia sub-centre was murdered. His dedication, selfless service, inspired leadership and growing popularity were too much for local quacks and vested interests to tolerate.

His death, though a blow, has only succeeded in causing the Kendra staff to be more determined and dedicated to the challenge they are entrusted with. His tragic death has been accepted as a symbolic expression of the meaningfulness of work that the Kendra has undertaken.

(f) This case also indicates that the politico-legal structure as institutionalised in the medico-health care system can be shaken up by the approach adopted by the Kendra.

The GK, as an organisation, can be represented as a developmental institution in a diagram (see Fig. 2.1).

A Reflection

It is now time to look back at the cases and the tentative conceptual framework outlined earlier in order to take stock of the processes of organising and mobilising as building blocks for effective rural voluntary organisations. In the context of the under-developed world, such cases as we took up are relevant, whether they offer negative, positive or mixed insights. At this stage, let us try to understand what Western theories about conflict and cooperation have so far sought to establish. Some of the more significant literature on the subject has been summed up in these words:

Figure 2.1

Gonoshasthaya Kendra as a System

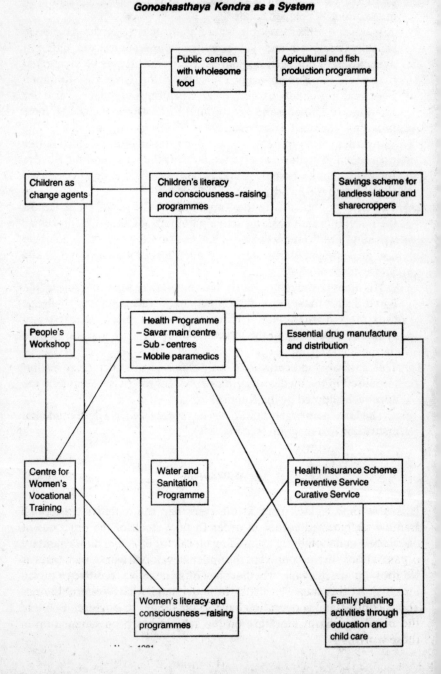

In short, these theories suggest that when groups are not already embedded in a clearly defined super-system that establishes inter-dependence and a structure of legitimate power relations, power asymmetries inhibit cooperation. Likely outcomes include exploitation by the powerful of an apathetic and passive powerless group or recurring and escalative conflicts around attempts to influence by consultant (Brown, 1977).

There is thus a recognition of the need for a widely-shared rationale for the continuance of a *specific* super-system. This we have sought to project in politico-legal realities as a reflection of the economic foundation. The distinguishing element between the powerful and the powerless is not the legitimacy of inter-dependent relations but the legitimacy or otherwise of forces of production in conjunction with the relations of production. As we see in the third world, the powerful are prone to strengthen the parameters of forces of production by continuously innovating and investing in more and more effective technologies. This is not only to create profitable markets for their wares, goods or services, but also to generate surplus to fortify their power base. The powerless when they seek to organise internally by creating homogeneous spearhead groups and externally by launching various types of movements, their primary task is to change the relations of production. Failing that, often in conjunction with an attempt at changing the relations of production in their own favour, they seek to influence the forces of production by resorting to subtle or overt restrictive activities. A tentative generalisation emerges from the cases.

A common perception of the superstructure is unlikely to emerge with basic contradictions persisting as also with differential strategies being adopted by the two confronting groups. One cannot but agree with the observation that the 'challenge of the century' lies in managing the relations between the powerful and the powerless (Blau, 1974). We suggest that relations cannot be isolated from the forces of production. Unless it is looked at from that perspective, evolution of a common framework in assessing superstructure is somewhat unlikely.

Our cases refer to natural entities rather than experimental situations as usually understood in social science research. We are supported by other evidences (Mozayeni, 1978; Masood, 1978) that where there is a comparatively homogeneous community on politico-economic and legal dimensions, it is possible to conceive of a cooperative model of community development as was done in these two cases in Iran and Nigeria. Here community revival has become possible along traditional values. The power distance created by property dynamics in both cases was far less severe than what we normally confront in a 'modernised' community. The Maliwada case which took to a cooperation model with some degree of success is a case of a comparatively less iniquitous economic foundation in the village, although the internal contradictions even in such a case did exist.

Another case in point is that of the village milk cooperatives in Kaira district, Gujarat, in India (Somjee, *et al*, 1978). Three village studies indicate interesting dynamics among socio-economic interest groups. At Asodar village, the two castes, Kshatriyas and Patidars were locked in a political struggle for control over the panchayat but when it came to running a milk cooperative, the socio-economically dominant Kshatriyas permitted the more business-minded Patidars to run the show as they were found to be more business-minded. The managerial leadership of the cooperative was left to 'efficient' hands. Ordinary members remained 'ordinary'. Business interests predominated over socio-political re-structure. A single-purpose institution acquired the trappings of traditional organisational design. The Ode village case is one of confrontation. The rich farmers, the Patels, were opposed to a milk cooperative. They could procure milk for their consumption from diverse sources as modernised agriculture provided them with enough resources. Not so with the Kumbis who came as migrant labour. By 1960s, the Kumbis got some vested land under the Land Tenancy Act and this newly acquired economic power pushed their case for a milk cooperative. They have been managing it so energetically that spin-offs came in the form of a cooperative bank and a cooperative consumer store. A less prosperous economic group has indeed benefited as an interest group. However, other lower level groups—economically and socially—are yet to benefit from this 'co-operative' venture. The Khadgodhara case brings out some other dynamics. In a backward village of 1,300 people, the women carried out the bulk of the burden of day-to-day chores for survival. Their appeal to the apex body, Amul Dairy, for a milk cooperative was turned down in 1964. However, the political leverage changed in 1967 when a woman was elected chair-person of the panchayat. The women were eager to organise, irrespective of caste and religious barriers—Brahmins, Venkars and Muslims. The reality of poverty was a levelling force. The women run the cooperative successfully and here male chauvinism did not, and in fact, could not, assert itself.

Several tentative conclusions emerge from these cases:

(a) So long as the milk cooperative is seen as a supplemental economic activity by the dominant class whose interests in modern agriculture remain unchallenged, the comparatively disadvantaged groups could organise themselves around such a new venture.

(b) While the cooperative is seen as a business venture, the leadership is coterie-based and power distribution is skewed. Consciousness raising effort remains a neglected activity.

(c) However, as in the last case, where a village is more homogeneous on account of its poverty-level and the women get organised in a co-operative, the cooperative enhances the cause of women's liberation acquiring additional components of health care and the need for planned parenthood.

Cooperation as an alternative form of the work system has been a subject matter of study by social scientists in different contexts (Nash, *et al*, 1976). The role of the state, i.e., the ruling class in cooperative and/or collective organisations has been studied in a number of countries. As an instrument of social change, the role of such institutions does not raise much controversy. What, however, is not clear is the direction and the purpose-seeking orientation of such an organisation system in a given socio-economic context. Manipulation by power-levers seem to be inevitable in most cases (Viqueira, 1976; Gagnon, 1976). Thus, popular participation remains a non-starter. Specific contexts and situations can, however, provide some hope. Viqueira documents the case of mutual cattle protection societies in Galicia in Spain where fifty family groups seem to manifest 'perfect social coordination and solidarity (which always occur with a minimum of formality or 'ritual' and which break up once their mission has been accomplished).' 'This has made us suspect on more than one occasion that the Galician peasant, far from lacking organising ability, has found a weapon of resistance in his apparent disorganisation, anarchism and excessive individualism' (p. 164).

Gagnon's investigation in Senegal, Cuba and Tunisia brought him to the conclusion that 'the cooperative system, even when it develops in a favourable context, does not preside over the birth of a new society but rather serves to facilitate the passage of marginal classes into the dominant mode of production ....' (p. 378). He does not make any distinction, in this regard, between a capitalist or a socialist system, an issue on which there cannot be an agreement unless one premises one's case on the bureaucratic–technocratic orientations of work organisation.

These cases also provide a range of tactics that the powerless did adopt, which might have resulted from a process of trial and error based on interplay of subjective and objective forces, to overcome passive and pathetic responses. All these cases are an expression acquiring a 'voice' through the process of horizontal mobilisation and the creation of a culture of homogeneity. A community, which is comparatively an 'unbound' system, can be brought with these tactical moves, to certain 'boundary' limits without which homogeneity cannot be attained. The internal organising process and environmental interaction through-mobilising are the means by which these have been attempted.

Yet another aspect is that, in certain cases, socially desirable ideals premised on future scenario are consciously cultivated throughout the developmental phases of organising and mobilising. In such cases, the organisational investment to strengthen the power base will be more effective. In the Maliwada case, ideals were comparatively restricted. In the case of Operation Barga, they were less visible. In the other three cases ideals were more pronounced and evenly shared. The new organisational crystal does not, however, emerge as purpose-seeking. What in effect happens is that the emerging actors anchor their behavioural modes of action including definition and reformulation of goals in a complex of ideals. The Chipko movement is quite distinctive as also the Gonoshasthaya Kendra. Maintaining an ecological balance in the reality of the Himalayan sub-region is an expression of maintaining a life-style to recreate a future not isolated from the realities of the present. The future is not embedded in regression but in progression. The territorial coverage in Uttar Kashi was comparatively limited. The relevance of such a movement need not be too strongly emphasised. There are authoritative official information to indicate that, over the past three decades, India has lost five million hectares of forest through relentless deforestation and denudation. There are indications that such activities are on the increase (Shah, 1979). The Himalayan region including the area around which the Chipko movement grew up, is exposed to more intensive exploitation. Commerce and profits are an inexorable logic. In the Kashmir Valley, ten million CFT of timber will be required to package exportable fruits by 1985. In Toukland in U.P., the State Forest Corporation is felling pine forests on hill tops to meet the growing demands. To overcome growing resistance from the local population, armed police are being deployed. The trinity of the State authorities, contractors and imported musclemen type labour are at it with determination. The Chipko movement's future is thus shrouded in uncertainty. What is the future of non-violent resistance? Perhaps, the mobilising process will lead to confrontation and bloodshed. Realisation of the ideals of GK in Bangladesh could not be conceived on the canvas of a nation state. Nonetheless, the spread effect cannot be lost sight of and the effect of the spread within manageable boundaries need not be under-estimated. In fact, it is not inconceivable that more and more of its members may be encouraged to start creating their own 'enclaves' in different parts of the country and the Kendra will continue to revitalise itself by fresh intakes. There are growing evidences (Arens and Bearden, 1977; Hartmann, 1979) that despite the commonality of religion, there are conflicts among classes, the struggle over land and the subjugation of women. It is also evident that the poorest women are sincerely keen on family planning, despite the superstitious myth, which is hopelessly frustrated by the bureaucratic labyrinth. In the inevitable conflicts of interest, the success of the Kendra may also lead to more intensive confrontation. What option can a purposeful organisation enjoy in such a growing reality, other than the organising and mobilising processes?

Voluntary organisations under discussion have their constraints just as bounded organisations, such as an industrial concern, have. There is, however, a qualitative difference. When a target group is powerless, the initial component of a shared sense of homogeneity is much too weak. That is why consciousness building within the cadre and then its extension to the peripheral members by relating it to their felt needs are so vital. The leaders' own consciousness about the liberation process perhaps begins with a search as to what extent they are liberated from the 'shackled' values of a system and to what extent they have been 'unchained' from these. Comprehension of this intra-psychic conflict within themselves is a building block for spearheading organising process. Liberation is a becoming process. It is more painful and tortuous when the actors are 'imprisoned' within the structure of a system. It is futile to use a surgical method to bring about an effective mobilising process without the sacrifice of human resources within the ranks of the powerless. Betrayal by some or many is not unexpected. But that the actors are likely to acquire the 'critical mass' for moving ahead is more relevant which may even ultimately bring the 'traitors' back into the fold. There are instances that 'dropouts' became useful elements in an organising process (Hinton, 1972).

Trist (1979) studied a number of community movements in the USA, Canada and the UK. Although these groups are different on many dimensions from our sample, we can still compare our experiences with his.

TRIST		DE
The Directions of Innovation		**The Directions of Innovation**
Outside:	Periphery, not centre	The powerless with leadership from within or without but essentially consisting of those who are not part of the establishment.
Below:	Bottom-up, not top-down	Top-down to begin with, but for effectiveness, the bottom asserts itself failing which organisational entropy ensues.

Middle:	Community, not national level	In a segmented society with significantly different power bases, we see segmented community mobilisation as a necessity.
Across:	Network leverage, not formal channels	Network leverage is relevant, but it seems to emerge after the powerless have acquired enough collective strength to give them adequate visibility even to establish linkage with potential supporters. 'Authenticity' appears critical for establishing linkage.

At this stage, it is necessary to comment on the Esman hypothesis (1978) based on the Cornell project covering sixteen rural studies in different Asian countries. His conclusion is that *constituency organisations* are necessary and desirable instruments for carrying out development administration among the rural poor. These organisations are seen as mediating agencies between the government institutions and the potential beneficiaries who are otherwise unorganised and unable to absorb and retain developmental gains. Our cases and analyses raise a number of issues in respect of such mediating type machinery. Who will constitute the *core* of such a social instrument? What is their class affiliation and what motivates them to undertake such a responsibility? These questions remain unconfronted in the Esman hypothesis. He believes that:

Effective constituency organisation is facilitated and may indeed depend on relative equity in the ownership and control of land, since this reduces the risk that they will be captured by established elites. Likewise, there is danger in including in the same organisation groups with inherently conflicting social and economic interests, such as incompatible ethnic groups as landowners and landless workers (p. 169).

Our analysis supports this contention. With certain provisos, ethnicity need not always be seen as a hindrance. However, he also propounds that constituency organisations should have *dual* accountability: *downward* to the membership and *upward* to governments. This proposition gives rise to our reservation. Should the character of the ruling caste be taken as the 'given' reality? Does it imply a collaborative type constituency organisation within an oppressive regime? Our contention about the need for changing the politico-legal structure whenever warranted has been neglected by Esman. In fact, an FAO study (Van Heck, 1979) conducted in countries of Asia, Near East and Africa confirms our thesis that collaboration strategy has its severe limitations.

Our study emanated from three possible ways of looking at an organisation system (De, 1979B). These are 'pre-modern', modern and 'post-modern' categories. A pre-modern organisation system is one which has been or is in a state of sub-optimum level mainly because of lack of knowledge, skills and predominance of ignorance. It does not imply that there is lack of opportunity. The tribals of Dhanbad before the organising process stirred up were probably at this stage and so were the hilly people in the Uttar Kashi area. The modern organisation, large or small, is hierarchic; it follows division of labour, under the suzerainty of technology, structured on impersonal or quasi-impersonal work relationships more or less reflecting instrumental measures of humans. Work is labour and labour is a marketable commodity subject to the dynamics of the prevailing economic system. A post-modern organisation opts for human development and not physical resource accretion on an alternative rationale of future oriented ideals.

We have tried to understand the genesis, growth and the stabilising process of rural voluntary organisations in the context of a scenario of the post-modern system. The cases offer elements of evidence that such an organisation tends to reflect some of the components of a post-modern human system. It is hypothesised that this trend is not culture specific or north-south confrontation specific. The potential exists in a poor country like Bangladesh as much as it does in a rich country. The paths that history will take for this kind of organisation to emerge may, however, be different in different contexts. Violence is not a distinguishing feature. There are evidences of violence while attempting to change a system as much in India as in the USA. What brings about the distinction is the content and the quality of ideals from which springs the motive-power to organise and mobilise.

3

Search Conference and Conscientisation Process in Building Institutions

In chapter 2, we have dealt with the organising and mobilising processes in evolving organisational entities in rural settings. There the intervention strategies employed are found to be diverse with varying degrees of effectiveness. In this chapter we shall explore and evaluate two known strategies. In a way, the spirit of these approaches are implicit in the work system redesign projects mentioned in the first chapter. The strategies discussed here refer to educational paradigms which can contribute to the cause of alternative social system designs.

We probe the prospect of a search conference as well as the conscientisation process as among the leading building blocks for the evaluation of institutions as *purposeful* systems. In this effort we shall confront two issues in the very beginning. *In the first place*, the way institutions have been differentiated from organisations cannot go unquestioned. It calls for validation. *Secondly*, the search conference as an action model has been bracketed with the conscientisation approach which is essentially a dialectic model of learning and changing (praxis). This observation too cannot go unchallenged. So, let us begin with the first issue.

Institutions and Organisations

Eisenstadt (1972), on the basis of his own work and a review of what he considered as relevant literature, reflected on social institution in terms of patterns of behaviour and regulatory mechanisms of behaviour which include norms, sanctions and stratifications. While he refers to collective goal-setting and norm-setting strata, he conceives of institutional dynamics essentially in terms of an exchange model. There is an acknowledged role for 'institutional entrepreneurs'. In his model there is room for basic 'Structural Core' and 'Coercive Core' even though there is a mention of the 'non-exchangeable' reality of human existence and endeavour. Emphasising the exchange model with appropriate distinction between 'mechanical solidarity' and 'organic solidarity', he has been led to the concept of an institution as an equilibrium state with a fabric of various frameworks, organisations and norms. Institutional parameters, such as (*i*) innovation and crystallisation of norms, articulation of goals and mobilisation of resources; (*ii*) clubbing together of certain values (though not explicitly spelled out), sanctions and organisations; and (*iii*) role performance, as identified by Eisenstadt, do not provide any significant insight into the futuristic *becoming* process of institutions. Rather, it seems to leave the impression that the elitist role, bargaining process and the concept of sanctions within the framework of the organisation structure and implicitly based on Weberian rationalistic model of bureaucracy.

In another context, Eisenstadt (1959) makes a distinction between bureaucracy as a tool for implementation of goals and bureaucracy as an instrument of power. But he does not deal with the dynamics of the debureaucratisation process other than introducing the element of clientele in his conceptual framework. It appears that an inability to distinguish between purposeful-system and goal-system has led him to equate institutions with organisations, despite his acknowledgement of the basic 'non-exchangeable' goals of human existence and endeavour.

The tradition that is discernible in Eisenstadt has been reflected in some other thinkers. Selznick (1966) makes a distinction between institutions as being responsive, adaptive organisms, as a product of social needs and pressures, and organisations as instruments of maximising efficiency and management. However, while deliberating on institutional leadership, he expresses the view that:

> he (the leader) must specify and recast the general aims of his organisation so as to adapt them, without serious corruption, to the requirements of institutional survival. This is what we mean by the definition of institutional mission and role.

To him, institution, organisational character and distinctive competence—all of these—refer to 'transformation of engineered, technical arrangement of building blocks into a social organism.' The concept of goal and goal-setting is still the predominant element in his framework.

Esman (1967) is more explicit when he defines institutions as a 'change-inducing and change-protecting formal organisation', a view which in some way or other is shared by Perlmutter (1965); Hill *et al* (1973); Pareek (1977); and Baumgartel (1976). It is no doubt fair to mention that some of them, as applied behavioural scientists, are concerned about the dysfunctions of bureaucratic organisations and as such are motivated towards planned organisation development strategies. Yet, there is an element of fuzziness and lack of clarity in discriminating between *ideals* and *goals*. Vickers (1973) has indeed been able to distinguish between values, norms and policies; however, he too perceives institutional roles and personal roles in organisational context, while emphasising the relevance of 'responsibility of every member of every system' in the pervasive process of management of conflict.

Recently, some scholars have been drawn towards value orientation of institutional designs. Bell (1976) in an analysis of the cultural contradictions of contemporary society mentions that: 'Western society lacks both the spontaneous willingness to make sacrifices for some public good, and a political philosophy that justifies the normative rules of priorities and allocations in the society.' Recognising the depersonalisation phenomenon in the contemporary bureaucratic system, the swing of developmental strategy from asceticism to hedonism, the contradictions and conflicts implicit in the dynamics between acquisitive culture, democratic policy and personal liberty that evade social responsibilities and sacrifices, he seeks to develop the idea of a *public* household 'within the explicit framework of social goals'. He perceives that the resolution, essentially, can come only from a 'consensual agreement on the normative issue of distributive justice in the balance to be struck between growth and social consumption'. In a critique of Weber, Satow (1975) has sought to introduce a concept of value-rational authority, thereby introducing a concept of ideology, essentially based on her insights into the working of professional organisations. Similarly, Weick (1976) has developed the concept of 'loosely coupled systems' for educational organisations.

While these efforts are an advancement in search for institutional rationale and forms, they are essentially an attempt at change 'within the system' by seeking to extrapolate some values and norms on which, however, a clarity is not easily discernible. Even Schein's (1970) 'role-innovative' role concept for professional career does not provide a futuristic gestalt for institutional ideals, even though his insight leads him to the observation that

the essence of role innovation is a rejection of some of the norms which govern some of the practices of the profession, combined with an interest in elucidating the true or ideal role of the professional in Society.

Sabatier's (1975) analysis of the phenomenon of domestication of regulatory agencies by the 'clientele capture' strategy spells out the critical role of the constituency support system. However, a dominant active constituency can create a regulatory mechanism to tame and weaken the intended beneficiaries of the regulatory agency to 'serve' the aborigines in Queensland (Australia) and the tribal population in India. Thus a hiatus between 'goal-seeking' and 'purpose-seeking' can be created. Similarly, Illich's (1969, 1970, 1976) allergy to institutionalisation of education, health and modern transport systems is understandable.

Two observations are in order at this stage. One, the hydra-headed organisational society has been rendering human agents into 'organisation men'. Those who accept this reality as inevitable, even desirable, view the institutionalisation process as one to eke out a constricted 'free space' role for human actors. Second, the searchers have developed their framework of enquiry within the context of what Emery, *et al* (1974) have identified as a type III social system: disturbed-reactive. Technological breakthrough since the turn of the century has sought to establish its hegemony over the human systems (Ellul, 1967). Understandably, then, the searchers have been seeking to 'humanise' organisation systems to ameliorate the 'bewitchment of technology' (Bell, 1967), not necessarily a radical departure from the current reality. The emphasis has thus been on organisation system reform. Management techniques, either in a packaged form or as a single-shot strategy, have been emphasised in the literature on institution-building approaches. Somehow human considerations have been sought to be 'added' to efficiency requirements of technological demands. It is relevant to mention, in passing, that Turner (1976) has sought to dichotomise self between *self-as-impulse* and *self-as-institution* to make the point that 'many standard sociological assumptions about social control are incompatible with the new pattern of self-identification.'

These binds, it is suggested, can be more adequately, if not comprehensively, dealt with if organisations are conceived as building blocks for the institutionalising process. Here some significant leads have been provided by interdisciplinary action-research-oriented scientists—Ackoff and Emery (1972), Emery and Trist (1972), Emery, *et al* (1974), Emery (1976A), etc.

Working on the premise of the type IV environment—*turbulence*—Emery and his colleagues have developed ideas about relevant response patterns for organisations. M. Emery's (1976) pictorial presentation is as given in Fig. 3.1.

Two significant aspects arising out of the approaches in Fig. 3.1 are (*i*) transition from goals to multi-goals to purposes to ideals (Ackoff,

Figure 3.1

Problem-puzzling Approach

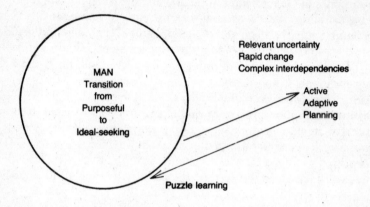

1971) and (*ii*) a shift from technique-laden, problem-solving learning to puzzle learning (searching process).

A noteworthy distinction arises here. Whereas an organisation system will operate on goal-seeking (rather, multiple goal-seeking) motivation with concomitant interests and corresponding behaviour patterns, thereby seeking to optimise results, an institution will seek higher level rationality to transform a human system from goal-seeking to purpose-seeking to ideal-seeking orientation. With this objective in view, problem-solving learning will call for a more open-system 'problematising' type of learning where human efforts are directed towards being 'with the world' rather than only 'in the world', a critical consciousness of reality with a view to changing the objective reality. Emery (1976A), proceeding further from previous work (Emery and Trist, 1972), has summarised the situation which can be presented in the format given in Table 3.1.

We sum up the position by stating that, for a clearer vision of the human universe and a desirable destiny, a distinction should thus be made between institutions and organisations. Creating an urge for ideals and designing conditions for members to aim at ideal-seeking is an Institution Building Process while multiple-goal-seeking is what the organisations are for.

Table 3.1
Human Ideals: Past, Present and Future

Parameters of Choice	Present Reality	Organisational Values	Human Ideals
Probability of choice	Selfishness	Transition from achievement to self-actualisation	*Nurturance* (cultivation and growth of people—self and others)
Probable effectiveness	Exploitation	Independence to inter-dependence	*Homonomy* (a sense of relatedness and belong-ingness to self and others)
Probability of outcome	Inhumanity	Self-control to self-expression	*Humanity* (man is the end measure)
Relative value of intention	Ugliness	Endurance of distress to capacity for joy	*Beauty* (aesthetic state)

While postulating this proposition we are aware of what Ackoff and Emery (1972) and Emery (1976A) have maintained. Emery has stated that 'only individuals can be ideal-seeking systems', that 'individuals can sustain the ideal-seeking state only temporarily' and that 'it is only within group life that ideals emerge'. Ackoff and Emery (1972) are of the view that

An ideal-seeking system or individual is necessarily one that is purposeful, but not all purposeful entities seek ideals. The capability of seeking ideals may well be a characteristic that distinguishes man from anything he can make, including computers.

While distinguishing between institutions and organisations, as we have sought to do, we are aware that human beings are common to both. The difference lies essentially in the reality that in the contemporary world (in our direct experience in the third world), human *agents* are primarily interests and goals-seeking entities in an organisation system while in an institution system human actors become capable of transcending interests and goals. They are potentially able to and seek consciously to create a social nexus so that inter-linking human work groups can become purposeful and ideal-seeking. In other words, we suggest that, in a futuristic context, an institution, as it is, is likely to be a habitat for human actors in ideal-seeking pursuits. As such, it may tend to move towards 'ideal-seeking if, on attainment of any of its objectives, it chooses another objective that more closely approximates its ideals' (quoted in Ackoff and Emery, 1972). In a sense an institution remains an *ideal* and yet sought after as something worth its while to create. (See Fig. 3.2.)

The essential point is that an organisation system is often conceived by its designers or its members as an open system in a limited context of environmental situations with the consequence that purposes and ideals are perceived vaguely and as remotely relevant. In the institution-building concept, organisations are seen as building blocks for ideal-oriented purposes. The boundary between organisations and institutions, in this approach, becomes permeable.

Search Conference

It will be our endeavour now to examine the role of the search conference as a modality for ensuring the initiation of institutional ideals. M. Emery's (1976) *Searching* has made a survey of the concept and a rationale of this strategy which, in a way, is an extension of Emery *et al*'s (1973) ideas contained in *Participative Design: Work and Community Life.* The first experiment with search conference design was attempted

Figure 3.2

*Configurational Representation of Transition from
Organisational Orientation to Institutional Orientation*

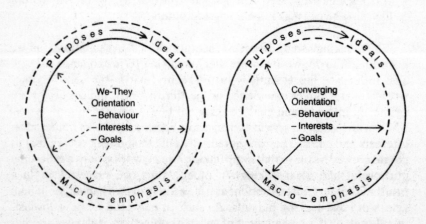

in 1960 (Trist and Emery, 1960). Since then, it has been utilised in a variety of situations. The strategy is seen as tentative and there is a conscious effort not to mystify it as *the* approach. The basic concepts can be identified as follows:

(*a*) Understanding of the social environment which both constrains and provides opportunities for the emergence of individuals as ideal-seeking systems.

(*b*) Learning situations within which an active adaptive planning task may be undertaken on the basis of such emergent individuals.

(*c*) A form of management to initiate group learning process so that it avoids those forces which inhibit learning and, hence, ensures that the capacity for future adaptive process and design is built into the search community itself. (M. Emery, 1976.)

M. Emery captures the situation of turbulent environment with clarity: 'Planning to produce a new state of affairs seems to presuppose that we know where we want to go, we know where we are now, we know what paths will take us from here to there and we know what means we have for traversing those paths.' For turbulent social environments this presumes an awful lot of knowledge. When the social setting and the human instruments of change are both changing, the knowledge we have today is increasingly less relevant. The dilemma is: 'how can we expect to improve our planning in the face of relatively decreasing knowledge?' From this and correlate diagnosis she tentatively concludes that the experts, knowledgeable on a project or programme, and the beneficiaries of the same, may create a work atmosphere where they can struggle together as co-producers of not only an effective planning process but also acceptable and better workable products.

Utilising these concepts, we can identify some leading parts of the design:

(*i*) To create conditions for collective learning processes for social planning to occur;

(*ii*) The structural scaffolding for learning is flexible enough to provide 'elbow room' to individuals to learn to work as a group and in search for viable alternatives 'converging in an understanding of a world which is self-directed towards the ideals of man'.

(*iii*) The staff role calls for elucidation. The staff, though knowledgeable, are not cast in a decision-making role. The *intrinsic* value of learning/exploring as a collaborative venture is their value-guide rather than an *extrinsic* motivation to act as a knowledgeable expert. The communication is polyarchical rather than uni-directional, dyadic. The staff members themselves work as a value-sharing group rather than as a multi-disciplinary team. The manipulative role, even in a subtle form, is unsuitable to the ethos of search.

(*iv*) There is an explicit commitment to the belief that the participants in a congenial learning-working situation can take responsibility for their own behaviour in responding to situational demands.

(*v*) A congenial work situation has several dynamics:
— Creating a non-threatening structure so that 'a framework of shared values and beliefs' can emerge through dialectics of agreements and disagreements in an experiential pedagogy.
— Use of simulation or game-playing techniques is avoided as these have a tendency to foster flight from reality orientation.
— Use of the selective approach in leaving out those participants who can be explicitly identified as hostile to learning-experiencing in an unstructured situation thereby acting as a barrier to progress.

Crombie (1976) sums up the approach: 'Any search conference is **found** to a large extent in the medium itself.'

In a sense, the search conference is a participative form of social planning where the end results are as vital as the opportunity to create the 'learning-planning community—experts and laymen together', with emphasis on joint learning. The search conference is thus a work-related education process which encourages the participants to reconstruct organisations and perhaps move these towards institutional forms.

It is also desirable to distinguish the search conference from the Delphi technique and committee working. Delphi considers an issue in depth, with specificity and technical details. As such, it does not enjoy the inter-connectedness, sweep and spontaniety of the search conference. Deviant views do not get lost in the search conference. The committees may tend to be propelled by power affiliation, rigid structuring seeking simpler solutions with the superficiality scenario (M. Emery, 1982).

The Gungahlin Experiment

M. Emery has documented several search conferences (1976). One such is the planning dynamics of a new town—Gungahlin. Gungahlin was conceived as a new town within metropolitan Canberra for a population around 1,00,000. It was felt by the Planning Division of the National Capital Development Commission (NCDC) that in order to bring the town to life in 1978, design activity was to commence in 1972.

A live-in search conference with active association of the Centre for Continuing Education (CCE) was organised at Guthega in 1974. Participation was decided on a voluntary basis from age-group 16–65 to ensure a mix of students and working people. There were 34 participants in the conference, although there was poor response from young married couples and members of lower socio-economic groups.

The objectives, briefly stated, were (*i*) community participation in social planning; (*ii*) participation in a meaningful activity intimately related to 'real-life' situations; (*iii*) an exposure, not necessarily to quantitative technological cobwebs, but to a qualitative sweep of a creative artist's overview; (*iv*) creation of a working-learning climate for young generations for reality orientation to adapt to competing values and goals; (*v*) provision of an opportunity to NCDC to clarify its role; and (*vi*) maintaining a stance of tentativeness so that the CCE search designers could acquire better insights into design problems.

M. Emery presents the overall structure of the search conference as given in Fig. 3.3.

While reviewing the conference a year hence, Angela Sands (M. Emery, 1975) of NCDC recalls her impressions immediately after the conference in these words:

1. The planner's role in society should be a more active advocate's role, in partnership with the community.
2. The environment is important, quite vitally so, and should be protected by controls if necessary. This includes encouraging a more modest use of resource, maximum covenants, public transport, wilderness conservation.
3. 'Community' only has meaning if people manage or control their physical and social environment. Schools, parks, creches, centres can only become meaningful and significant if those who use them make the important decisions regarding their use and management. As social interaction and social networks are the bases of community, an imperative of physical planning must be to plan, not to leave to chance, opportunities for the meeting and association of people.
4. The plurality and diversity of our towns and cities was recognised as a positive attribute.

Opportunities for increasing a choice in life style was advocated, although the centrifugal effects of this were also recognised.

After a year, her review reads as follows:

It is difficult to measure carefully the effect of such an occurrence,

Figure 3.3

Gungahlin Search Conference Gestalt

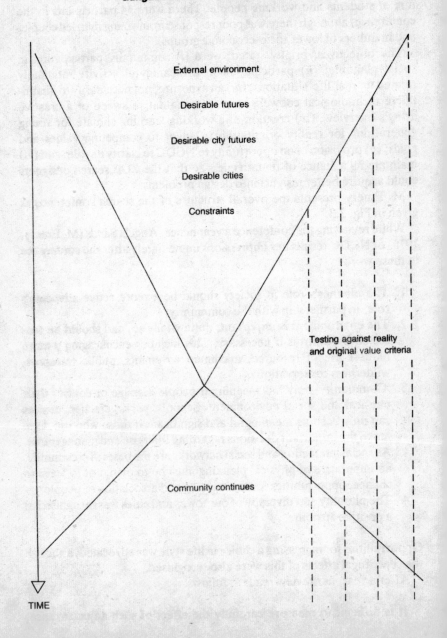

External environment

Desirable futures

Desirable city futures

Desirable cities

Constraints

Testing against reality
and original value criteria

Community continues

TIME

particularly by diffusion in the general community. It was a meaningful important occurrence for those who participated, it fulfilled the objectives of involving, in a creative positive situation, a group of young persons in the planning of Gungahlin New Town. The effectiveness of the search conference structure was fully satisfied, the recommendations were listened to by the official bodies with some real sympathy. As a first attempt at serious consultation with the community there is no doubt of its success.

Some of the essential elements that have motivated the innovators of the search conference are:

(*a*) a basic faith in human worth for reaching out towards an ideal-seeking system and in order that it becomes feasible.
(*b*) 'you cannot build a viable creative human community unless you build into it some room for the community to start taking over its own planning. That is, a community is only that when it can generate itself.'
(*c*) a sense of relief from avoidable constraints of learning structures so that freedom-prone reality search becomes possible to sensitise an involved community to discover and experience the institutional ideals as spelled out by Emery (1976A).

There will be further comments on search conference strategy at a later stage.

Conscientisation Process

Paulo Freire started his work in north-east Brazil by actively associating himself with poor, exploited, superstition-ridden peasantry in an effort to liberate themselves from a 'culture of silence' and marginal existence through a literacy programme linked with an appreciation of objective reality and changing that reality to a state of desirable futures. This strategy of education and action for the 'children of darkness' was carried out in Chile, Peru and more recently in Guinea-Bissau and other countries through the efforts of the Institute for the Development of Peoples in Paris, the Institute of Cultural Action in Geneva, the Education Programme Unit of the World Council of Churches and others.

The basic themes of the approach have been documented primarily by Freire (1972A, 1972B, 1974, 1978). The core element in the conceptual framework is the idea of *conscientisation*.

Conscientization refers to the process in which men, not as recipients, but as knowing subjects, achieve a depending awareness both of the socio-cultural reality which shapes their lives and of their capacity to transform that reality. (1972B).

The reality refers to social, political, economic and cultural contradictions inherent in the contemporary disturbed-reactive human environment. 'There can be no conscientization of the people without a radical denunciation of dehumanising structures, accompanied by the proclamation of a new reality to be created by men' (1972B). In a later exposition, Freire has restated his position not in terms of two stages of development—awareness of current reality and then an attempt at transformation of the same—but as a *becoming process*. 'It is ... important that in the conscientization process the uncovering of social reality be grasped not as something which is, but as something which is *becoming*, as something *which is in the making*' (1975).

This becoming dynamics, not necessarily a new concept to humanistic psychologists, such as Maslow, Carl Rogers and Rollo May, have been anchored in the concept of *praxis* by Freire. Drawing on the insights of Marx (1966) who wrote that 'the materialist theory that men are the product of different circumstances and a different education, forgets that the circumstances are actually transformed by men, and that the educator himself needs to be educated', he has sharpened his thoughts by highlighting the inner contradictions of splitting *action* from *reflection*.

.... If action is emphasised exclusively, to the detriment of reflection, the world is converted into *activism*. The latter ... negates the true praxis and makes dialogue impossible. Either dichotomy, by unauthentic forms of existence, also creates unauthentic forms of thought which reinforce the original dichotomy. (1972A).

Proceeding further.

Praxis is involved in the concrete situations which are codified for critical analysis. To analyse codification in its 'deep structure', is ... to reconstruct the former praxis and to become capable of a new different praxis. The relationship between the *theoretical context*, in which codified representations of objective facts are analysed, and the *concrete context* where these facts occur, has to be made real. (1972B).

.... Only human beings ... who work, who possess a thought-language, who act and who are capable of reflection on themselves and on their own action ... only they are beings of praxis. They are praxis. (1974).

Praxis thus acquires a futuristic orientation. A futuristic orientation calls for objectives.

Our pedagogy cannot do without a vision of man and of the world. It formulates a scientific humanist conception which finds its expression in a dialogical praxis in which the teachers and learners together in the act of analysing a dehumanising reality, denounce it while announcing its transformation in the name of the liberation of man. (1972B).

Praxis is thus linked with liberation—the creation of a desirable future.

I consider the fundamental theme of our epoch to be that of *domination*. This implies that the objective to be achieved is *liberation*, its opposite theme .... In order to achieve humanisation, which presupposes the elimination of dehumanising oppression, it is absolutely necessary to surmount the limit situations in which men are reduced to things. (1972A).

The change-proneness pregnant in the concept of praxis to convert contemporary human degradation into a desirable future leads to the *dialogical process*—the medium through which praxis has been sought to be realised. This process starts with a departure from the 'Banking' and 'Digestive' predilection to knowledge acquisition (1972B). It challenges the authenticity of extension education; it favours communication as more efficacious (1974). Dialogue essentially involves the elimination of the teacher-taught dichotomy (or status hierarchy) in that both become *subjects* in search of an object (or theme, problem, i.e., exploration and transformation of reality). There is thus a praxical relationship among human actors (the teachers and the taught as subjects in a common quest) and between the subject and the object (objective reality and its transformation).

The de-elitisation of the knowledgeable (the staff) in a dialogical relationship involves some parameters of ideals: 'a profound love for the world and for men', a sense of humility and 'an intense faith in man.' (1972A).

'Authentic education is not carried on by A for B or by A about B, but A with B, mediated by the world—a world which impresses and challenges both parties, giving rise to views or opinions about it.' The act of extension, whether in relation to 'transmission, handing over, giving, missionism, mechanical transfer, cultural invasion, manipulation, etc.,' negate the search for reality and its transformation. The staff role is 'communication, not extension' (1974). This sentiment is in consonance with Fromm's

(1964) observation: '... knowledge means that the individual makes his own way, learning, feeling, experimenting with himself, observing others, and finally coming to a conviction without having an irresponsible opinion.' The leadership role of staff, unless it takes dialogical, praxical relationship, may lapse into dangers of 'massification' resulting in dehumanisation and alienation.

The dialogical process is for a purpose. This purpose is *problematising* or developing *critical* consciousness. Problematising is 'problem-posing education' with a futuristic (hopeful) orientation. The objective is to explore the historical role of humans, to identify the dynamics of regress and progress, segmentation and integration and then to build the praxical modes.

> We must realise that the aspirations, the motives and the objectives implicit in meaningful thematic or generative themes that have critical relevance to them, are human aspirations, motives and objectives. They do not exist out there somewhere, as static entities: they are occurring. They are as historical as men themselves; consequently, they cannot be apprehended apart from men. To apprehend these themes and to understand them is to understand both the men who embody them and the reality to which they refer. (1972A).

Thus, problem-posing activity involves people's thinking about reality as it *affects* them, whether these are superstitious or naive rethinking about them.

> In the process of problematisation, any step made by a subject to penetrate the problem-situation continually opens up new roads for other subjects to comprehend the object being analysed....Problematisation implies a critical return to action. The process...is basically someone's reflection on a content which results from an act, or reflection on the act itself in order to act better together with others within the framework of reality....Transcendence must take its point of departure from discussion on the *here*, which for humans is always a *now* too. (1974).

What does problem-focusing do? The objective is a series of action-reflection dynamics leading to, hopefully, a state of critical consciousness. However, reality consciousness in a type III environment—disturbed-reactive—is likely to be in a state of *semi-intransitivity of consciousness*—a state caused by a massified culture imposed by the elite group that sits on the top of the socio-economic-politico-cultural pyramid, causing constricted, introverted and closed social structures. Kennedy (1975) expresses it this way:

> ... oppression involves subjugation to overarching 'myths' which prevent people perceiving clearly their actual condition. Freire analyses the introjection of the dominating value system of society into its people, so that they lack the structural perception necessary to see that their values reflect their dominators' advantage rather than their own. These cultural myths often supported by religious teaching immerse people in an ideology that limits their ways of reality. This 'mythification of reality' results in a falsification of consciousness.

Dialogical processes with subjects (who are *in* and *with* the world) pursuing the search for the meanings of generative themes (objects), 'amplify their power to perceive and respond to suggestions and questions arising in their context' (1974) adding further to the quality of dialogue leading to a stage of *transitivity*. 'Transitivity of consciousness makes man permeable' (1974). However, this stage in a developmental epic is still a state of naive transitivity (consciousness). '....It is the consciousness of men who are still almost part of a mass in whom the developing capacity for dialogue is still fragile and capable of distortion' (1974). Unless it develops into the next higher level of the epigenetic stage of consciousness, it may be deflected by sectarian irrationality into fanaticism. This may be called *fanaticised transitivity*. The progressive step, however, will be *critical transitivity* (or consciousness) which is symbolised by authenticity, democratic culture (i.e., people-orientation), permeability (i.e., flexibility), culture of centrality (as opposed to the culture of silence) and a continuous dynamic equilibrium of man-world balance.

> Critical consciousness is integrated with reality; naive consciousness superimposes itself on reality and fanatical consciousness whose pathological naivete leads to the irrational, adapts to reality...critical understanding leads to critical action: magic understanding to magic response. (1974).

The pedagogy of learning, in Freire's concepts, aims at 'the practice of freedom.' This concept of freedom is central to the cognitive map. He makes a distinction, depending on the character of historical reality, between cultural action and cultural revolution. While one is called for in a limiting situation of dominating forces, the other can operate in a comparatively more liberating situation where the reality of marginality has been surmounted, at least, halted and weakened.

Before we proceed to the examination of concrete cases on conscienti-sation strategy, let us present the thoughts expressed so far in a schematic form, as shown in Fig. 3.4.

BIRLA INSTITUTE OF TECHNOLOGY AND SCIENCES [BITS] AND GUINEA-BISSAU CASES: TRANSITION OF TRANSITIVITY

We shall now study two cases—one a micro-level experiment in India and another at a macro-level in a newly liberated country—in order to relate our understanding to the Freirean approach.

BITS

In 1964, BITS, located at Pilani in Rajasthan, acquired University-level status and gradually it shifted its approach to higher education. Its Chairman, G.D. Birla, expressed his vision in these words, in 1965:

> ... The time has come when we should revolt against all out-of-date ideas, and acquire new knowledge, acquire new dreams, think in a new method and be prepared to face the problem of 1985 .... For this purpose, we have to change our concepts, we have to change our visions and angles, and we have to be prepared for future.

The change process could take a more visible shape in early 1970s when a new Director was inducted into the system. His induction and urge for action initially created a stir within the system—the faculty and, perhaps with their implicit encouragement, the students. The management stood by him. He survived and started developing a new approach to structuring education programmes leading to an action plan.

The *first* step was to create a common base for a discipline-based programme: engineering (different branches), natural sciences, pharmacy, management, social sciences and humanities by making the first year of the 5-year programme (4-year for pharmacy) with common inputs. *Secondly*, at the end of the first year, provision was made for flexibility for students to seek movement from one stream to another, although certain obvious limitations are there. A student of humanities may not qualify for an engineering stream. Even in the second year, a certain common base is maintained for all streams while initiation to knowledge specialisation comes in. *Thirdly*, a concept of practice school has been introduced in the third year for a period of 2½ months which goes on increasing in the fourth and fifth year when it becomes 5½ months. Practice school is meant to cover all streams including humanities. The concept applies to master level engineering education and even at the doctorate level.

Figure 3.4

Dynamics of Critical Consciousness

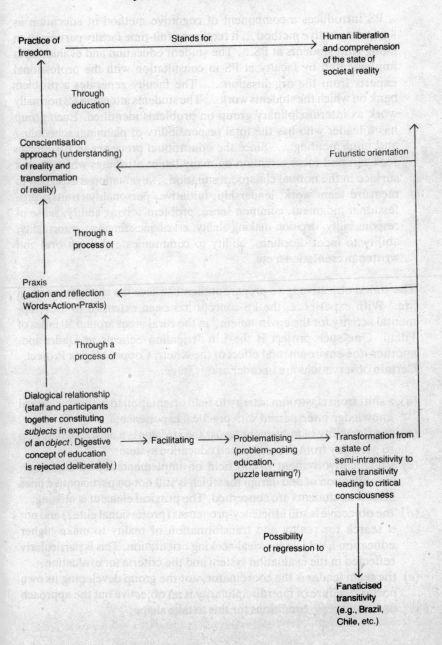

The motivation for and approach to practice school (PS), in the words of Mandke (1975) are as follows:

> ...PS introduces a component of cognitive method of education as against narrative method ... it requires a full-time faculty participation along with students at PS.... The student education and evaluation is implemented by faculty at PS in consultation with the professional experts from the organisation .... The faculty generates a problem bank on which the students work.... The students attending PS normally work as interdisciplinary group on problems identified. Each group has a leader who has the total responsibility of planning, scheduling and implementing .... Since the educational processes in PS courses seek out and focus attention on many latent attributes which do not surface in the normal classroom situation, ...evaluation is designed to measure team work, leadership, initiative, personality (traits), professional judgment, common sense, problem-solving ability, sense of responsibility, decision-making ability, art of guesstimation, punctuality, ability to meet deadlines, ability to communicate through oral and written presentations, etc.

The stated objective is 'to prepare students to face the challenges of real life.' With experience, the PS concept has been extended to 'developmental activity for the environment,' in the rural areas around 50 miles of Pilani. One such project is the Lift Irrigation Scheme at Dadri and, another, the environmental effect of the Khetri Copper Mining Project. Certain observations are in order at this stage:

(a) a shift from classroom activity to field orientation to make theoretical knowledge interspersed with practical experience;

(b) the flexibility of movement across the streams is a desirable first step to get away from the segmented education system;

(c) student involvement in the field on implementation of a project, identification of and design for which is still not on participative lines insofar as students are concerned. The praxical element is missing;

(d) the objective is still efficiency-proneness (professional elite?) and not a search for reality and transformation of reality to make higher education a vehicle for ideal-seeking orientation. This is particularly reflected in the evaluation system and the criteria for evaluation;

(e) the team leader is the coordinator, not the group developing its own norms. Culture of interdisciplinarity is an objective but the approach does not create conditions for this to take shape;

(f) the responses of students who have volunteered for PS, indicate that quantum of stipends they receive from the host organisations is an important incentive for going in for PS. Exposure to realities of life has been defined with hedonistic orientation;

(g) rural exposure in order to change reality in the form of development of appropriate technology has not yet become a priority.

Guinea-Bissau

Guinea-Bissau, on the western coast of Africa, has a population of 800,000 of which 90 per cent of the working age group is involved in agriculture, particularly paddy cultivation. There are more than 20 ethnic groups with more than that number of languages. The country was dominated by Portugal for centuries. The liberation struggle mobilised with Amilcar Cabral at the vanguard of the movement was hard and bitter. In early 1973, Cabral was murdered but the struggle went on with Luis and Mario Cabral filling up the vacuum. In September 1973, independence was declared by the African Party for the Independence of Guinea and Cape Verde (PAIGC) and, in 1974, the country joined the comity of free nations.

In the spring of 1975, IDAC of Geneva and Paulo Freire were invited by the Education Commissioner, Mario Cabral, to 'participate in the development of the national adult literacy programme' for the country. There is a little piece of history behind the priority given to education within a year of national liberation. Amilcar Cabral had close empathy and priority for children. He used to begin his struggling day with the morning spent with children in the schools. 'The children are the flowers and the reason for our fight.' In the words of Oliveira and Oliveira (1976), 'Children (there) represented the future.' Freedom thus provided the spark to use education as a strategy for building the new society. Within a year, the people's government asked a conscientisation-oriented group to join this venture.

The group adopted a dialogical approach from the very first contact with the government and continued the spirit of conviviality with the education authorities and the people. The exploration together encountered two broad streams of culture: a culture of gut-level nativity and a culture of colonised elitism. The first group, the vast majority 'may not all possess sophisticated technical know-how or super specialisation, they may not always have the answer to every question but they do have a visceral, daily and practical knowledge of their country and its people. They know why they do things....' (Oliveira, *et al*, 1976). The other culture as nurtured by the colonial school system for urban areas had no other goal than teaching the Africans how to be more useful to the Portuguese.

The dialogical pursuit gradually identified the challenges for 'reinventing education' in Guinea-Bissau (recreating the issue as Wertheimer (1945) would have it).

(*a*) 'To permit the re-examination and theoretical elaboration of all political and cultural experience which the freedom-fighters accumulated during the independence struggle.

(*b*) To assist their political development and technical training for new tasks, either inside the army or, for those to be demobilised, when they re-enter the rural setting.'

One aspect is apparent. Literate or not, in their context, words such as struggle, unity, land, work and production are loaded with both existential experience and political context for the people. 'Each of these words contains *a theme for discussion* in such a way that the progressive mastering of the language can be accomplished at the same time as the group reflects on its concrete situation and real problems.

Learning a linguistic code, then, goes together with developing political awareness and receiving technical preparation for accomplishing immediate tasks.'

(*c*) The realisation that a failure of massive literacy campaigns is primarily due to its isolation, an end in itself and not related to everyday reality leading to the transformation of current reality.

With these diagnostic insights, the group began its task with a spirit of experimentation. The staff expertise was not taken or given as a major input. The very fact that the first visit of the group in September 1975 was followed by the second visit in February 1976, is indicative of the reality that the homework of learning/experiencing was being locally rooted and generated.

The tasks, unlike the tradition-hallowed concept of education, began with re-emphasising the positive aspects of African culture with equal emphasis given to confronting the dynamics of negative aspects leading to an awareness of and action flowing therefrom in transforming those aspects. Some of these were: *marginalisation of women, feeling of powerlessness and paralysis when encountering natural phenomena and 'submission to oppressive authoritarianism' of tribal chieftains*. At the political level, the significance of organising production activities on non-bureaucratic lines, highlighting the need for cooperation and solidarity through group work, making learning as an active component of work-life, making the emerging educated integrated with the common people's life and work became the highlights. Oliveira, *et al* (1976) sum up the approach in these words:

On a blank sheet, everything is possible; you can write or draw what is the most new and the most beautiful. This is even more so in relation to literacy.

The approach adopted took two directions:

— towards the group's past and present social practice, encouraging a critical understanding;
— towards the future, stimulating the group to conscious and creative involvement in bettering the reality around them.

A later review of the Guinea-Bissau national level change process by Freire (1978) highlights the context of experiments undertaken. The foothold of a continuing learning-changing culture has its own character-istic grip. The Brazilian experiences could not be shipped to Chile. And Chilean experiments could not be transplanted to Guinea-Bissau. It was realised in the instant case that the liberating struggle was 'a cultural fact and a factor of culture', and so the consciousness sharpening process was mooted in the dialectics of unity of learning through working.

The new knowledge, going far beyond the limits of the earlier knowledge, reveals the reason for being behind the facts, thus demythologizing the false interpretations of these same facts. And so, there is now no more separation between thought, language and objective reality. The reading of a text now demands a 'reading' within the social context to which it refers. In this sense, literacy education for adults becomes an introduction to the effort to systematise the knowl-edge that rural and urban workers gain in the course of their daily activity—a knowledge that is never self-explanatory but must always be understood in terms of the ends that it serves. (Freire, 1978).

The process (means) has to complement the spirit of the ends. The collective approach enlivens and enriches the individual effort. Ackoff and Emery (1972) make the distinction among *observation, perception, sensation* and *consciousness*. We postulate that the dialogical process as collectively utilised in re-shaping this African community, sharpened and expanded the dimensions of observation, perception, sensation and feeling to redefine the context and the content of critical consciousness.

All in all, the tentative assessment

demonstrates very clearly that a people's *total existential experience* can become a fundamental source of new knowledge. Within such a context, the school can play only a complementary role, and even then only to the extent that it succeeds in systematising the general experience being lived and brought to life by the people's social practice. (Oliveria, *et al*, 1976).

The BITS and Guinea-Bissau experiences have been presented together with a view to appreciating the emphasis, in an historical context of a social system setting, that underscores the differential approaches. This is not to suggest that the BITS experiment lacks the potential of finding out extended free space to build bridges between higher education and the transformation of reality. But for that to happen it is apt to realise that professional education and the realities of on-going life of the people do not necessarily converge. The excellence in the learning role is not as if development matters but that development is desirable as if people matter. This shift is, we believe, a *sine qua non* on using organisations as building blocks for ushering the ideal-seeking systems.

Search Conference and Conscientisation Process: An Overview

We shall seek to view the two approaches as a contribution to institution-building efforts.

In order to do that, let us present our understanding of the two modalities, quite unique in many ways, breaking away from conventional wisdom in terms of their emphasis, priorities and process. (See p. 177 ff.)

A. *Explicit Common Elements that Distinguish the Two Approaches*

Search Conference (SC)	**Conscientisation Process (CP)**
1. Futuristic orientation with emphasis on man as ideal-seeking system.	1. Futuristic orientation with emphasis on 'practice of freedom' as man's destiny.
2. Seeking a productive alternative to type III environment: disturbed-reactive, characterised by competition-prone, 'satisficing' type organisation system and alienated human beings, leading to type IV strategy.	2. Seeking a viable alternative to massified, dehumanised social system that subsists on dominating culture and 'mythification of reality'. Cultural action is the focus for type III reality whereas cultural revolution for type IV reality.
3. Basic faith in persons: common men who are otherwise treated as 'faceless', inexperienced, uninvolved (e.g., participants in the Gungahlin experience).	3. Basic faith in men—the historically ordained victims of 'culture of silence'. (Hence, concern for getting involved with the poor peasants and the oppressed.)
4. Learning as an experience of freedom and understanding of reality (puzzle learning). This will lead to creation of desirable futures through adaptive social planning and action.	4. Learning as an enriched experience of reality leading to involvement in transformation of reality (action-reflection based change orientation; problematising).
5. Group as a vehicle of search and change (individual orientation negated).	5. Group as the basis for praxical experience—critical consciousness to be internalised by individuals, but in a group context.
6. Staff role is not seen as elitist, expertise-based role. They are fellow explorers.	6. Staff and participants become *subjects* in exploration of an object.
7. There is an exclusion principle involved in that those who are not oriented towards seeking new ways, new alternatives for human futures, are not encouraged to stand in the way of those who want to.	7. The members of dominating forces who generate and foster the massification culture are not the target of change exploration.

I

8. Confrontation with reality is emphasised. Simulations or games are seen as diversionary for learning experience.

9. Extension as a form of education is rejected. Direct criss-cross communication is preferred. That is why there has been a critical attitude towards TV as a vehicle for education (Emery, *et al*, 1975).

10. The approach oriented towards social system change has set its course against the current of esoteric, quantitative bias, social science research which, according to this approach, counts trees missing the forest—the totality of man in relation to his world.

8. Learning from day-to-day on-going themes and their codification and decodification is crucial. Concrete context and theoretical context are inseparable from human experience.

9. Communication is direct, exploration-oriented. Dialogical process.

10. Conscientisation approach takes the man-reality nexus as its focal issue, and numerical configuration which cannot but measure the reality in segments, is discarded.

B. *Implicitly Common Elements that are Perceived in the Two Approaches*

Search Conference (SC)

1. Apparently the action-orientation is not evident in this approach to a point of criticality. However, the participative design which has led to SC has action orientation on democratising a system (Emery and Thorsrud, 1975).

2. Emphasis on process in the statement of 'medium is the message' does not reflect the purpose-orientation of SC. Content is equally significant while considering not only the issues, but also the purposes behind the processes moving towards institutional ideals.

Conscientisation Process (CP)

1. Action-orientation is explicitly emphasised. But not activism at the expense of reflection.

2. Process is a major message in the new pedagogy but the objectives of human liberation (negation of falsified life and living) are in the forefront all the while.

3. In Freire, the objectives of liberation and practice of freedom visualise social system arrangements where the ideals that Emery has identified can be anchored.

3. Institutional ideals as spelled out by Emery (1976A) stated in the form of ideal seeking are explicit.

4. Although futuristic vision is there, the orientation towards the present is not neglected. More explicitly, work-system redesign to debureaucratise and reduction of rigidity of hierarchical formalities are seen as the beginning of the building blocks for designing the future.

5. Implicitly, SC modality rejects messianism. No doubt, Fred Emery's pioneering role is acknowledged but others do not feel constrained in their thoughts and action in pursuing the change strategy utilising their skills and appreciation of realities.

4. Orientation towards the present may be less explicit in CP. In reality it is not so. The emphasis on educational pedagogy to change the present education system is an example of the building block for approaching desirable future. Exploration of existing myths and culture is yet another example.

5. Freire has potentially all the elements of being canonised. He himself expressed concern about mythification of conscientisation and that 'I have become a sort of pilgrim of the obvious.' (1975). On the other hand, continuous emphasis on socio-cultural context of an historical epoch or a country ensures the openness of approach negating dogmatism.

C. Differential Elements in the Two Approaches

Search Conference (SC)

1. The socio-economic context of SC is the first world—UK, Australia, etc.—the metropolitan countries with predominantly industrial culture.

2. The socio-economic-politico-cultural context of change (transformation of reality) is still to play its appropriate role in SC. Maybe it will emerge as Emery, *et al* have done in the chapter on China (1974).

Conscientisation Process (CP)

1. The socio-economic context of CP is the third world—the satellite countries where rural economy still dominates.

2. The accent is on reality search and identification of the forces that constitute the reality. So, there is unmistakable emphasis on political consciousness and role of education.

3. Cultural change and cultural revolution are dichotomised in

3. Gradualness ot change may be implicit in both micro-level and macro-level change. Emphasis on the diffusion-process in a democratic context where mobilisation is a persuasive-voluntary effort.

the context of social realities. However, cultural action is premised on mobilisation principle in a dialogical framework where semi-intransitive consciousness is to lead to critical consciousness for basic structural change. Time element acquires a sense of urgency here.

CONCLUDING OBSERVATIONS

Perhaps, at this stage, it may be appropriate to reflect further on the search conference and the conscientisation process. Our interaction in August 1976, with the colleagues in the Centre for Continuing Education, Canberra, who are in the forefront of the search conference in Australia, leads us to some of these reflections:

(*a*) M. Emery spells out her vision of search conference on the basis of her accumulated experience in terms of mobilisation of people, particularly, the young generation, whose identity with the decision-structure for creating desirable futures, has not been, historically, legitimised in the traditional concept of the formal decision-process. The same dynamic of work-alienation of industrial workmen is at work in respect of the school kids, housewives, unemployed youth, the dropouts, young administrators and managers. The mobilising process has been essentially conceived as organising strategy outside the boundary of a formal 'Organisation System'. Instead, the model has evolved out of adaptation of the Chinese *wei-ch'i* game. The essential thrust of the game is that one cannot control 'the future state of the board (on which the game is played) by any degree of power one builds up over the centre of the board. If one wants to win, one must move to, and control, the edges of the board and in particular to find and control the corners.' (Emery, *et al*, 1974). So, in a neighbourhood, the search conference will have actor-groups—interacting in a meaningful way to transform reality (see Fig. 3.5).

Figure 3.5

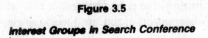

Interest Groups in Search Conference

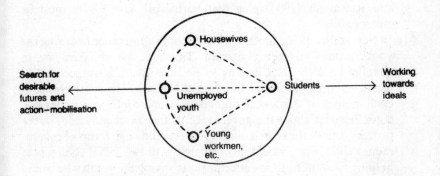

(b) While the strategy is still on trial, there are instances of positive first stirrings. At Geelong, where a search conference for neighbourhood planning was held, the unemployed kids who attended the conference got together with other kids with the question, 'What are we going to do about us?' These activities moved some officials of NCDC to a positive orientation; however, the NCDC as a bureaucratic organisation was yet to be responsive. The organisation was embedded in goal-seeking pursuit while the youth were getting oriented towards purpose-seeking pursuit.

Similarly, 12 months after the Gungahlin search conference, a group of young kids became active (the process has been an on-going one) and put up an action-plan seeking broad-based, autonomous self-management of the neighbourhood, rather than creation of layers of representative government.

Yet another case is the Aranda Primary School where the kids-teachers-parents are seeking to create a new, desirable model of learning community for all, rather than for school kids only.

(c) Somewhat on a different focus, although on the basic tenets of the search conference, have been the experiments with cooperative leisure industry of which there are 1,500 voluntary clubs in New South Wales. These clubs, financially viable, could, through the search process, successfully examine their choice options of activities resulting in a quest for a higher quality of life (not necessarily different kinds of excitement). Besides, each club originally was a self-contained enclave but the conferences helped them to extend their horizon in the form of a 'network' (Caldwell, 1973). That this effort can be a potential intervention in the transformation of working men and women from a state of semi-intransitive consciousness is relevant in the context of Bell's (1960) observation of the tired working class behaviour in the form of 'conspicuous loafing', Friedman's (1961) observation that 'fragmentation of labour ... may tend to disorganise the rest of life' and Riesman's (1964) plea that both work and leisure must be meaningful.

(d) In September 1976, another type of search conference involving the youth groups was being planned. This time the objective was to develop an awareness leading to positive action in respect of 212 municipal organisations in the state of Victoria. The youth groups in each municipal area would organise a search conference to develop consciousness about the governance of the community and, in the process, utilise the search mechanism on municipal forms of government. The Centre would involve itself with two initial conferences helping to identify 18 resource persons among the youth who would then fan out to organise more conferences in other areas and gradually help in identifying more and more resource persons, a diffusion strategy which did not need to rely on the original two staff members from the Centre for Continuing Education.

(e) Without multiplying further examples, we could appreciate that the search conference utilising a significant section of the community, essentially urban, is seeking to mobilise meaningful socially relevant action which has the potential of relating to reality and changing the reality—primary education, neighbourhood locality, social planning, municipal organisation and so on. It has the potential of movement from a state of semi-intransitivity linked to hedonistic reality to higher levels of consciousness. Whether it will reach the state of critical consciousness is a matter on which even a tentative formulation will be a speculation. Whether in the socio-economic and structural realities in Australia, the search conference can find a meaningful expression in mobilising the 'oppressed'—the aborigines in northern territories, and Queensland in particular*—is still an open issue.

On the other hand, the conscientisation approach, oriented toward action for liberation of man, has suffered a setback in Brazil and Chile and could not yet show signs of recovery. In Guinea-Bissau, however, the progress was obvious. A question may, therefore, arise whether the conscientisation process is essentially bound by the characteristics of socio-economic and political structures whereas the search conference is 'less threatening' in its strategy even though the objective is ideal-seeking in terms of practical freedom for all.

---

*One survey report in August 1976 indicated that per capita weekly income of an aborigine was between A$6 to 8 while the national average for a non-aborigine worker was A$145 to 150.

What strikes as relevant in both approaches is the value of openness and tentativeness and as such a critical comparison of the two in terms of relevance is yet premature.

Emery (1976B) has clarified the ethos of the search conference in an exposition where he pleaded for participative forms of governance in the future as more appropriate than what the 'Westminister' model has so far been able to offer. No doubt, a direct, dialogical participation is his model but he appreciates the difficulties involved. Thinking of a developing country, he said that

> ...the crux of the problem is at the narrowest span of interest, e.g., where the village development officer is face to face with the villagers, the police constable face to face with the local citizens. If, at this point, there is no effective communication leading to shared understanding there is not likely to be much shared understanding when broader spans of interest are involved.

It seems that the search conference is an approach appropriately designed to deal with social themes so that realities at the grassroots can be understood and transformed.

TOWARDS INSTITUTIONAL MOORINGS

Our discussions bring us back to the issue of creating and sustaining the institution system as a suitable habitat for ideal-seeking persons. How do the search conference approach and conscientisation process together, or as separate strategies, facilitate the process?

Let us begin with a favourable situation: the second world. These centrally planned socialist countries have brought about the end of economic exploitation of labour based on the logic of a 'free market' economy. Yet, these countries and the political parties in other countries struggling for socialist order, are not nearer to the 'practice of freedom'. Interpersonal conflict, power struggle, personality cult with a Messiah as a reference point marshalled in support of conflicting stances (e.g., Marx, Lenin, Mao, Kim) often taking the cloak of ideological conflict, do not lead to the ideals of nurturance, homonomy, humanity and beauty. This has, perhaps, motivated Freire to emphasise the role of cultural revolution in such social context. Similarly, the participative design approach seeks to democratise work culture, because, in the second world, the vagaries of market forces having become inoperative, the work process assumes a central role in life and yet the work system design in the world of socialism has not succeeded in resolving the dialectics of work-life and the wholeness of the human self.

That we are not harsh in our assessment of the second world can be substantiated by what we find in the approach of a well-known ideologue, Gyorgy Lukacs (Kolakowski, 1978). The proletariat, in his view, in the process of involvement in the class struggle develops a level of consciousness which coincides with the interest of the humanity. That becomes possible through the acceptance of the supreme role of the Party. No wonder that Lukacs became an apologist for the Stalinist era, which he meekly sought to undo in the post-Stalinist days. More fundamentally, this *a priori* justification for the omnipotent role of the Party elites is empirically untenable and in fact is an inevitable denial of the practice of freedom which praxical experiences offer to human beings. The treatment meted out to Andrei Sakharov by the C.P.S.U. leadership is a negation of the vanguard role of the Party as facilitative of the ideal-seeking venture (*The Guardian Weekly*, 20 and 27 December 1981). It appears that the concept of critical consciousness has a more solid foundation in Freire than in Lukacs.

The relevance of the two approaches will, no doubt, be evident in the structural and cultural realities of the first and the third worlds.

Another relevant issue here is the philosophy of planned change. The majority of social scientists have adopted the digestive approach to education leading to insight impartation to the participants in a change activity (students, social workers, managers, trade union leaders, church missionaries, administrators, etc.) orienting their researches and teaching accordingly. A minority of applied behaviour scientists have, however, without giving up their scholastic orientation, taken recourse to change-prone management techniques, such as group dynamics method, organisation development (OD), transactional analysis, etc., which enjoy a certain degree of action potential but not the totality of focus on man-in-social context. Their approach, covertly, if not overtly, is efficiency-prone with man acquiring an instrumental value.

It is thus not surprising that emphasis has been on behaviour change or modification. Fromm (1974) from his psycho-social insights has been led to make a distinction between *behaviour aspects* and *character aspects* of man. Giving an illustration from the feeling of boredom, he cites several stimuli which can control or overcome this behaviour and its symptoms but 'the whole person...his deeper feeling, his imagination, reason,' his culture, his traditional moorings remain unaffected. There is a relief, not a cure. The more basic issue is the aspect of character.

Character is the specific structure in which human energy is organised in the pursuit of man's goals; it motivates behaviour according to its dominant goals .... Character is a human phenomenon in more than a rudimentary sense.

The complex aspect that is implied in the expression 'more than a rudimentary' refers to the social structural realities that shape human character. 'The life-thwarting syndrome' versus the 'life-furthering syndrome' is just not a product of instinct but a concatenation of forces: economic, social, cultural and political. Researches are available, for example, to support the contention that protein-deficiency and other environmental factors have a 'direct influence on the growth of the brain'. It is often the experience of many field-unit administrators in India (apart from those who intend to rationalise the perpetuation of the practice) that a landless rural labourer in a state of bondage (a variation of serfdom or slavery) is reluctant to seek freedom even though legal sanctions are in his favour. The weight of heritage, submission to socio-economic domination resulting in a sense of its inevitability and cultural myths and taboos institutionalised to stabilise the bonded labour system throughout the course of history (Pandhe, 1976; Herbst, 1976), cannot but evoke the response of option for serfdom. Fromm and Maccoby (1970) in a study of a Mexican village confirmed that social character, vis-à-vis individual character, was conditioned by structural differentiation caused by socio-cultural and politico-economic forces. Waddington, in his book *The Ethical Animal* (1960) has taken the position that

...cultural communication between generations is the main mechanism of human evolution. Changes in society do not depend on changes in genetic constitution, but on changes in what is transmitted culturally. (Smith, 1976).

In that context, the critical role of ethics and its contents has been emphasised.

Given these parameters, we may now see the significance of the search conference and the conscientisation processes as a way of puzzle-learning, opening up of free space for exploration, movement from a semi-intransitive state of consciousness (bondage of falsified myths) to a critical consciousness state through a dialogical approach, through problematising and demystification of reality. It is suggested that these approaches have a potential for restructuring social character, not just behaviour, and thus ensure the ethical influences that can generate forces for an ideal-seeking state. The applied behaviourists fall short of this insight and commensurate orientation.

One more observation: the institution-building process is a *becoming phenomenon*. Ideals are ideals because their dynamics are infinite. As such, no one modality or two can have the quality of finality. The relevant issue is whether the search conference and the conscientisation approach as a meaningful symphony can create new music for the exploration of institutional ideals for the human universe—segmented today among the first, the second and the third world. Faith in man demands a corresponding hope for the discovery of viable forms of fulfilment.

II

TRANSCENDING THE PRESENT: EXPLORATION INTO THE FUTURE

Introduction

This section is premised on expansionism paradigm of the eternal quest
for socially productive knowledge so that a better future can be sought for
humanity. Socially productive knowledge has acquired 'criticality' in the
context of the deployment of a large number of scientists and technologists
in the arms and armaments race. Data indicate that about 40 per cent of
these knowledge scientists are engaged in military research. Their motivation to work for military establishments vary widely—from a sense of
self-importance to misplaced national glory to pecuniary gains. That such
gigantic strides in resource diversion creates a mega-structure of socially
harmful, and in human terms of fearful consequences for the human race,
do not strike the knowledge workers as perverse and repulsive.

In the perspective of this contemporary scenario, Chapter 4 seeks to
spell out the historic need to identify the elements of alternative principles
of global policy planning. The supreme challenge, it is suggested, lies in
creating new structures for alternative forms for planning for human
beings for the three world systems. In the process, the chapter offers
some criteria for an enriched quality of life, which have remained comparatively unexplored in the burgeoning literature on the quality of
work-life. The pioneering work of Emery, Ackoff, Trist, Thorsrud,
Maccoby and a few others has influenced us to situate the quality of life
components on a global canvas.

Chapter 5 is an exercise in looking at our future from the design
perspective. Two abiding human considerations are the hope for a better
human future and the concern for initiating concrete action *now* to instal
it tomorrow. Based on this premise and accepting the ideals enlisted by
Emery, we have sought to proffer and explore the meta-ideal of

Samaj-Siddhi, which we believe will be hailed upon and imbibed by an increasing number of human beings at a time when the elites at the apex of the power-pyramid are confronted with the deepening crises in the human systems they have designed in their conventional wisdom.

4

---

*A Perspective on
Global Policy Planning for
Development: Towards the Quality
of Life*

> Neither a wise man nor a brave man lies down on the tracks of history to
> wait for the train of the future to run over him. .
>
> Dwight D. Eisenhower

> It is not true that suffering ennobles the character; happiness does that
> sometimes, but suffering, for the most part, makes men petty and
> vindictive.
>
> W.S. Maugham

Introduction

To begin with, let us confront two preliminary issues. While dealing with
global policy planning for development, we have to decide upon the
approach. The approach to planning, any type of planning, is concerned
with the future. Planning is an exercise in the future and, as such, the past
is not the only substance of history on which one can rely. Emery (1977)
has pointed out that we have to depend on an overlapping temporal
gestalten in planning for the future. When, over time and space, comparatively independent processes of change take place, overlapping one
another, a new process may and does emerge. A class of events may
evolve which is thus independent of any precedent and unknown when
the processes were unleashed. This is an exorable logic of unfolding
history.

At the risk of appearing somewhat abstract, we seek to postulate that
human motivation as reflected in behaviour and cognition is basically
interest/goal-directed. Goal-directed activities respond to, in numerous

forms, on the strength of the information profile. Since an individual, by and large, functions in a social context, he is likely to develop sensibilities which specifically relate to the spatio-temporal and informational conditions which such systems presuppose and to the degree of integration the individual has accomplished. This potential purposeful behaviour is what Sommerhoff (1974) describes as *directive correlation*. It refers to 'any goal-seeking activity which is characteristically matched to the environment in a manner which raises the occurrence of the goal-event above the level of change-coincidence.'

There are three types of directive correlation. Instant adaptability belongs to the *executive* process. At the other extreme, we find the long-term and slow *phylogenetic* adjustments of evolution. At the intermediate level are *ontogenetic* adaptations, the gradual adaptations through which the individual organism adjusts during its lifetime to the special circumstances of its existence. Adaptations essentially refer to the environment which can also be influenced by human actors thus making it *enacted* environment. Environment also refers to the *domain* of direct correlation.

The challenge for the global planners lies in expanding the boundary of the domain by undertaking purposeful behaviour. Active intervention is warranted over passive adaptation.

The other aspect that is relevant to the complex planning process is the orientation of those who are involved in the study and action about planning. Terms, such as evaluation, trends, scenarios, forecasting and prediction, are likely to create confusion. We are somewhat more comfortable with evaluation techniques provided we know why we want to evaluate, what we want to evaluate and how we undertake the exercise as we deal with the past. It is more difficult to study trends because trends are a study of process and not of the past. Yet, without trend analysis, it is difficult to develop scenarios (prognosis) which are a beginning of the exercise of looking at the future. Mesarovic, *et al* (1975) define a scenario as a consequence of possible events and socio-political choices which encompass economic aspects as well. Forecasting deals with uncertainty while prediction implies exactitude in time, nature and magnitude of future events. We can present a linkage of these issues in the manner given in Fig. 4.1.

The global planning process will indeed encompass all these aspects but the present exercise will deal with some selective aspects only.

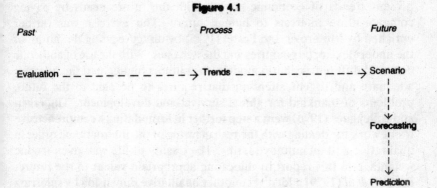

Figure 4.1

Discounting the Future: The Predominating Scenario

One major issue in respect of global planning related to development is concerned with the discount rate of the future. As per the logic of Gresham's Law, immediate problems predominate over the likely future issues whether it is in the arena of macro-planning or micro-planning. The result is that even if one is aware of future problems concerning future generations, the current burning issues receive immediate attention. When the major global powers are locked in massive arms and armaments development (the arms race cost in every four hours which is equal to the annual UNICEF budget; Grant, 1982), the discount rate for retaining their power and influence in order to maintain their bargaining strength, the security of their country and the areas of their influence is much lower than what they do about the problems that beset the third world countries, be these unemployment, poverty, malnutrition, health care of the marginal population of these countries. When the technology of the green revolution receives a high premium, the discount rate is obviously low. DDT is one such example. To the extent that certain pesticides are seen as useful inputs to raise agricultural production, they receive high priority in terms of investment. That the same pesticides, like DDT have weighty evidence against them—that the after-effects in the future can cause considerable damage to plant life and, directly or indirectly, to the consumers causing unintended health hazards—are given low premium. A recent report mentions that the Yamuna in Delhi is polluted by DDT factory wastes and that it swallows 200 million litres of sewage daily of which 20 million litres are industrial effluents. It has been pointed out that 'over 60 per cent of economic and industrial activity is supervised by the government—sewage disposal, drainage, power generation, mining, transport, railways, steel and housing—all these together account for 90 per cent of the effluence discharged into the system.' (*India Today*, 16–31 January 1981).

The successive reports commissioned by and submitted to the Club of Rome is an educative precedent-setting example. Meadows, *et al* (1972) for the first time brought out dramatically the need for balancing the present trends of economic growth with the future needs by paying commensurate interests to human future. The exercise was further enriched by Mesarovic and Pestel (1975) by disaggregating the future of the under-developed countries and the rich ones. With the use of authentic data and different scenario models, the authors highlighted the need for adequate and urgent attention that requires to be paid to the future problems of mankind for global survival and development. Tinbergen and colleagues (1976) went a step further in formulating a comprehensive framework for dealing with the restructuring of the international order in qualitative and quantitative terms. The quality of life was given its due weightage in this report by allocating appropriate values to the future. Botkin, *et al* (1979) added yet another qualitative dimension by referring to the untapped element of the human potential for learning, growth and development so that the present can be reshaped in order to accelerate a qualitative transformation of human society through the process of tapping human resources for establishing desirable values for the future generation where men, women and children can live with the fulfilment of their needs—physical and mental.

Many policy-makers and activists are indeed concerned with the task of shaping the current course of history. In the process they influence, even determine, the contours of the future, consciously or otherwise. However, in the contemporary world, with few exceptions, the architects of the globally relevant policies and practices, discount* (or devalue) the human future at a disconcertingly high rate. Thus the mission of the Club of Rome, in a way, is yet to gain acceptance.

To discount the future at a high premium, there has emerged a counter-culture of environmentalists, eco-development protagonists and sensitive members of the young generation organised in voluntary groups and societies spread all over the world. They seek to reassert the need for reversing gear by putting a higher premium on the future of human generations. Sahal (1977) has dramatised the predominating culture by mentioning that 'reduction is inherent not in nature but in our methods of conception.' Complex problems and issues of today and tomorrow, through the logic of entertaining a high discount rate for the problems of the future, have propelled global planners to take the course of reducing the issues to such a level that these can, at least through their limited rationality, be dealt with, so they believe, by comfortable means and methods with which they are so familiar. By delinking the present from the future, these national and global policy-makers tend to forget that a continuous and sustained action can produce a variety of discontinuous

* In our context, discount implies a lower degree of premium or concern than objectively desirable.

and unintended effects, which ironically render the task of fruitful global planning more complex and frustrating.

Clive Simmonds (1977) suggests a way out by first developing the perception of the future from which a definition of problems as perceived can emerge. Even the definitions that emerge can be tested against feedback loops to monitor the results of feed-forward thinking and to plan and further refine the perception of problems. Once the problems are perceived the next step is to structure the problems which is an appropriate management function, first for formulation of choices for decision-making and then for effective implementation of the emerged decisions.

This is a simplified version of the Simmonds case but it indicates that the starting point should be a scenario of the future action which is a dire need today. The diagram given by him is presented in Fig. 4.2.

Figure 4.2
Perceptual Model for Planning

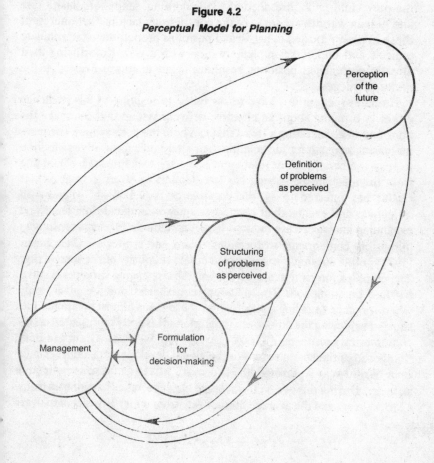

In this diagram it appears that a comparatively undistorted mapping of *social reality* is a major challenge to global planners.

Managing Complexity: A Challenge to Planners

A challenge to planners, particularly to global planners, is to face up to the complicated task of managing complexity. Complexity arises out of a variety of situations. Generation of knowledge, advancement of technology, political and economic forces creating new challenges and equally intriguing crises, globalisation of human problems including poverty, lengthening shadow of unemployment, exploitation of the poor nations, marginalisation of urban and rural poor and continued neglect of the poor children in dire need of food, clothing, sanitation, health care and human warmth are some of the contributing factors. Self-interest of those in power located in privileged positions propels them to formulate policies and undertake implementation with a view to fortifying their already entrenched positions resulting in an unethical neglect of the under-privileged.

Human organisations have so far failed to respond to this challenge either in bringing about an effective delivery system that can reach the poor and in accelerating a trend that can help the poor acquire adequate mobilising strength for formulating their alternative forms of organisation to reap the benefits of development projects. A simple logic emanating from the machine-age-gestalt has led planners to resort to what Ackoff (1974) has referred to as 'the doctrine of reductionism' whereby all objectives and events, their properties and accumulated experience and expanding knowledge are reduced to certain ultimate elements constituing indivisible components to formulate plans and strategies. Churchman (1977) points out that it is not easy to create simplicity out of complexity. The complex interaction among innumerable changing variables is still a baffling phenomenon. The planners nonetheless prepare plans, but, when it comes to facing up to reality, these plans almost invariably fall short of achieving the objectives. This dilemma is aptly represented in the contemporary writings of Grant (1981A, 1981B, 1982). Grant presents 'tempered optimism' in regard to the global developmental efforts made since World War II, through the process of what we may call segmented strategy. During this period the average life expectancy has gone up from 42 to 54 years and the average literacy rate from under 30 per cent to over

50 per cent. More land has been brought under cultivation in Asia, Africa and Latin America. In addition, about 25 per cent of the global population have moved from material well-being to unprecedented affluence. These are impressive records (Grant, 1981B). But let us observe the other side of the picture. Some 35,000 children die every day; of them nearly 10,000 in India alone (1981A). One child in four suffers from malnutrition; four out of five children have no modern health care and an equivalent number in the rural areas do not have adequate water or sanitation (1982). The 32nd round of National Sample Survey in India reveals that 21 million persons in 1980 joined the unemployment market on an average per day with a backlog of 11.31 million, thus making an aggregate of 42.58 million (in the age group of 15–59 years) by the year 1984–85 (*Mainstream*, 2 January 1982). By A.D. 2000 South Asia is likely to remain the home of over half of the world's population and that about 13 per cent of the global inhabitants 'will still be left behind in absolute poverty, their lives dominated by frequent malnutrition and ill-health, *by lack of opportunities* ... and by early deaths of three out of every ten of their children.' (Grant, 1981B, emphasis added). This global split phenomenon is a testimony to the failure of the existing policy planning and its implementation.

An analytical framework helps to understand why it happens. Maruyama (1963; Linstone, 1977: 140–42) in his concept of the second cybernetics, seeks to deal with the complexity embedded in a system. He has argued for moving from a deviation-counteractive mutual casual paradigm (maintenance of entropy) to a differentiation amplifying mutual casual paradigm (decreasing entropy). The second approach has been mentioned as the second cybernetics. It possesses both the multiplier effect and the trickle effect. An initial investment may, arising out of high profits in a company, generate more income and more profits, market conditions remaining as effective. There can be some amount of trickle-down benefits to employees—permanent, casual and temporary and similar level of employees in other beneficiary organisations. A second situation is that the profits, through manipulative methods, are siphoned off to smuggling operations which will provide a spurt to such activities. The minor minions engaged in the trade with increased activities will reap more benefits and more persons may join the trade and so on. Many such illustrations from diverse activities can be provided in favour of the deviation amplification mutual casual relationship principle.

The latter principle argues in favour of self-organised systems in which complex patterns so generated can be managed by simple rules of interaction, a path that the planners and policy framers hesitate to take.

The differentiation-amplifying mutual casual paradigm approach is premised on individual sensitivity and validity-based social reality, two values which do not necessarily go together with the global planners who operate from a position of privilege and power.

Social complexity is something which one can live with or cope with or, as a compromise, partly live with and partly seek to cope with, which is what pragmatically-inclined global planners aim at achieving. Michael (1977) argues that planning ought to be a way of moving with complexity so that the complexity becomes enriching rather than destroying. Social complexity has two aspects: one that can be regulated and the other that has the turbulent aspect. The regulative aspects can be controlled and handled by developing and maintaining certain relationships through time and space. There will naturally be some amount of continued expectations, reliability and stability although there will be, hopefully, a forward movement, and that is the tradition-based concept of progress.

Turbulence is both objective and subjective. The subjective aspect lies in the state of ignorance from which a planner operates. Ignorance may arise out of lack of valid information and/or on account of inability to come to grips with the available information in an imaginative manner. The source of turbulence lies in the unpredictable aspects of changing circumstances whereby various events and processes of happenings interact in a variety of ways whose outcome can neither be confidently anticipated nor predicted. Lack of appreciation of how to deal with disturbance-amplifying situations and problems has led the planners and implementors to a reactive mode of approach to contain the problems rather than to deal with them in a manner that can encompass the internal dynamics of a system along with the external dynamics of the environment which interact with a system. Emery (1977) argues that the bureaucratic mode of organisation system is itself generative of transition to turbulence as the world moves towards the twenty-first century. There is comparative insensitivity as well as the inability to innovate alternative modes of human organisations which can offer non-bureaucratic forms of human organisations. Instead, the predominating mode of global planning as carried out by experts and specialists aims at implementing plans with such organisation models as are characterised by superficiality, segmentation and retreatist modes. No doubt, in such a situation, the cynics are polarised towards a doomsday scenario and the optimistic resort to expediency-based pragmatic, but essentially *status quo* oriented action. Either way, the basic problems which confront the global majority remain unresolved.

The adaptive orientation, it has been argued (Emery, 1977; De, Chapter 5) depends upon the acquisition of certain meta-ideals of which, according to De, the acquisition of *Samaj-Siddhi* through collective liberation can be the objective. Human beings are potentially ideal-seeking even though the reality of social forces in an inequitable world system does not help to germinate some future oriented desirable ideals.

Samaj-Siddhi is not individualism even though implicit in it is a concept of individuation. It is indeed a negation of non-productive orientation. Non-productive orientation generates the value of self-seeking, self-centred and one-dimensional aspects of individual behaviour fostering distorted views of global problematique. *Samaj-Siddhi*, on the other hand, is an assertion of a productive culture in establishing a new social order which cannot be brought in and conceptualised by expert planners and efficient minority implementors of plans. It requires a liberating sense of commitment which can encompass the deprived majority of population in the third world and their counterparts living in comparative deprivation in the rich world. Liberation needs to be embedded in collective thinking and collective action.

Peter (1977) provides evidence that the Tangue tribe of New Guinea has developed a culture of a popular game called 'take-tak' which consists of throwing a spinning top in groups of six into the ground. Each of the two teams of players tries to touch as many stakes with their tops as possible. The participants play not to win but to draw. The game continues until an exact draw is achieved. The message of this game is one of equity-based social ethics which we term as the concept of *Samaj-Siddhi*. Collectivity is not a problem of a number of people coming together but a quality of relationship that is premised on the collectivity moving towards an objective of creating a better world so long held out by many as either a dream or a utopia. Berger and Luckmann (1967) have persuasively argued the case in the following manner:

> The decisive question is whether man still retains the awareness that, however objectified, the social world was made by man and, therefore, can be remade by man.... Typically, the real relationship between man and his world is reversed in consciousness. Man, the creator of a world, is apprehended as its product and human activity as an epiphenomenon of non-human processes. Human beings are no longer understood as world creators but as being in turn products of the nature of things.

Samaj-Siddhi seeks to negate this conscious and unconscious global myth. This is a major qualitative challenge to global planners. Vickers (1977) provides an insight to the concept of culture. Utilising his idea, one way of generating *Samaj-Siddhi* is to seek a comprehensive definition of the concept of the neighbour. An inward-looking system has a narrow concept of neighbour which stands in the way of collective thinking and action. A broader concept, though it gives rise to complexity, extends the concept of neighbour. In the contemporary world, the dichotomy of relationship between North and South, South and South, North and North, Region and Region, Country and Country and one interest-group and another, are constrained concepts of neighbourliness. Global planners will have to rise above this artificially imposed limitation of the global planning process. The planners at a global level, who seek to deal with global problems with enriched knowledge and wisdom, have to continuously beware of seeking to solve the wrong problems. They must be aware that their responsibility lies in solving the right problems. For this to happen, we begin with value as 'preferred outcome' (Laswell, 1976). The selection of options for human development from a spectrum of possible futures requires conscious formulation of policy, which will spell out the framework within which a human organisation can work towards developing its future. The policy thus states the 'ought' aspects of an organisation's intentions. Strategy is the art of choosing the instruments for implementing, and directing these instruments to achieve policy ends. Thus, strategic aspects refer to an achievable 'can'. Tactics refer to management of resources needed to achieve the strategy and this spells out the 'will' aspects of an organisation (Jantsch, 1974A, 1974B). A schematic presentation of this is made in Fig. 4.3.

Figure 4.3

Value/Norm Hierarchy

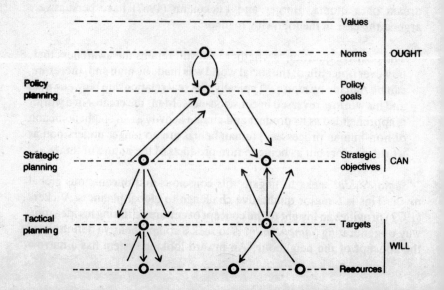

Johanson (1980) has formulated and forcefully argued in favour of a concept of global humanism. Global humanism posits itself as the most needed and a viable alternative to global *super-powerism*, or the global hegemony of super-powers. Our life today presents us as victims of double-think and double-speak reducing human race to the status of a pseudo-species. There is thus a need to undertake a transformation process to make us *homo-humanus*. Ethnocentric values are reflected in a negative, divisive, parochial and distorted vision of the human race segmented into different groups and clusters. The compulsions of the global situation demand that we overcome, by collective citizen action, these ethnocentric failings. The ethical and moral urges of the mute majority of population all over the world should find articulation in creating and accelerating by an alternative global planning process to establish a long range interest in developing a global system aimed at realising the values of global humanism. Johanson argues that 'the unifying and mobilising potential of a vision of human liberation and positive innovation depends on a popular movement fuelled by our own imagination and willingness to act.' This urge has been adequately articulated in a more concrete action plan by Paulo Freire, as mentioned in Chapter 3.

There are two concrete issues that we want to mention here in connection with the management of complexity in the global context. The present day society has fashioned for itself a productive system which is based on a devouring culture. The products of nature are converted through human labour to offer goods and services that can continuously propel the human society to run for slick, artificial and excitement-promoting wares of which a monumental example is what the media-pandered leisure industry seeks to achieve in the rich world. A child in the USA uses 25 to 50 times as much of the earth's resources as an African or an Indian child.* The quantum that a child uses is a reflection of the parents' orientation to consumerism. The global planning process, it is suggested, is to work towards the provision of goods and services which will re-build the intrinsic worth thereby enriching human life and not degrading it. The social relation of production will then indicate a qualitative change which will put an end to not only the exploitative instrumental value of human labour, but will assert the use-value of human labour, for the purpose of creating positive results for all humanity. In that context, the use-value will predominate over a power-based inequitable exchange value (Illich, 1975).

The other aspect refers to the children of the earth. When we refer to future planning in the interest of development, our primary focus is on the present and the future generations. Without detracting from the urgency

* US examples are only illustrative. The rich in all the three sectors of the globe (the first, second and third worlds) suffer from the same malaise.

of attending to the adults and the old to enrich the quality of their life so as to strengthen their ethical core in day-to-day transactions with fellow human beings, the primary focus, so long painfully neglected, should be on the children of today and of tomorrow. Gabriala Mistrala, a nobel laureate, has expressed the sentiment in a poignant manner:

> We are guilty of many errors and many faults, but our worst crime is abandoning the children, neglecting the fountain of life. Many of the things we need can wait. The child cannot. Right now is the time (when) his bones are being formed, his blood is being made and his senses are being developed. To him we cannot answer 'tomorrow', his name is 'today'.

The relevance of this call for action becomes evident when we take into account the officially disclosed fact that 118 million children in India live below the poverty line—99 million in rural areas and 19 million in urban areas (*Patriot*, 26 February 1981). India is one among the LDCs. Blueprints for global planning and national action cannot escape this urgent responsibility on the plea of other priorities.

Global Problems Confronting Global Planning

On the basis of the assessment of the required values and approaches in handling the complexity that confronts the human race today, we would wish now to mention some of the urgent, priority-based global problems which do not brook further evasion or procrastination. To begin with, let us take the case of *arms and armaments*.

Barnaby (1980) has shown that in 1980 over $500 billion, roughly 6 per cent of the total world output, was devoted to military expenses. In 1983, it exceeded $600 billion. This works out at about 1.3 million every minute spent on the armament race. Among the countries, the primary positions go to the USA, the USSR, France and Britain. The proposals formulated by the US Administration dramatises the fact that in order to put the USA on the path to economic recovery, the US Administration would resort to drastic cuts in social services while the Pentagon budget would go up. In fiscal 1981, the military spending was $171 billion which went up to $215.9 billion in 1983 and $228 billion in fiscal 1984. It is indicated that in 1985, the budget may reach a figure between $284 and $291 billion. It is also proposed that there will be a cut of $633 million in the basic internal programme and economy in workforce provision to the tune of $171 million in 1985 (Facts on Files, *World News Digest*, 1984; *IDSA News Review*, 1984; *The Times of India*, 19 October 1983 and

9 June 1984). It is pertinent to mention that military spending is a poor employment generator. The $1 billion spent on public services would yield 51,000 more jobs in a major industrialised country than if it were spent on the military sector (*New Internationalist*, May 1984).

With limited resources, as is the reality of the economic crisis, it is but natural that more funds available for one purpose will deprive other objectives of necessary funds. In this case the other objective, which is being sacrificed, is naturally social service and social welfare within the country and outside for those who need food, shelter, clothing and health care and not bullets and bombs. What applies to the USA, applies, with equal force, to other super-powers. Ironically enough, this also applies to the resource-hungry third world countries. Of the 56 nations producing major weapons, 24 are in the third world. The military budget of the third world countries is on the increase.

Galtung (1981) has documented that, in between 1945 and 1976—a period of 32 years—of the 120 armed conflicts (or wars) involving 84 countries that took place, only 5 were in Europe and the rest in the third world. In 64 instances, the developed capitalist countries actively intervened. The developed socialist countries were involved in 6 and the third world in 17 conflicts. The major intervening powers have been the USA, the UK, France and Portugal, in that order. The first three happen to be permanent members of the UN Security Council.

What this boils down to is that, as an espoused cause, the global forums, formal and informal, are vocally committed to the alleviation of human misery and creating a better world for the deprived and under-privileged. In practice, however, more and more scarce resources are being devoted to an industry whose objective is only to create a depraved culture, which is a negation of the quality of life. The tragic aspect apart, the armaments race can be seen as a major enemy of global understanding and human development for a better world. We see this as a major challenge.

In the second place, we refer to the population problem. In 1974, in the Bucharest Conference, China and some other radically-oriented countries argued vigorously on ideological grounds that the population problem was not a major global threat and that the bogey of population explosion was a super-power diversionary tactic intended to confuse all about the major global problems. With scientific and technological breakthroughs, it was possible, thus went the argument, that the projected population of the world in the coming few decades could be fed, clothed and supported adequately. China's own policy in population planning and control since then has shown that this was a hollow ideological stance. There has been remarkable progress in China's population control which during the period 1975–80 shows an average growth of 1.33 per cent in contrast to India's 2.30 per cent.

From the beginning of the Christian era, it took 1,830 years for the world population to reach one billion. It took another one hundred years to reach the two billion mark in 1930. For the third billion the period taken was 30 years. In 15 years, from 1960 to 1975, the world population reached 4 billion. It is projected that it will take another 12 years to reach 5 billion in 1987 and the prediction is that in another 10 years, i.e., by 1997, the world population will touch the 6 billion mark. As against this number, let us note that about 40 per cent of the population of the under-developed countries is under 15 years. Half of them are eking out an existence which crushes their rights as children today and their potential as adults tomorrow. It is estimated that out of 100 children born each minute in the under-developed countries, 15 will die within one year. Of the 85 who survive, 75 will have no access to modern medical care in childhood. About 25 per cent will suffer from malnutrition during the crucial weaning age. During this period, their chances of death will be 30 to 40 times higher than if they had been born in Europe or North America. Of those who will survive to the school age, ony six out of 10 will ever enter a classroom. Not even four of six will complete their elementary schooling (*Asia Year Book*, 1981).

James Grant (1979) has mentioned in an analysis that the basic human needs of 800 million people are not being met, which number undoubtedly has swelled by the beginning of 1981. With the trends that we have indicated about armaments proliferation rather than armaments deceleration, it is doubtful whether these very basic human needs programmes could keep heart and soul together and sustain this most deprived population to enable these people to gain, for themselves, the minimum. of human dignity. It is in this context that a more imaginative and practical population policy is to be formulated and acted upon. Scientific methods of population control by themselves are useless. As the Chinese experiences indicate, population planning establishes inter-linkages with sustained productive employment and provision of health care, shelter, functional literacy, offer of opportunity to the poor to raise their level of consumption and availability of potable drinking water. Population planning is part of a comprehensive package of economic development for which the measures adopted so far by the global planners are *ad hoc*, peripheral and patently inadequate.

The third aspect that calls for global planning refers to the theme of technology. The importance of technology in the generation of productive output is indeed phenomenal. As a matter of fact, technological development can play a role more significant than capital investment. Recent studies (Haeffner, 1979) indicate that technology development accounts for 68 per cent of the growth of GNP in the USA. For Sweden, the corresponding figure is 59 per cent in the whole of the post-war period and 74 per cent during the period 1949-59. In other words, technology and its use is a productive venture provided the social purpose of the use of technology is borne in mind.

The global planning of technology development continues to be lopsided as is evidenced from the fact that, on the basis of published statistics of 1972, close to half a million scientists and engineers, almost half of the world's scientific and technical manpower, have devoted their talents and skills towards military research and development. Then again data from various third world countries, particularly South Korea, Brazil and India indicate that technological innovation and its utilisation can have a positive impact on income generation but not on its distribution. These are among the many other dysfunctional aspects of global technological planning (De, 1981B). Galtung (1981) has mentioned the hidden, and not so hidden cost, of technology transfer from the Western world. *Culturally*, it is a transfer of a hidden social code (Westernisation). *Socially*, it strengthens the group of elites who handle the new technology within their social fabric. *Politically*, it 'will serve to homogenize the world elites'. *Economically*, it creates an industrial culture that destroys the artisan's craftsmanship.

The issue seems to be to develop a distinctly different global paradigm in converting appropriate forms of technology both for the first and the third world in accordance with which there is a need for adaption of technology to its appropriate utilisation for the benefit of the majority of global population. The social characteristics of adaptation for each nation may better be conceived in terms of diversified, pluralistic and flexible organisation systems developing and implementing technology diffusion processes. Then again this cannot be divorced from the politico-economic structure of a country.

That technology development has to face a major challenge in its futuristic orientation can best be documented by referring to certain facts of life. An average American discards 540 pounds of paper each year as a result of which the forests disappear. The use of cloth napkins and towels with minimum washing soap and water will be a desirable alternative which will save many trees being felled and forests being destroyed. US citizens buy 70 million tons of packaging materials each year and an average of about 660 pounds of paper, plastics, glass, metal and other packaging materials is consumed per person. 90 per cent of this is discarded. As someone put it: 'Willful taste brings woeful want'. Earlier, we made a reference to the extravagant use of DDT and its contribution to overall environmental deterioration. Recent findings indicate that DDT has far reaching consequences even at a long distance. The Canadian Arctic carries a high concentration of DDT which has affected the polar bears adversely. The toxic chemicals have infected them like lethal poison. There are evidences that the Soviet Union is also insensitive to environmental degradation.

> Lake Baikal is poisoned by a factory making hardened cord for bomber wheels; the general disregard of ecological regulations by the defence industries; shoot-up of wild life by high-ranking military (personnel)— helicopter hunting for polar bears; troop-carriers assaulting the Black Sea wild-fowl. (Thompson, 1981).

Nearer home, in India, 1 per cent of cultivable land is lost to the desert because of deforestation and the consequent erosion every year. The rate at which crop lands are being extended to the forest areas, the next 30 years will witness that half of the global forests will be denuded. The 1952 forest policy of India provides for reserving at least 33.3 per cent of the land for forests. Since then deforestation has taken a toll of 3.4 million hectares. At this rate, not even 22 per cent of the land is under forest now and in many Indian states the figure is lower than 18 per cent (Nadkarni, 1976). The lessons are obvious. Conversion of scientific knowledge into technological use is now more and more devoted to consumer-oriented goods and services. This is all in the name of progress to provide more comfort and pleasure to life. Forest produce are used for constructing roads and tasteful buildings including summer houses in the hills. The long-range effect on physical ecology, has, however, brought about manifold miseries to the people residing in and around forest lands through frequent visits of floods and erosion of fertile soil.

Secondly, the wasteful use of non-renewable resources as reflected in an ever-increasing variety of consumer goods is gradually eating into the vitals of the earth's resources so as to pander to the self-centred existence of the present generation who command an adequate purchasing power to take care of their immediate needs and interests. Sciences and technologies need to be reoriented—for which the responsibility rests as much with the builders of knowledge as with the policy-makers who operate nationally and internationally. Put another way, the real challenge in the development and management of technology lies in a cultural revolution in that if the future is not to be discounted at an alarmingly high rate, these elites will need to strike a balance between the present consumption trends and provision for the future. This seems to be a major challenge to global planners.

Related to this is the issue of energy management. Thanks to the oil price hike since 1974, human search and ingenuity have, for the first time, been devoted to alternative sources of energy. Hydel energy is still untapped in many third world countries including India, Nepal and the Mekong belt. Solar energy, still in an experimental stage, can be harnessed for a variety of purposes, though not yet for major power generation. Shale-oil is yet another source of production. Coal liquefaction and gasification can lead to 15 million barrels of fuel per day by the turn of the century in the USA (Madison, 1980). Should technologists succeed in considerably reducing the dangers of nuclear hazards—fission and fusion technologies can go a long way by the twenty-first century. Tidal waves hold potential promise.

Here again a dilemma is apparent. Scientific talents, technological skills and massive investments are available to the rich countries who are in a better position to mobilise all these. The poor countries will be left behind in the race. This will repeat the history of the industrial revolution. In order that the tragedy does not assert itself by making the third world more and more dependent on the rich countries, it is essential that global policy emerges not necessarily on the strength of political bargaining and *real politik*, but does so in a manner that the sum total of benefits flow in an equitable fashion in the overall interests of global development. Unless that happens one can safely predict that the disparity that exists today between the first and the third world, which contributes to the destabilisation of global peace and prosperity, will be further accentuated. After all, the rich world is still dependent on the contribution of some basic materials from the third world to maintain a standard of living at a price which is high for the third world and comparatively low for the rich countries. The exchange rate of goods and services is patently iniquitous. If global peace is indivisible, so too are the gains in sharing the fruits of technological advancement.

We have touched upon three aspects of global issues confronting global planners today. Issues in respect of aid and trade, bilateral and multilateral, and terms of trade and diffusion of cultural hegemony are no less important but we have been selective in the choice of the issues for the purpose of expounding the theme.

What emerges out of this discussion is that global planning is to contend with global problems not by resorting to a sectoral or reductionist approach but by taking recourse to the broader spectrum of a newer paradigm taking into account the complexity of issues involved.

An Epilogue

Towards the end of our journey on global planning challenges, we refer to certain values which, we believe, are the *sine qua non* for ushering in a new paradigm of the planning process at the turn of the century. Kaje (1977) believes that there is need for a value shift towards the feminine mode into the forecasting exercise. The Chinese make a distinction between the Yin (feminine) and Yang (masculine) aspects of human behaviour. Out of the list that she provides, one can identify the different characteristics of the two insofar as these are related to our theme. We present a shorter list below:

Yin	Yang
Feeling	Thinking
Eros (the principle of relatedness)	Lagos (the principle of fact and logic)
Oral tradition	Western science
Myths	Guidelines
Rituals	Games
Comprehensive	Analytic
Natural knowledge	Conventional knowledge
Sense of community	Competition
Diffused awareness	Focused consciousness
Soul, Body	Head, Intelligence
Intuition	Sensation
Mediator	Inventor
Relaxation	Concentration, Determination
Consequence	Result
Love, Forgiveness	Right/Wrong, Hate, Revenge
Earth and Moon	Sun
Warm soil, Sea	Seeds, Ideas

This is not to suggest that women are necessarily Yin-oriented and men are *ipso facto* Yang-oriented. But these are two broad parameters of human comprehension. Kaje believes that, for a qualitative reorientation towards human futures, an insight of forecast needs to complement the scientific bent of mind through enriched qualities of imagination, mediation and dialogue. There is a need to see and believe; intuitive and diffused awareness should be encoded in the domain of a future scenario. We too share this view that the culture vacuum reflected in the mass alienation of global planners and their colleagues needs to be overcome to create a healthy climate for a more humane and effective global planning strategy. The challenge is implicit in a message that Konrad Lorenz offers: 'Our planet could feed many more people than it can support in dignity and freedom. The spatial requirements for a mentally healthy life are much larger than the requirements set by food production.'

In the same vein, Robertson (1978) offers a value-oriented approach for the design of human futures. There are, in his view, five options to today's humanity: business-as-usual; disaster; the totalitarian, conservatist future; the hyper-expansionist (HE) future; and the sane, human ecological (SHE) future. Understandably, he opts for the SHE alternative as a sign-post to a self-fulfilling future. The transformation involves six modes of action:

1. *Life-style*: Changing one's personal way of life so that it is most consistent with the SHE future.
2. *Enabling* (*Liberation*): Fostering new growth points which help people to liberate themselves from dependence, to become more self-reliant and to develop their autonomy.
3. *Enabling (Decolonisation)*: Managing the breakdown of existing institutions, relationships, etc., so as to help previously dependent people to become more self-reliant and to develop their own collective autonomy.
4. *Metaphysical Reconstruction*: Creating new visions of the SHE future, developing new paradigms and communicating them.
5. *Strategy*: Mapping the transition to the SHE future; identifying pitfalls and unresolved problems; providing opportunities for communication, information exchange and cross-fertilisation.
6. *Opposition*: Opposing and attempting to obstruct activities which discriminate between man and man, groups and groups, nations and nations and in addition tend to counter the four alternatives whose relevance to the future world is palpably questionable.

These rules apply to global planners. The knowledge acquisition process itself is a liberating role which, it appears, can partially emanate from an ability to inculcate a larger and sharpened vision of social reality and partially from the pressures that will generate from the under-privileged. Jean Piaget (1972) has suggested that the world of empirical facts are indeed to be critically examined so that, from a structural orientation, human beings can emerge as capable of establishing meaningful relationships and interlinkages, which go beyond the world of empiricism. Without a purpose, causal relationships cannot be established and that brings us back to our preference for meta-ideals. Jantsch (1972) emphasises the need for education for self-renewal which is to be premised on a *joint system* of society and technology. All these ideas and insights offer value premises to global planners. From one-level multi-goal, the planners will have to move towards multi-level multi-goal, with a view to reaching a higher level of coordination in the human society with a common purpose. Inter-disciplinarity, however, remains the close preserve of a few minds. At the level of integrated teleology of expanding spectra of knowledge, there are rare specimens like Gregory Bateson. At the interface of political planning and administrative insight, the level at which global planners operate, an extended enmeshing of comprehensive knowledge-based thinking and reflective action-based forward movement is new music. It has no comforting parallel to draw upon, other than reverting for insights to socially purposeful organisational systems.

In operative terms, Herbst (1974, 1976A) has proposed an orientation towards non-hierarchical work design to bring closeness and fit between planning and action. At one level these are value prescriptions; at another level, these are the logical options for global planners who are in search of optimum means and who also seek global humanism. We cannot put it any better than what Albert Einstein did years ago: 'Perfection of means and confusion of ends seem to characterise our age.' This is the challenge before the global planners of today to plan for the future.

Let us now bind our thoughts to a perspective of the quality of life (QL) for a desirable third world. It is, at best, a tentative formulation of a paradigm.

Element I: Inter-society
Element Ia: *Third World Perspective*
Components:
1. Orientation towards futuristic development scenarios versus fulfilment of immediate, expedient short-term goals.
2. Movement towards collective domain versus trends towards sectoral dominance.
3. Increasingly active cooperation on development front with priority on eradication programmes against poverty, unemployment, malnutrition, endemic diseases, paucity of drinkable water, unhygienic housing, illiteracy, exploitation of women and children, desertification, paucity of food, etc., versus collaboration on arms, armaments and repressive technology development.
4. Movement towards autonomous society versus propensity towards acceptance of military-economic dominance of hegemonic powers.
5. Increased emphasis on cultural/educational exchange to appreciate and tolerate the relevance of diverse norms of traditions, mores and beliefs versus imitation of those aspects of the rich world 'culture' which value consumer-oriented life-style.
6. Trends towards interdependent and complementary utilisation of

non-renewable physical resources versus dependence on 'exports' of primary commodities to the rich world.

7. Strengthening a culture of non-confrontation emphasising equitable terms of trade with the rich world versus tendency to cultivate bilateral, bloc-wise 'favoured clause' treatment from selective countries of the rich world.
8. Strengthening the forums for defusing and resolving inter-state potential tension/actual conflict within the third world versus dependence on the rich country intervention.
9. Creation of the third world forums for technology assessment/choice for the countries versus dependence on the rich world assessors.
10. Development of a third world news media to voice facts including reporting on internal dissent and public debates and not falsehood/doctored data versus dependence on mass media emanating from the hegemonic powers.
11. Economic boycott of countries escalating/destabilising global peace whether these belong to the rich world or the third world versus secret deals with them.

Element Ib: *Bilateral/Bloc-level Perspective*
Components:

1. Development of operative values to conform to the third world consensually validated norms versus tendency towards 'deals' with divisive forces vis-à-vis other third world countries/groups.
2. Active joint action on development programmes to optimise natural resource utilisation for mutual benefit; reciprocity on a broad range of mutually beneficial projects without strings of hegemony. Soil preservation, afforestation, eradication of poverty-related diseases, electricity generation, irrigation and foodgrains production, etc., can lay claim to joint action versus dependence on technologies to bolster the interests of the ruling elites.
3. Mutual arms limitation programme and joint programme of defence against external aggression versus arms build-up, border disputes and making scapegoats of neighbouring countries.
4. Withdrawal of support to foreign aggressor versus diplomatic silence/secret alliance.
5. Freer movement of citizens across the countries versus restrictive practices fostering misunderstanding among people.
6. Joint programme to protect ethnic groups, their culture and tradition versus repression of their life-enriching traditions including language/literature.
7. Joint programme for family planning and increased care for the children, widows, older generation versus neglect of their priority needs resulting in marginalisation of such specific groups.

8. Initiation of cultural/education projects to curb the flush of pseudo nationalism and hatred of neighbour nations versus distortion of history and culture.

Element II: Nuclear Society

Element IIa: *Politics and Government*

Components:

1. Trends towards *purposeful* political ethos in accordance with which the political elites will inculcate the spirit of insuring the interests of the present and future generations of population versus self-oriented, self-serving and power-retaining short-range policies being pursued.

2. Management of the political system, complex as it is, to seek to integrate two components: informed and enlightened knowledge as well as expression of priority needs of the muted majority of the population versus elite-based people-insensitive administration system.

3. Introduction of such socio-economic programmes as will foster distribution of income and wealth equitably, reduce disparities between the urban and rural areas and between the top 25 per cent and the bottom 25 per cent of the nation's income groups versus maintenance of economic *status quo* with policies tinkering with symbolic manipulation of change by rhetoric exhortation.

4. Initiate policies to generate productive employment of those who enter the labour market by devoting budgetary allocation to appropriate programmes versus catering to dominant interest groups' vocal demands.

5. Initiate policies to gradually reduce unproductive use of resources including arms reduction measures versus the build-up of agencies for repression of people (militarist orientation).

6. Encourage down-up/participative forums/agencies free from control by vested interests to mobilise human commitment to family planning, health care, conservationist programmes versus provision of incentives for proliferation of conspicuous and wasteful consumption.

7. Right to people to recall politicians in power through exercise of secret ballot versus manipulations of elections/referendum.

8. Administration of justice to be 'just', fair, simple and quick versus cumbersome, procedure-oriented, time-consuming and elitist.

9. Support to popular, voluntary organisations with grassroots base for development projects versus administrative bureaucratic-initiated programmes and action.

10. Policies devoted to crime-control, prison and police administration, law and order maintenance to become elevating and humane in action versus counter-productively regulative/repressive.
11. Joint optimisation of growth and human development versus blinding faith in rate of ascending GNP.

Element IIb: *Productive Organisations*
Components:
1. All human organisations tend to move towards productive orientation, be they economic, educational, research-based, related to art, culture, leisure, sports, regulatory, preventive and so on to optimise the committed utilisation of human energy versus tending to become parasitic, lumpen and static.
2. Trend towards goal-directedness enriched by purposefulness emanating from certain basic ideals/meta-ideals versus hardware-based, efficiency-prone, management techniques oriented insensitive artefact of production.
3. Advocate of authority and power being utilised for differentiation amplifying mutually accommodative human system.(innovation-prone) versus protagonist of deviation-counteracting mechanisms oriented impersonal system (control-fostering prone).
4. Propensity to generate learning culture in work situation fostering rewards of intrinsic and extrinsic varieties versus fostering narrow-band 'specialist' culture with demarcation between thinking/planning and doing.
5. Environment sensitive type (internal and external) versus environment atrophy type.
6. Oriented towards growth with conservation scenario (doing more with less) versus the squander society scenario (doing less with more)/the *status quo* scenario (doing more with more)—(Henderson, 1978).
7. Work ethics to become synergistic with QL in terms of societal transformation for a better future world versus immediacy-prone, effort-inducing exploitative relations of production.
8. Organisational commitment is premised on hierarchy of societal purposefulness versus a system of hierarchy of organisations motivated by elitist interests.
9. Movement towards interlinkage of human institutions on pluralistic complementary perspective versus 'enclave', self-propelling, and 'on-one's-own' compelling logic of existence.
10. Internal system of work based on integrated tasks, interdependence of colleagues, semi-autonomous group work, internally evolved

work norms versus externally ordained segmented roles, plurality of controls and authority-based regulative functions.

Element III: Primary/Secondary Groupings
Components:
1. A range of family groups—nuclear to joint to extended—based on cultural mores, traditions and sustained by social ecology of economic and emotional needs versus the rich country practice of fostering the nuclear family as a mono-culture.
2. Inter-family cooperative, communal living/working as a conserver, viable group versus ascriptive, divisive-prone caste groups with 'we-they' ties and loyalties.
3. Spatial distribution of families on an egalitarian basis so as to strengthen ties of ethnic, cultural, work-diverse family groups, in a homogeneous area with common social services, facilities and constraints versus income-group, profession-based group, ethnic group, caste group and region-based group spatially segregated.
4. Family activities organised on reciprocally responsive collective norms versus sex-role, parents' dominated children, male dominated division of labour.
5. Family as life-sustaining, life-enriching unit of social purpose versus a bankable vault of accumulated economic surplus.
6. A delicate purposeful balance of the autonomy of members and interpersonal interdependence versus a unitary structure generative of tension, escape-mechanism, double-standards of loyalty resulting in breakdown of relations/rootedness.

Element IIIa: *Voluntary Groups*
Components:
1. Temporary or quasi-temporary socially desirable objectives oriented groups versus acquisitive/*status quo* maintenance groups.
2. Organisation innovation-prone human system as a 'third force' versus imitation-prone groups secondary to the government system and bureaucratic work organisation system.
3. Membership is value-based and self-nourishing versus membership is obligatory.
4. Productive of cultural maturity versus cradle for irrational demands fulfilling.
5. Nurturer of the sane, humane and ecological future scenario strengthening the roots of family groups versus 'instant' needs-meeting pressure groups sub-optimising utilisation of societal resources.

6. Tend to ensure the future generations' needs by action today versus aiming at consumption of resources to maintain socio-economic privileges enjoyed by the present generations.

Element IV: Person
Components:
1. A person's domain is socially purposeful versus 'do-your-thing' syndrome of cultural insolvency.
2. A continuum of social-self epigenetic unfolding from child to adolescent to adult to old versus disabling, disjointed growth from one life stage to another.
3. Inheritor of a human system as well as a transformer of the inherited culture versus conformer and guardian of the predesigned social systems.
4. Manager of stability and change versus protagonist of unexamined tradition or iconoclastic propensity to destroy the rich creation of the past.
5. Liberating self-learner versus passive receptacle of knowledge.
6. Cooperatively interdependent versus meekly submissive or aggressively counter-dependent.
7. Actor versus cog.
8. Hope in collective action for creation of desirable future versus faith is externally-ordained human destiny.
9. Respector of human differences versus engineer for constructing uniform types.
10. Conversion of own motive structure into explict, observable behavioural modes versus remaining a victim of the 'iceberg' complex of motives with hidden components predominating.

We shall now present our framework in the form of an unfolding lotus flower as given in Fig. 4.4.

The symbol of a lotus is deliberate. The lotus as a flower with unfolding petals grows in water. That is where its mooring is. We do not visualise a third world as an entity by itself. It is an integrated part of the globe. We do not visualise that its self-sustaining and sane growth in terms of the quality of life with futuristic mission can be isolated from what will happen to the rest of the globe.

We have chosen the third world to illustrate our main theme of global planning for development. To begin with, the third world is inhabited by a vast majority of the global population. Its problems and prospects are, on the one hand, mind-boggling and, on the other, a matter of deep concern rooted in a sense of utmost urgency. We do visualise, however,

Figure 4.4

Quality of Life: The Third World Perspective

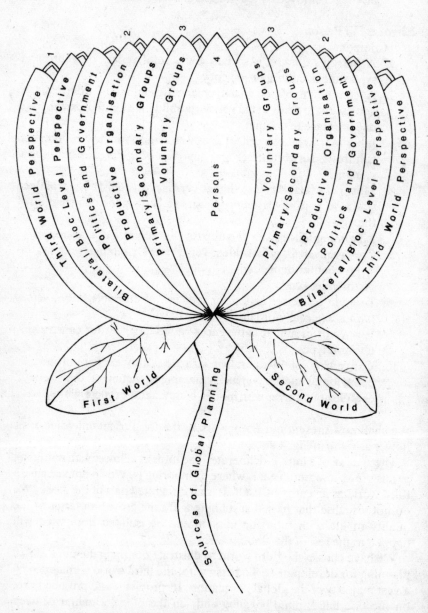

that complementary movement elsewhere towards the quality of life is a *sine qua non* for emphasis on QL.

At this stage it is worthwhile to consider the studies carried out in the field of quality of work-life criteria (QWL): Kanter, 1977; Stein and Kanter, 1980; Maccoby, 1975; Seashore, 1976; Walton, 1974. While our framework of QL has a global perspective, we have been directly influenced by the experiences in the third world and the impact of the rich countries on this sizeable global segment. Except for Maccoby, the other authors have their perspective derived from the rich countries. Their search for indicators is also confined to organisational life-space. It is perhaps implicit in their attempt at developing criteria that democratisation of work-life in the organisational galaxy will influence the national and global policies.

The Walton thesis has been summed up by him in the way given in Table 4.1.

The Seashore scheme can be presented as follows:

Stage 1:	Manpower orientation	*Gainful employment *Optimum skill level
Stage 2:	Economic man orientation	*High pay level with collateral rewards
Stage 3:	Welfare orientation	*Maintenance cost of the unemployed *Reduction of occupational illness *Equity among population categories, etc.
Stage 4:	Employee attraction orientation	*Capacity to attract and retain qualified employees *Capacity to elicit adequate work role performance
Stage 5:	Life-enhancement orientation	*Delayed harm or benefit experienced *Compatibility of the job characteristics with requirements of non-job social roles *Job contributions to learning and self-development *Opportunity for expression, individuality and creativity
Stage 6:	Future orientation	*Productive work to have voluntary character

Kanter's paradigm stands as follows:

I. Individual effectiveness	*Position-location in the system *Individual abilities

| II. Organisational power | *The level of opportunity
*Availability of the amount of power to a person in a position |
| III. Generativity | *Motivation to perform
*Use of knowledge and skills
*Performance level |

Maccoby's work spans a range of work situations. However, he has used four criteria:

1. Security	*Job security *health *safety
2. Equity	*fair rules, regulations *compensation
3. Democracy	*more opportunity *thinking and expressing
4. Individuation	*the goal of stimulating the fullest possible development of an individual's creative potential

There are four striking features in these explorations. In the first place, there is the recognition that organisational context and the employee context are organically interlinked. The nature of the interplay between the two sets of forces being complex, some have highlighted these more than others. However, none has ignored the essential unity of the two, even if, for analytical purposes, a distinction has been maintained. Secondly, in the studies referred to and elsewhere, there is a recognition that the larger social context of QWL cannot be ignored. However, in Seashore, Walton and to a lesser degree Kanter, the societal fabric in terms of economic, political and social forces have not been adequately acknowledged. They tend to tilt their orientation to the rich country-focused organisational life. Maccoby, influenced by the work of Fromm (Fromm and Maccoby, 1970), has exhibited somewhat more sensitivity to the social character of individuals shaped by socio-economic as well as psychological dimensions of social reality. Thirdly, the key criteria presented in our model which refer to persons, voluntary groups, primary/secondary groups and productive organisations are consistent with their thoughts. This convergence of ideas provides an insight that the global perspective of persons-in-organisations need not be segmentally looked at and examined. Lastly, we have sought to comprehend and brought into our framework the burning issues which refer to international, regional and national forums upon which organisational scientists are still slow to respond.

Table 4.1

Level for Conceiving and Measuring QWL

Level 1		Level 2		Level 3
Organisational Conditions	→	Employee Attitudes	→	Behavioural Symptoms (Associated with negative feelings)
1. Adequate and fair cooperation.	→	Security-insecurity in economic sense. Adequacy-inadequacy as a provider.		Alienation-passive aggressive response:
2. Safe and healthy working conditions.	→	Safe-vulnerable in physical sense.		*turnover, absenteeism, tardiness
3. Immediate opportunity to use and develop human capacities.	→	Stimulated-apathetic about work content. Influential-powerle's regarding work-related matters.		* accidents, mistakes *lower energy, motivation *passive resistance to rules
4. Future opportunity for continued growth and security.	→	Optimistic-apprehensive regarding career.		
5. Social integration in the work organisation.	→	Related-isolated from other people.		Alienation-active aggressive response:
6. Constitutionalism in the work organisation.	→	Sense of justice-injustice or inequity. Freedom—controlled or constrained.		*militancy in grievances, negotiations and strikes *wildcat strikes, failure to ratify contracts *individual acts of violence against people, property
7. Work relative to the total life space.	→	Satisfaction-guilt regarding balance or imbalance between career and family.		
8. Relevance to larger society.	→	Pride-shame regarding social significance of product and employer.		Low self-esteem: *lower mental, physical health *harm to family, community

The components mentioned can be subjected to measurements. Criteria and sub-criteria can be developed and, in fact, they exist in some form in respect of several items in different countries. (One may refer to PQL as spelled out by the Overseas Development Council.) By presenting a polarised picture in respect of each component we also recognise the reality that we do not aim at a utopia. Both the positive and negative components can be measured which then may constitute a composite index. In between different components allocation of *inter se* weightage is not a simple job. A measure of value judgment will indeed be involved. Depending on the orientation of the students of QL, there would be differences in priorities and, as such, reflected in measurements. Thus, each of the four major clusters and seven sub-clusters will present different cumulative values. On the basis of these different values, it is possible to map out somewhat of a gestalt with different sets of values. Over a period, the movement, postive or negative, can be assessed. We do believe that some exercise is necessary for monitoring our progress towards emerging scenarios of QL in the third world. A similar exercise with different sets of elements and components can be undertaken for the first world and the second world.

While such an exercise can provide a direction, no major change towards QL can emerge without deliberate human intervention. In the third world, interventions by political and administrative elites have so far yielded unsatisfactory results. Perhaps, the monitored picture will help sharpen the consciousness of the ruling elites. The major thrust, however, will come from the poorer strata of the society who are currently experiencing the deeply felt need to change the societal arrangements in order to emerge out of the long shadow of continued neglect and suffering. What is, therefore, required is to help them organise and mobilise upon a new paradigm for human organisations with their active membership. They should acquire abilities to organise and mobilise effectively with successive degrees of sophistication and effectiveness. This has been articulated in Chapter 2.

5

Meta-Ideals-Based Futures Design

Those who cannot remember the past are condemned to repeat it.

George Santayana.

In earlier chapters there has been recurrent reference to meta-ideals. We shall take up this theme for exploration here. While doing so, we shall focus on these propositions: that there is a future for humanity; that the design of the future, a conscious process, should take stock of the on-going endeavours of today to create better tomorrows; that the vision of the future should be premised on unassailable meta-ideals; and that the shape of the human futures be consistent with these meta-ideals. The task is not to prepare a blueprint for survival of the pseudo-species but to design a framework within which systems for ideal-seeking humans can be installed.

Hope Overtakes Despair

A random survey of literature conveys a distinct flavour of hope even as the distinguished authors are incisively clinical about the contemporary scenarios. Lorenz (1974) lists civilised man's eight deadly sins but does not fail to note the 'silver lining' that a growing number of people are 'really concerned about the predicaments of humanity'. Further, after an analysis of human aggression, he (1968) commits himself to an 'avowal of optimism'. Heilbroner (1975) portrays the present as harsh and grim history and yet seeks rays, however diffused and hazy now, to take us beyond doomsday; in the end he exhorts us to be the inheritors of Atlas, to unfalteringly master courage, fortitude and will if we are to resurrect humanity. Stavrianos (1976), while presenting a historical perspective on the accumulated garbage of human enterprise, does not foresee degradation, rather a 'transcendence of *Homo sapiens* to *Homo humanus*', sprouting of green grass through the concrete. Emery (1977) assesses the present as social fields composed of turbulent environments where maladaptive strategies prevail but rejects the doomsday scenario in favour of a vision of adaptive social futures. Birch (1975) begins with an image of the tunnel of darkness but assembles substance to foresee light at the end of the tunnel—a 'sustainable society'. Buckminister Fuller (1972) visualises man's success as transformation from a national myopic to a 'world man', for whom, he approvingly quotes a scientist: 'the world has become too dangerous for anything less than Utopia'. Gabor (1972), at times betraying naivety in his approach, visualises a society through 'the engineering of hope'. We end the recital by referring to Fromm and Maccoby (Maccoby, 1976; Fromm and Maccoby, 1970). From a concept of human energy posited in character traits which form a sort of bee-hive, as a social character responding to socio-economic functions of specific groups; they add other elements, such as, mode of relatedness to others and relationship to parents, to constitute the 'whole syndrome (of a person with) full interaction of character, socio-economic conditions and cultural traditions'. The dominant class would seek to maintain its *status quo* through the stability of its social character. However, the hope for creating a desirable future lies in 'social selection'. Multi-faceted environmental changes cause disequilibrium in the structure for the minority dissenters to assert and establish a new order through their 'social character'. A synergy of the qualities of head and heart, finite limits to which are yet to be established, is the *raison d'etre* of desirable change.

To sum up, thoughtful persons such as these echo the eloquence of many more, that hope for the future lies in the simple premise: the human mind is a living testimony to the negation of the entropy law. The body decays but the biophilic contributions of the mind as a reflection of many concrete and achievable realities continue. Herein lies the root: the future has a present.

Tomorrow-Today Scenario

Today's efforts to create a desirable tomorrow are significant for at least two reasons: (*a*) a test-out of ideas, tools and strategies offers reflection, clarity and teleological insights in what could otherwise be a socially expensive leap in the dark; (*b*) they foster a spirit of an 'invisible college' that facilitates a global network of social designers without the trappings of an over-burdened organisation. Basically, the success experiences reinforce faith and hope in humans' capability to undertake and sustain change. Cook, *et al* (1971) and Nash, *et al* (1976), for example, summarise a wide range of social experiments around the world, at once, a reflection of the urge to design better human systems translated into action.

We shall briefly recount two cases of organisation renewal and one case of local community innovation. Elden (1978) reports an interesting case of a district banking office in Norway. Let us assume two branches similar in size, technology, market, employee characteristics and so on. In one case, the decision-making task on computer use, manpower planning, work allocation, supervision of work and so on is concentrated at the top. Employees see the bosses as aloof and distant. They complain about the rigidity of the system, feel harried. Autonomy of the branch is fragile. Initiative lies with the head office. In the second case, there is openness and trust all around. The president included the subordinates in a task force to redesign his own role. Employees organised the work system with provision for time-off for study and self-improvement. Flexi-time was working well. The 'interesting' aspect is that it is the same office and the same people—the story of a radical change in two years. It is a fine example of participatory action-research, where *concerned* people reflected on their reality, gathered data, decoded the message and with collective responsibility redesigned a new human system of work.

The Bolivar Case (Maccoby, 1975; 1978; Duckles, *et al*, 1977) is unique in that, in a multi-racial factory operating in a highly competitive industry in the USA, the management and the union together worked out a plan of total participation of employees in order to redesign a production sytem to realise the values of *security, equity, individuation* and *democracy*. Evaluation conducted after five years indicates not only productivity gains but more significantly, stimulation and reinforcement of healthy character development with attainment of the employees' personal happiness and social responsibility. *A work system can become a continuing learning system.*

A work organisation is vital for bringing meaning to life, but nourishment of life demands that the social nexus too becomes an object of social action. There are growing examples of local community action to redeem this promise (Ackoff, 1974; Campbell, *et al*, 1977; De, 1977; Haugen, *et al*, 1977; etc.). Let us offer one case illustration. Trist (1978) reports on Jamestown in New York State which suffered an economic slump in the early 1970s with an unemployment rate at about 10 per cent. Industrial relations were bad and the place earned notoriety. A dedicated mayor stepped in resolutely. He mobilised the labour conciliation machinery to bring management and unions together. A year's labour brought about a

climate of dialogue. That was the start of a community renewal programme with community participation. An area union-management
committee went into action. Skills development programmes for dominant
industries were undertaken. The local community college was brought in.
State extension education services came forward. As the story spread
around, industries started coming up. The work-systems were planned
with a view to providing not merely a livelihood but a way of life that
could add dignity and engagement to people at work. The success story
acquired a national stature. Jamestown today, after seven years, is just
not a production centre but an all-absorbing, vibrant, participative,
ecologically balanced community.

These are but a glimpse of how the present has been put to use to pave
the way for a better tomorrow. What are the forces at the core of such
endeavours? That brings us to the concept of meta-ideals.

Meta-ideals: Acquisition of 'Samaj-Siddhi' through Collective Liberation

An overwhelming concern for a work system is to achieve its goals. The
same is the case with humans. For humans, however, the motive force of
behaviour lies in social character and personal interests (a reflection of
character traits). This becomes a source of conflict. Systems goals spring
from hierarchical, power-dominated decision-makers. The peripheral
members' interests may not necessarily coincide with these goals. This is
one contributing element to widespread alienation phenomenon. This is
as true of organisation systems as of a larger system usually structured in
the shape of nation-states.

We need to extricate ourselves from this bind. Ackoff and Emery
(1972) sought a new formulation in *purposes* which transcend as well as
include multiple goals. A goal or goals may change within the framework
of a purpose. A step forward and we come to *ideals*. Purposes can,
likewise, be transposed in the context of an ideal or ideals. We thus reach
a stage where human systems are purposeful and members are *ideal-
seeking*. Ideals may not be attained but these are, nonetheless, sought
after. Emery's (1976A) later formulation can be diagrammatically presented
with modifications as in Fig. 5.1.

It is necessary to refer to the modification proposed. Ackoff and Emery
(1972) use the concept of omnipotence as a meta-ideal. Let us examine
their justification. They cite Singer (1923): '... The condition for attaining
any end in the world is such control of the world's machinery as shall give
you power to get what you want.' From this they draw the inference that

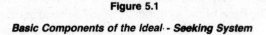

Figure 5.1

Basic Components of the Ideal - Seeking System

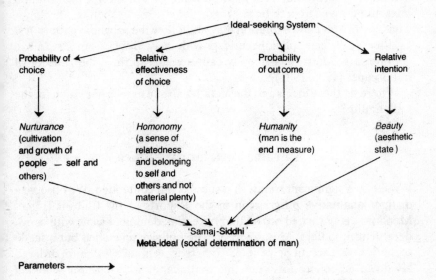

…the ability or *power* to satisfy desire is universally desired and must be desired at least as much as anything else is…. Little wonder that in every conception of God—man's formulation of an ideal being— omnipotence is one of his attributes (p. 240, emphasis in original).

We differ here from Ackoff and Emery. They themselves mentioned that Singer felt that the *nature* of the desire was a key to the issue.

We conceive the *nature* somewhat differently. Ideal-seeking persons are aware that by keeping an eye on the ideals they *seek*, they cannot necessarily attain them. Such persons, by virtue of their orientation, are indeed aware that human beings cannot be omniscient nor can they be omnipresent. Similarly, too, with omnipotence. Reality-orientation is likely to be the strength of ideal-seeking humans. In our view, *Samaj-Siddhi* is a more acceptable form of a meta-ideal. In organisational/ institutional set-ups, self-determination of the members can take place in the context of fellow human beings bound by certain ideals, as identified by Emery, in order to create a continuously improving human society as an unfolding design. *Samaj-Siddhi* seems to enjoy operational relevance not apparent in the concept of omnipotence.

We shall also mention that the ideals of nurturance, homonomy, humanity and beauty, on a global perspective, will be heterogeneous and diverse on the basis of the multiplicity of the cultural heritage. The paths to ideals as well as the contents of ideals will take to morphogenetic dynamics (Maruyama, 1981). The meanings will incorporate cultural hues and derive strength from progressive myths, symbols and heritage. The North American evolution may not follow the Japanese pattern just as the Norwegian phylogenetic growth may differ from its Indian counterpart. Maruyama happily captures this spirit in the concept of mindscapes (1980, 1981).

Where do these ideals and the meta-ideal take us to in our vision for the millennium?

A Framework for the Future

We see two significant trends that support our contention. We observe a distinct qualitative progression in the Reports to the Club of Rome. Meadows, *et al* carried out an undifferentiated number game with considerable forebodings; Mesarovic, *et al* do not give up models but bring in scenarios with accent on people; Tinbergen, *et al* shift further in order to lay down guidelines for a new international order. *Goals for Mankind* (Laszlo, 1977) has conceived the future in the language of goals, aspirations and values. Botkin, *et al* (1979) highlight learning, social apprenticeship and development. The other milestone is the recent establishment at MIT, the mecca of science and technology, of a college devoted to study the humanistic aspects of the technological society: its culture, the lives of people, their attitudes, perceptions, problems, goals and prospects, hopefully, a step towards a purposeful system.

Inevitably, our centrepiece is the human being with all the potential of human development, rooted in human groups, a point emphasised in Chapter 4. While we do expect further contributions emanating from trans-disciplinary research in the genetic code field, we believe that the redesigned human systems will act as a counterpoint to the misdirected use of these contributions.

We shall briefly touch upon four aspects of future society.

First, organisation systems will essentially be composed of social humans. The Bolivar experiments will no longer be hothouse pieces. They will even be improved upon, given the ingenuity of the human mind. Work organisations will be much smaller because people are not numbers. Viability will not be a function of competitive survival. The harshness of competition will be replaced by an urge for excellence. Creative acts in whatever fields will be shared property. The multinationals will go out with their avarice, arrogance and ugliness (Stavrianos, 1976: 1970–173). Internal management will be democratised and be consistent with socio-physical ecology. We visualise module one to cover all human systems. Hoarding or parasitic orientation will be rendered redundant. (Fig. 5.2.)

Secondly, the technology-resource scenario will be free from the obsessive exploitative mode. Science (a product of concrete experiences and creative urges) will march ahead to develop such sophisticated technology as will conserve scarce resources, recycle today's non-renewable items and offer meaningful work to all. The cult of consumerism will give way to labour engaging technology. Science and technology will subordinate themselves to human dimensions. The military-industrial complex, too frightening today, will be scrapped as unnecessary (Leontief, 1978; Dhawan and De, 1978). Instead, education and health, shelter and food challenges will engage science and technology to human use.

Thirdly, the media will acquire quality. The concepts of leisure and entertainment will assume a human meaning. TV will no longer be the 'third parent' fostering passivity. The cultural hegemony of Donald Duck will be replaced by two trends: the best in the tradition of civilisation will rekindle interests; at the same time, creative urges will seek finer, sensible, wholesome experiences of newer and newer variety. Violence as a vicarious pleasure propped up by the media will yield ground to those that can strengthen the meta-ideal of *Samaj-Siddhi*.

Lastly, the rich-poor division of the world will go. Nation states will continue with a qualitative transformation. The super-power status, trade and aid manoeuvrings, power-blocks confronting ideologies and xeno-phobia will acquire benign, productive sublimation in global, ecological

Figure 5.2

Typology of Adaptive Institutions

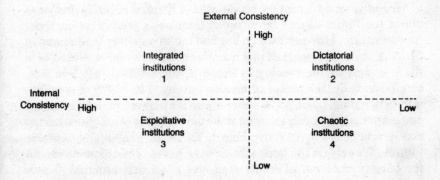

concerns. The enemies will be scourge and degradation, products of many ages, not men and nations. A network of regional collaborative ventures will unleash the contributions of science and technology to confront any challenge to human dignity and growth. Bargaining strategies will be replaced by the mobilisation principle to activate collective benefits. Power-needs will be converted to service-need. Men and nations will put an end to socio-economic exploitation of men and depredation of nature. Negative sanctions will yield grounds to superordinate positive, social action. Essentially, human energy will be propelled by a spirit of eternity rather than by the finite concept of time. Life-styles will be rich but simple. A sense of the numinous will supercede material profligacy.

Clarifying Comments

In the end, we owe it to ourselves and the readers that our assumptions and approaches do not convey any meanings which are contrary to our intent.

In the first place, our approach is not utopian. Utopias, as discussed by Winthrop (1978: Ch. 3), have historically acquired certain associative characteristics from Plato's *Republic* to Thomas Moore's *Utopia*, Bellamy's *Looking Backward*, H.G. Wells' *A Modern Utopia* and B.F. Skinner's *Walden Two*. Apart from the static, deterministic character of these social orders, there is an assumption—explicit or implicit—about the administrative arrangements for the new social order. An exclusive elite caste of brahmins or samurai would emerge as the guardians of the system. We do not share such a meritocratic world-view. We believe that the people are not inert masses nor can the Hitlerite extreme of a superior race, with its numerous variations, ever succeed in mastering the complexity of the future.

Secondly, we do accept the proposition of Kahn, *et al* (1972) that views about the future cannot be divorced from one's preconception about human nature. However, we do not find ourselves either in the camp of St. Augustine who believed that man was basically sinful or wicked or in the company of the theologian Pelagius who asserted that man was, single-handedly, the maker of his own destiny. The reality of complex, interpenetrating, open, social systems with the network of flows of energy and matter continuously gnawing at the ultra stability of the global human eco-system calls for collective human action for establishing desirable futures. We rely on the hope that growing human consciousness can tilt the balance in favour of reality as against historically acquired illusory myths.

Thirdly, we are reluctant to prescribe any specific futuristic models as the state of our knowledge about the enormously growing complexity in our environment does not permit such a venture as yet. Rogers (1967: 260) has captured the drama of management complexity by pointing out that with the addition of two states to the USA, the number of political interfaces on the state level can increase almost 2,500-fold. Yet another example is that a new cabinet post added to the existing ten increases the number of departmental interfaces eleven-fold, not by 10 per cent.

Here we are in accord with the views of Prigogine, *et al* (1977: 58) that 'complexity is limited by stability which, in turn, is limited by the strength of the system-environment coupling'. However, stability is not a mechanical entity. Shifting and turbulent quasi-equilibrium states will be an inevitable reality in the management of the future. Statistically predictable cause-effect relationships will not hold unless we collectively and deliberately decide to go back to the mythical but idyllic habitat of the Vedic era of the Hindu saints. Our hope is predicated on the evolution of meta-ideal, as spelled out earlier, which will provide the choice of tools for designing the future for human supremacy.

Fourthly, our future orientation is normative and not 'extrapolative'. Extrapolation has its limited use in that it *informs* as in Kapur (1975) and Malgavkar, *et al* (1977). But it does not provide illumination which can emanate from the roots of ideals. The choice of options for action is not value-free. So, we need direction from the beacon of a meta-ideal.

Fifthly, we carry the conviction that future design is not a matter of planning as is traditionally conceived. The adaptive planning process encompasses planned action as well. Our presentation has emphasised this issue when we deliberated on the 'tomorrow-today' theme with illustrations. To the extent that the Delphi technique is elitist and selective, it is inadequate for designing the human future. We also believe that participation in a planning process may not necessarily lead to concrete planning of action in basic social system design, in which case it will become a self-defeating exercise. Let us get to the heart of it by referring to Carlson (1977: 294). An exercise on the state of Washington for designing its alternative future went on as follows:

A 150-person task force initially generated new information about alternatives for the State. 1,500 persons participated in regional conferences reviewing the findings of the task force. 2,400 people participated in a Delphi poll.... With the information collected, the task force identified 11 alternative futures for the State.... Through an effective media campaign and a unique call-in programme, over 60,000 people participated in the programme, with 1,00,000 to 2,00,000 persons watching programmes on public television.

There was, however, no follow-up action. The result of such a well-intentioned plan could as well be 'an overall increase in frustration and alienation'.

We do believe that the basic challenge in such a situation lies in people-mobilisation in order that the collective will can gather momentum in the shape of power to acquire a voice for action. This is how we visualise active, adaptive planning.

Sixthly, we have not specifically responded to the deepening feeling among many socially sensitised fellow humans in the rich world that the powers-that-be are propelling people to a 'termination course' of high consumption and low, emotionally-rich life-styles. We do not deny the existence of this danger. In fact, we see its galloping, viral spread to the richer sections of the third world. Without going into the sustained structural instability of such a socio-economic order on account of the interplay of numerous contradictions, we pin our hope on the possible historic role of the rebels, the deviants, the minority whose ideals will help them to acquire a voice through the people.

Lastly, in Chapters 1 to 3 we have offered some concrete approaches as to *how* the meta-ideal-based human systems design will take shape. None can deny the importance of the issue. However, the operative process is a challenge by itself, not to be mixed up, in our view, in the outline of a framework for relevance of *specific* ideals in the human system design. In the days of contemporary nation-builders such as Marcos, Park, Bokassa and Pinochet, it is but human to reiterate the obvious.

Works Cited

ACKOFF, R.L. 1971. 'Towards a System of Systems Concepts', *Management Sciences*, 17, 11.
———. 1974. *Redesigning the Future*, New York, John Wiley.
———. 1981. *Creating the Corporate Future*, New York, John Wiley.
ACKOFF, R.L., and F.E. EMERY. 1972. *On Purposeful Systems*, Aldine, Chicago.
ARENS, J., and J.V. BEURDEN. 1977. *Jhagrapur: Poor Peasants and Women in a Bangladesh Village*, Amsterdam, Paupers' Press Cooperative Limited.
ARGYRIS, CHRIS. 1972. *The Applicability of Organizational Sociology*, Cambridge, Cambridge University Press.
BAHRO, RUDOLF. 1978. *The Alternative in Eastern Europe*, London, N.L.B.
BANDYOPADHYAY, D. 1979. *Land Reforms in West Bengal: A Few Operational Issues* (mimeo), Calcutta.
BARNABY, FRANK. 1980. 'World Arsenals in 1980,' *The Bulletin of Atomic Scientists*, September.
BAUMGARTEL, H. 1976. 'Some Notes on Institution-Building,' *National Labour Institute Bulletin*, July.
BELL, D. 1960. 'Work and its Discontents,' *The End of Ideology*, New York, Free Press.
———. 1967. 'The Year 2000—The Trajectory of an Idea,' *Daedalus*, Summer.
———. 1976. *The Cultural Contradictions of Capitalism*, London, Heinemann.
BERGER, L.L., and T. LUCKMANN. 1967. *The Social Construction of Reality*, quoted in D.N. Michael, *op. cit.*
BIRCH, C. 1975. *Confronting the Future*, Harmondsworth, Penguin Books.
BLAU, P.M. 1974. 'Presidential Address: Parameters of Social Structure,' *American Sociological Review*, 39, pp. 615–35.
BOTKIN, J.W., *et al.* 1979. *No Limits to Learning*, New York, Pergamon Press.
BOULDING, KENNETH E. 1966. 'The Economics of the Common Spaceship Earth,' in *Environmental Quality in a Growing Economy*, Baltimore, Johns Hopkins Press.
BRADLEY, K., *et al.* 1981. 'Motivation and Control in the Mondragon Experiment,' *British Journal of Industrial Relations*, July.
BRAVERMAN, HARRY. 1974. *Labour and Monopoly Capital*, New York, Monthly Review Press.
BROWN, DAVE L. 1977. 'Can Haves and Have-nots Cooperate: Two Efforts to Bridge a Social Gap,' *Journal of Applied Behavioural Science*, 13, 2.

BUCKMINISTER FULLER, R. 1972. *Utopia or Oblivion*, Harmondsworth, Pelican Books.

BURNS, T.R., *et al.* eds. 1979. *Work and Power*, London, Sage Publications.

CALDWELL, G. 1973. *The Future of Clubs*, Canberra, Centre for Continuing Education, The Australian National University.

CAMPBELL, A. 1976. 'Subjective Measures of Well-Being,' *American Psychologist*, February.

CAMPBELL, A., *et al.* 1977. *Worker–Owners: The Mondragon Experience*, London, Anglo-German Foundation for the Study of Industrial Society.

CARLSON, R. 1977. 'Public Feedback for the Club of Rome,' in E. Laszlo, *et al.* (eds), *Goals in a Global Community*, Vol. 1, New York, Pergamon Press.

CHATTOPADHYAYA, D.P. 1973. *Lokayata, A Study in Ancient Indian Materialism*, New Delhi, Peoples' Publishing House.

———. 1975. *The Indian Philosophy*, New Delhi, Peoples' Publishing House.

———. 1976. *Individuals and Worlds*, London, Oxford University Press.

CHERNS, ALBERT. 1977. 'Can Behavioural Science Help Design Organizations?' *Organizational Dynamics*, Spring.

———. 1979. *Using the Social Sciences*, London, Routledge and Kegan Paul.

CHOWDHURY, ZAFRULLAH. 1978A. 'Basic Service Delivery in Underdeveloped Countries,' *Human Futures*, Summer.

———. 1978B. 'The Paramedics of Savar: An Experiment in Community Health in Bangladesh,' *Development Dialogue*, 1978, 1.

———. *et al.* 1982. *Essential Drugs for the Poor: Myth and Reality* (mimeo), Savar, Bangladesh, Gonoshasthaya Pharmaceuticals Ltd.

CHURCHMAN, C. WEST. 1977. 'A Philosophy for Complexity,' in H.A. Linstone, *et al.* (eds), *Futures Research*, London, Addison-Wesley.

CLIVE SIMMONDS, W.H. 1977. 'The Nature of Futures Problems,' in H.A. Linstone, *et al.* (eds), *op. cit.*

COATES, KEN, *et al.* 1972. *The New Unionism: The Case for Workers Control*, London, Peter Owen.

COLMAN, A.D. 1976. 'Operant Conditioning and Organisational Design,' in E.J. Miller (ed.), *Task and Organization*, London, John Wiley.

COOK, T.E., *et al.* 1971. *Participatory Democracy*, San Francisco, Canfield Press.

CROMBIE, A. 1976. *Post-industrialism and the World of Work*, Occasional Paper No. 10, Canberra, Centre for Continuing Education, The Australian National University.

DAS, ARVIND N. 1979. 'Field Notes on Visits to Gonoshasthaya Kendra' (typed), New Delhi, Public Enterprises Centre for Continuing Education.

DAVIES, ALAN. 1980. 'Some Notes on the Application of Political Concepts to the Power Relationships within Organizations,' *Towards Continuing Education*, August.

DAVIS, LOUIS, and A.B. CHERNS, 1975. *The Quality of Working Life*, Vols. 1 and 2, New York, Free Press.

DAVIS, LOUIS, and E.L. TRIST. 1974. 'Improving the Quality of Working Life: Socio-technical Case Studies,' in James O'Toole (ed.), *Work and the Quality of Life*, Cambridge, MIT Press.

DE, NITISH R. 1976. 'An Approach to Research Methodology on Employee Motivation,' *National Labour Institute Bulletin*, New Delhi, 2, 11, November.

———. 1977. *Adaptation of Traditional Systems of Agriculture in a Developing Economy*, Occasional Paper Series, 2/77, New Delhi, National Labour Institute.

———. 1978. *Initiation Process in Designing New Forms of Work Organisation: Tentative Experiences from India* (mimeo), New Delhi, Public Enterprises Centre for Continuing Education.

———. 1979A. 'India's Agrarian Situation: Some Aspects of Changing the Context,' in A. Das and V. Nilakant (eds), *Agrarian Relations in India*, New Delhi, Manohar.

———. 1979B. 'A Note on Understanding Participation Process in Organisation System Design,' *IFDA Dossier*, 10, August.

———. 1981A. 'Personnel Implications for Management of New Forms of Work Organisation,' in Nitish R. De, *et al.*, *Managing and Developing New Forms of Work Organization*, Geneva, I.L.O., Second Edition.

———. 1981B. 'Some Thoughts on Technology and Economic Development,' *Human Futures*, Spring.

DHAWAN, S.K., and NITISH R. DE. 1978. 'Arms and Aid: An Exercise in Hegemony Versus Development,' *Human Futures*, 1, 4, Winter.

DORAISWAMY, R. 1982. *Quality of Working Life—Experience at Kotagiri Post Office* (mimeo), paper presented at the National Seminar on Improving the Quality of Working Life held in New Delhi.

DOVBA, A.S., *et al.* 1979. 'USSR,' in *New Forms of Work Organization*, Vol. 2, Geneva, I.L.O.

DUCKLES, M.M., *et al.* 1977. 'The Process of Change in Bolivar,' *Journal of Applied Behavioural Science*, Summer.

DUNCAN, K.D., *et al.* 1980. *Changes in Working Life*, New York, John Wiley.

Ecodevelopment News. 1981. Progress Report No. 7, Gonoshasthaya Kendra, March.

EISENSTADT, S.N. 1959. 'Bureaucracy, Bureaucratisation and Debureaucratisation,' *Administrative Science Quarterly*, 4.

———. 1972. 'Social Institutions,' *International Encyclopaedia of Social Sciences*, 13, 14, New York, Macmillan.

ELDEN, M. 1978. *Three Generations of Work Democracy in Norway*, Trondheim, Technical University.

ELLUL, G. 1967. *The Technological Society*, New York, Vintage Books.

EMERY, F.E. 1959. *Characteristics of Socio-technical Systems*, London, Tavistock Institute Document No. 527.

———. 1970. *Freedom and Justice Within Walls*, London, Tavistock Publications.

———. 1976A. *In Pursuit of Ideals*, Canberra, Centre for Continuing Education, The Australian National University.

———. 1976B. *Adaptive Systems for Our Future Governance*, Occasional Paper No. 4/7, New Delhi, National Labour Institute.

———. 1976C. *The Assembly Line—Its Logic and Our Future*, Canberra, Centre for Continuing Education, The Australian National University.

———. 1977. *Futures We Are In*, Leiden, Martinus-Nijhoff.

———. 1981. 'On Inventing Theory,' paper presented at the International Conference on the Quality of Working Life, Toronto, 30 August–3 September.

EMERY, F.E., *et al.* 1974. *Futures We Are In*, Canberra, Centre for Continuing Education, The Australian National University.

EMERY, F.E., *et al.* 1975. *Choice of Futures: To Enlighten or Inform*, Canberra, Centre for Continuing Education, The Australian National University.

EMERY, F.E., *et al.* 1978. *The Emergence of a New Paradigm of Work*, Canberra, Centre for Continuing Education, The Australian National University.

EMERY, F.E., and M. EMERY. 1973. *Participative Design: Work and Community Life*, Occasional Papers in Continuing Education No. 4, Canberra, The Australian National University.

EMERY, F.E., and M. EMERY. 1974. *Participative Design-Work and Community Life*, Occasional Papers in Continuing Education, No. 4, Canberra, Centre for Continuing Education, The Australian National University.

234 Alternative Designs of Human Organisations

EMERY, F.E., and E. THORSRUD. 1975. *Democracy at Work*, Canberra, Centre for Continuing Education, The Australian National University.

EMERY, F.E., and E. THORSRUD. 1976. *Democracy at Work*, Leiden, Martinus-Nijhoff.

EMERY, F.E., and E.L. TRIST. 1960. 'Socio-technical Systems,' in *Management Sciences Models and Techniques*, Vol. 2.

EMERY, F.E., and E.L. TRIST. 1972. *Towards a Social Ecology*, New York, Plenum.

EMERY, M. ed. 1975. *Planning our Town*, Canberra, Centre for Continuing Education, The Australian National University.

———. 1976. *Searching*, Occasional Paper No. 12, Canberra, Centre for Continuing Education, The Australian National University.

———. 1982. *Searching*, revised edition.

ENGLAND, G.W. 1975. *The Manager and His Values*, Cambridge, Ballinger Publishing Co.

ESMAN, M.J. 1967. *Institution-building Concepts: An Interim Appraisal*, University of Pittsburg.

———. 1978. 'Development Administration and Constituency Organisation,' *Public Administration Review*, March–April.

ETZIONI, A. 1968. *The Active Society*, New York, Free Press.

FLASSATI, DOMINIC. 1981. 'i Viva la Co-operativa!' *New Internationalist*, December.

FREIRE, P. 1972A. *Pedagogy of the Oppressed*, Harmondsworth, Penguin Books.

———. 1972B. *Cultural Action for Freedom*, Harmondsworth, Penguin Books.

———. 1974. *Education for Critical Consciousness*, London, Sheed and Ward.

———. 1975. 'Pilgrims of the Obvious,' *Risk*, 2, 1.

———. 1978. *Pedagogy in Process*, New York, Seabury Press.

FOSTER, MICHAEL, *et al.* 1970. *An Overview of Industrial Democracy and Worker Participation*, London, Tavistock Institute of Human Relations.

FOY, N., and H. GADON. 1976. 'Worker Participation: Contrast in Three Countries,' *Harvard Business Review*, May–June.

FRIEDMAN, G. 1961. *The Anatomy of Work*, London, Heinemann.

FROMM, E. 1964. *The Heart of Man*, New York, Harper and Row.

———. 1974. *The Anatomy of Human Destructiveness*, New York, Holt, Rinehart and Winston.

FROMM, E., and M. MACCOBY. 1970. *Social Character in a Mexican Village*, Englewood-Cliffs, Prentice Hall.

GABOR, DENNIS. 1972. *The Mature Society*, London, Seeker and Warburg.

GAGNON, G. 1976. 'Cooperatives, Participation and Development: Three Failures,' in J. Nash, *et al.* (eds), *Popular Participation in Social Change*, The Hague. Mouton Publishers.

GALTUNG, JOHAN. 1981. 'Global Processes and the World in the 1980s: Prolegomenon I for a GPID World Model,' Tokyo, The United Nations University.

GETLER, MICHAEL. 1981. 'Spending Plan Accelerates Military Outlay,' *International Herald Tribune*, 20 February.

G.K. 1977. *Progress Report No. 6* (mimeo), Savar, Bangladesh, Gonoshasthaya Kendra.

GORZ, ANDRE. 1965. 'Capitalist Relations of Production and the Socially Necessary Labour Forces,' *International Socialist Journal*, August.

GRAMSCI, A. 1973. *Selections from the Prison Notebooks*, New York, International Publishers.

GRANT, JAMES. 1979. 'Central Issues in the North–South Dialogue,' *OECD Observer*, January.

———. 1981A. 'Health for All by the Year 2000: Sincere Commitment or Empty Rhetoric?' The H.R. Leavell Lecture, World Foundation of Public Health Associations.

————. 1981B. 'The State of the World's Children, 1980–81,' New York, United Nations Children's Fund.

————. 1982. 'Children in Dark Times,' *The Economic Times*, 10 April.

GVISHIANI, D. 1972. *Organization and Management*, Moscow, Progress Publishers.

HAEFFNER, ERIK A. 1979. 'The Innovation Strategies for Industrial Corporations and for Satisfying National Needs,' in H.J. Baker (ed.), *Industrial Innovation*, London, Macmillan Press.

HAIRE, MASON, *et al.* 1966. *Managerial Thinking*, New York, McGraw-Hill.

HAMPTON, CHRISTOPHER. 1981. *Socialism in a Crippled World*, Harmondsworth, Penguin Books.

HANSPACH, HEINZ, *et al.* 1979. 'German Democratic Republic,' in *New Forms of Work Organization*, Vol. 2, Geneva, I.L.O.

HARASZTI, MIKLOS. 1977. *A Worker in a Worker's State*, Harmondsworth, Penguin Books.

HARTMANN, B. 1979. Review article on 'Jhagrapur: Poor Peasants and Women in a Bangladesh Village,' *Bulletin of Concerned Asian Scholars*, 11, 2.

HAUGEN, R., *et al.* 1977. 'Self-initiated Community Development,' *National Labour Institute Bulletin*, January.

HEILBRONER, R.L. 1975. *An Enquiry into the Human Prospect*, London, Calder and Boyars.

HELLER, AGNES. 1976. 'Theory and Practice from the Point of View of Human Needs,' in A. Hegedus, *et al.* (eds), *The Humanisation of Socialism*, London, Allison and Busby.

HENDERSON, HAZEL. 1978. *Creating Alternative Futures*, New York, Berkley Publishing Corporation.

HERBST, P.G. 1962. *Autonomous Group Functioning*, London, Tavistock Publications.

————. 1974. *Socio-technical Design*, London, Tavistock Publications.

————. 1976A. *Alternatives to Hierarchies*, Leiden, Martinus-Nijhoff.

————. 1976B. *A Note on Rural India* (mimeo), New Delhi, National Labour Institute.

HILL, T.M. 1973. *Institution-building in India: A Study of International Collaboration in Management Education*, Harvard, Boston, School of Business Administration.

The Hindu. 1979. 'What Happened to Vested Land?' 13 August.

HINTON, W. 1972. *Fanshen*, Harmondsworth, Penguin Books Ltd.

HODGKIN, THOMAS. 1981. *Vietnam: The Revolutionary Path*, London, Macmillan Press.

HOPWOOD, A.G. 1979. 'Economic Costs and Benefits of New Forms of Work Organization,' in *New Forms of Work Organization*, Vol. 2, Geneva, I.L.O.

I.C.A. 1976. *Maliwada: Human Development Project*, Bombay, Institute of Cultural Affairs.

————. (no date). *Human Development Training*, Bombay, The Institute of Cultural Affairs.

ILLICH, IVAN. 1969. *Celebration of Awareness*, Harmondsworth, Penguin Books.

————. 1970. *De-schooling Society*, Harmondsworth, Penguin Books.

————. 1975. *Conviviality*, Geneva, International Institute for Labour Studies.

————. 1976. *Medical Nemesis*, Harmondsworth, Penguin Books.

I.L.O. 1979. *New Forms of Work Organization*, Vols. 1 and 2, Geneva.

————. 1980. *Work and Family Life*, Geneva.

JANTSCH, ERICH. 1972. 'Towards Interdisciplinarity and Transdisciplinarity in Education and Innovation,' *Interdisciplinarity*, Paris, OECD.

————. 1974A. *Technological Planning and Social Futures*, London, Associated Business Programmes.

————. 1974B. 'Social Responsibility and its Effects on Technological Innovations: Roles for World Corporations,' University of Sussex/University of Stirling Seminar, September.

JENKINS, D. 1974. *Job Power*, London, Heinemann.

————. 1981. *QWL—Current Trends and Directions*, Toronto, Ontario, Ministry of Labour.

JOHANSON, ROBERT. 1980. *The National Interest and the Human Interests: An Analysis of US Foreign Policy*, Princeton, Princeton University Press.

KAHN, H., *et al*. 1972. *Things to Come*, New York, Macmillan.

KAHN, R.L. 1974. 'Work Module: A Proposal for the Humanisation of Work,' in James O'Toole (ed.), *Work and the Quality of Life*, Cambridge, MIT Press.

KAJE, RITVA. 1977. 'Bringing the Feminine into Forecasting: Foreseeing and Learning,' in H.A. Linstone, *et al*. (eds), *op. cit*.

KANTER, R.M. 1973. *Communes*, New York, Harper and Row.

————. 1977. *Men and Women of the Corporation*, New York, Basic Books.

KANTER, R.M., and B.A. STEIN. eds. 1979. *Life in Organizations*, New York, Basic Books.

KAPUR, J.C. 1975. *India in the Year 2000*, New Delhi, India International Centre.

KENISTON, KENNETH. 1972. 'The Varieties of Alienation,' in A.W. Finifter (ed.), *Alienation and the Social System*, New York, John Wiley.

KENNEDY, W.B. 1975. 'Pilgrims of the Obvious or the Not-so-Obvious,' *Risk*, 2, 1.

KHAN, M.H. 1979. *Sind-Hari Committee, 1930–1970: A Peasant Movement*? (mimeo), Geneva, I.L.O.

KHANDELWAL, G.K., and V. NILAKANT. 1976. 'Work Reorganisation in State Bank: A Preliminary Report,' *National Labour Institute Bulletin*, 2, 7, July.

KLEIN, L. 1976A. *New Forms of Work Organization*, Cambridge, Cambridge University Press.

————. 1976B. *A Social Scientist in Industry*, London, Gower Press.

KOLAKOWSKI, L. 1978. *Main Currents of Marxism*, Vol. 3, Oxford, Clarendon Press.

LAMMERS, C.J. 1974/1975. 'Self-Management and Participation: Two Concepts of Democratization in Organizations,' *Organization and Administrative Science*, 5, 4, Winter.

LASWELL, HAROLD, *et al*. 1976. 'The Continuing Revision of Conceptual and Operational Maps,' in H. Laswell, *et al*. (eds), *Values and Development: Appraising Asian Experience*, Cambridge, MIT Press.

LEONTIEF, WASSILY. 1978. 'Observations on Some World-wide Economic Issues of the Coming Years,' *Challenge*, March/April.

LOGAN, CHRIS. 1982. 'Do it Yourself Socialism?' *The New Statesman*, 16 April.

LORENZ, KONARD. 1968. *On Aggression*, London, Methuen and Co.

————. 1974. *Civilised Man's Eight Deadly Sins*, London, Methuen and Co.

LOW, I. 1976. 'One Thousand Up,' *New Scientist*, 13 May, pp. 354–55.

MACCOBY, MICHAEL. 1975. 'Changing Work: The Bolivar Project,' *Working Papers for a New Society*, Summer.

————. 1976. *The Games Man*, New York, Simon and Schuster.

————. 1978. 'The Bolivar Project—Productivity and Human Development,' *Human Futures*, 1, 4, Winter.

MADALA, M.K. 1982. *Action Research Project at Srinagar Post Office, Jhandewalan: Some Reflections* (mimeo), paper presented at the National Seminar on Improving the Quality of Working Life held in New Delhi.

MADISON, C. 1980. 'You Know that Synfuels are for Real when the Big Boys Enter the Picture,' *National Journal*, 13 September.

MALGAVKAR, P.D., *et al*. 1977. *Towards an Industrial Policy: 2000 A.D.*, New Delhi, Centre for Policy Research.

MANDKE, V.V., *et al*. 1975. *BITS Practice School* (mimeo), Pilani, BITS, August.

MARKUS, M., and A. HEGEDUS. 1976. 'Community and Individuality,' in A. Hegedus, *et al*. (eds), *op. cit*.

MARUYAMA, MAGOROH. 1963. 'The Second Cybernetics,' *American Scientist*, June.
———. 1977. Quoted in H.A. Linstone, *et al.* (eds), *op. cit.*
———. 1980. 'Mindscapes and Science Theories,' *Current Anthropology*, October.
———. 1981. 'Mindscapes: Meta-principles in Environmental Design,' *Garten and Landschaft*, 10.
MARX–ENGELS. 1966. 'Thesis on Feuerbach III,' *Selected Works*, Moscow.
MASOOD, M. 1978. 'The Traditional Organisation of a Yoruba Town: A Study of Ijebu-O,' *Ekistics*, July–August.
MEADOWS, D.H., *et al.* 1972. *The Limits to Growth*, New York, Universe Books.
MEDAWAR, C. 1979. *Insult or Injury?* London, Social Audit Ltd.
MESAROVIC, M., and E. PESTEL. 1975. *Mankind at the Turning Point*, London, Hutchinson and Co.
MICHAEL, D.N. 1977. 'Planning's Challenge to Systems Approach,' in H.A. Linstone, *et al.* (eds), *op. cit.*
MILLER, E.J. 1975. 'Socio-technical Systems in Weaving, 1953–1970: A Follow-up Study,' *Human Relations*, 28, 4, pp. 349–86.
MILLER, E.J., and A.K. RICE. 1967. *Systems of Organization*, London, Tavistock Publications.
MISHRA, A. 1979. 'The Forest Cover,' *Seminar*, May.
MISHRA, A., and S. TRIPATHI. 1978. *Chipko Movement*, New Delhi, People's Action.
MOZAYENI, M. 1978. 'In Praise of Indigenous Manmade Environments: Mossuleh in Iran,' *Ekistics*, July–August.
M.R. 1978–79. *Monthly Review*, July–August and May respectively.
M.V.D.P. 1978. *Status Report: Maliwada Demonstration Village and 24 District Pilot Villages*, Bombay.
NADKARNI, V.C. 1976. 'Greening of India,' *The Illustrated Weekly of India*, 20–25 June.
NASH, J., *et al.* eds. 1976. *Popular Participation in Social Change*, The Hague, Mouton Publishers.
NOVACK, GEORGE. 1976. 'The Problem of Alienation,' in E. Mandel, *The Marxist Theory of Alienation*, New York, Pathfinder Press, Third Printing.
OLIVEIRA, D.D., *et al.* 1976. *Guinea-Bissau*, IDAC Document No. 11/1, Spring, Geneva.
O'TOOLE, JAMES. 1973. *Work in America*, Cambridge, MIT Press.
———. ed. 1974. *Work and the Quality of Life*, Cambridge, MIT Press.
PANDHE, M.K. ed. 1976. *Bonded Labour in India*, Calcutta, India Book Exchange.
PAREEK, U. 1977. 'Institution-building: The Framework for Decision-making,' in U. Pareek, *et al.* (eds), *Institution-building in Education and Research*, New Delhi, All India Management Association.
PERLMUTTER, H.V. 1965. *Towards a Theory and Practice of Social Architecture: The Building of Indispensable Institutions*, London, Tavistock Publications.
PETER, L.J. 1977. *The Peter Plan*, New York, Bantam Books.
PIAGET, JEAN. 1972. 'The Epistemology of Interdisciplinary Relationships,' *Interdisciplinarity*, Paris, OECD.
PIVEN, F.E., and R.A. CLOWARD. 1979. *Poor People's Movements*, New York, Vintage Books.
PRADEEP, P., and ARVIND N. DAS. 1979. 'Organisation of the Future: A Case Study of the Bihar Colliery Kamgar Union,' *Human Futures*, Autumn.
PRIGOGINE, I., *et al.* 1977. 'Long-term Trend and the Evolution of Complexity,' in Laszlo, *et al.* (eds), *Goals in a Global Community*, Vol. 1, New York, Pergamon Press.
QUINN-JUDGE, PAUL. 1982. 'A Vietnamese Cassandra,' *Far Eastern Economic Review*, 26 February–4 March.
RAO, V.R. 1975. 'Quality of Life in an Industrial Township: An Initial Survey,' *National Labour Institute Bulletin*, 1, 10, October.

————. 1976A. 'Shishu Vihar: An Evolving Learning System,' *National Labour Institute Bulletin*, 2, 6, August.

————. 1976B. *Identification of Training Needs for Supervisory Personnel at Hardwar Unit* (mimeo), New Delhi, National Labour Institute.

RICE, A.K. 1958. *Productivity and Social Organization: The Ahmedabad Experiment*, London, Tavistock Publications.

RIESMAN, D. 1964. 'Leisure and Work in Post-industrial Society,' *Abundance for What?* London, Chatto and Windus.

ROBERTSON, JAMES. 1978. *The Sane Alternative*, London.

ROGERS, W.L. 1967. 'Aerospace Systems Technology and the Creation of Environment,' in W.R. Ewald (ed.), *Environment for Man: The Next Fifty Years*, Bloomington, Indiana University Press.

ROKEACH, M. 1973. *The Nature of Human Values*, New York, Free Press.

RUSSELL, RAYMOND, *et al*. 1979. 'Participation, Information and Worker-Ownership,' *Industrial Relations*, Fall.

SABATIER, P. 1975. 'Social Movements and Regulatory Agencies: Toward a More Adequate and Less Pessimistic Theory of "Clientele Capture",' *Policy Sciences*, September.

SAHAL, DEVENDRA. 1977. 'Conception of Futures in a Systems Framework,' in H.A. Linstone, *et al*. (eds), *op. cit*.

SALAMINI, L. 1981. *The Sociology of Political Praxis*, London, Routledge and Kegan Paul.

SARAN, K.M. 1957. *Labour in Ancient India*, Bombay, Vora and Co.

SATOW, R.L. 1975. 'Value-Rational Authority and Professional Organizations: Weber's Missing Type,' *Administrative Science Quarterly*, March.

SCHEIN, E.H. 1970. 'The Role Innovator and His Education,' *Technology Review*, October/ November.

SEASHORE, S.E. 1976. *Indicators of the Quality of Working Life* (mimeo), Institute for Social Research, University of Michigan.

SEEMAN, MELVIN. 1972. 'Alienation and Engagement,' in A. Campbell, *et al*. (eds), *The Human Meaning of Social Change*, New York, Russell Sage Foundation.

SELZNICK, P. 1966. *Leadership of Administration*, Tokyo, Harper International Edition.

SEN, K.M. 1961. *Hinduism*, Harmondsworth, Pelican Books.

SHAH, K. 1979. 'Denuding the Himalayan Ranges,' *Indian Express*, 6 November.

SHARMA, K.C., *et al*. 1978. *Participative Redesign of the Work System*, New Delhi, Department of Personnel and Administrative Reforms, Government of India.

SINGER, E.A. 1923. *On the Contented Life*, New York, Henry Holt.

SINGH, J.P. 1979. *New Forms of Work Organisations* (mimeo), New Delhi, National Productivity Council.

SMITH, B., *et al*. 1972. 'Cross-cultural Attitudes of Managers: A Case Study,' *Sloan Management Review*, Spring.

SMITH, J.M. 1976. 'Ethics and Human Evolution,' *New Scientist*, 15 April.

SOHR, RAUL. 1982. 'Will Capital Break the US Blockade?' *The New Statesman*, 23 April.

SOMJEE, A.H., *et al*. 1978. 'Cooperative Dairying and the Profiles of Social Change in India,' *Economic Development and Cultural Change*, 26, 3, April.

SOMMERHOFF, GERD. 1974. *The Logic of the Brain*, London, John Wiley and Sons.

SRINIVASAN, S. 1982. *Role of the Postal Staff College in the Improvement of the Quality of Working Life in the Indian Post Office* (mimeo), paper presented at the National Seminar on the Quality of Working Life held in New Delhi.

The Statesman. 1982. 'The Poverty Debate,' 9 May.

STAVRIANOS, L.S. 1976. *The Promise of the Coming Dark Age*, San Francisco, W.H. Freeman and Co.

STEIN, B.A., and R.M. KANTER. 1980. 'Building the Parallel Organisation: Creating Mechanisms for Permanent Quality of Work Life,' *Journal of Applied Behavioural Science*, 16, 3.

TANDON, R., *et al.* 1980. *An Organisational Analysis of Trade Unions in India* (mimeo), New Delhi, Public Enterprises Centre for Continuing Education.

THOMAS, JOHN M., and WARREN G. BENNIS. 1972. 'Introduction,' in J.M. Thomas and W.G. Bennis, *Management of Change and Conflict*, Harmondsworth, Penguin Books.

THOMPSON, E.P. 1981. 'Beyond the Superpowers,' in *The New Statesman*, 6 March 1981 (referring to Boris Komarov, *The Destruction of Nature in the Soviet Union*, Pluto Press).

THORSRUD, E. 1976. 'Democracy at Work and Perspective on the Quality of Work Life in Scandinavia,' Research Series No. 8, Geneva, International Institute for Labour Studies.

TINBERGEN, JAN, *et al.* 1976. *Reshaping the International Order*, New York, E.P. Dutton.

TRIST, E.L., 1976. 'A Concept of Organizational Ecology,' *National Labour Institute Bulletin*, 2, 12, December.

———. 1978. 'A New Approach to Economic Development,' *Human Futures*, 1, 1, Spring.

———. 1979. 'New Dimensions of Hope,' *Human Futures*, Autumn.

———. 1981. *The Evolution of Socio-Technical Systems*, Toronto, Ontario, Ministry of Labour.

TRIST, E.L., *et al.* 1951. 'Some Social and Psychological Consequences of the Longwall Method of Goal-getting,' *Human Relations*, 4, 3–38.

TRIST, E.L., *et al.* 1963. *Organizational Choice*, London, Tavistock Publications.

TRIST, E.L., and F.E. EMERY. 1960. 'Report of the Barford Conference for Bristol/Siddley Aerospace Engine Corporation,' London, TIHR 598, Tavistock Institute of Human Relations.

TURNER, R.H. 1976. 'The Real Self: From Institution to Impulse,' *American Journal of Sociology*, March.

UMADIKAR, R.H. 1969. *The COCC Story* (mimeo), Bombay, Life Insurance Corporation of India.

Unit for Industrial Democracy. 1978. *Industrial Democracy*, Sydney, CCH Australia Ltd.

VAN GROENOU, W.W. 1976. 'Sociology of Work in India,' in G.R. Gupta (ed.), *Main Currents in Indian Sociology*, Vol. 1, Delhi, Vikas Publishing House.

VAN HECK, B. ed. 1979. *Participation of the Poor in Rural Organisations*, Rome, F.A.O.

VARDAN, M.S.S., *et al.* 1976. *An Opinion Study of the Component Centre System at HMT* (mimeo), Bangalore, HMT Centre for Manpower Development and Research.

VICKERS, G. 1973. *Making Institutions Work*, London, Associated Business.

———. 1977. 'The Future of Culture,' in H.A. Linstone, *et al.* (eds), *op. cit.*

VIQUEIRA, J.P. 1976. 'Change in the Traditional Forms of Collectivism in Spain: Theoretical and Methodological Considerations,' in J. Nash, *et al.* (eds), *op. cit.*

WALTON, R.E. 1974A. 'Innovative Restructuring of Work,' in J.M. Rostow (ed.), *The Worker and the Job*, London, Prentice Hall International.

———. 1974B. 'QWL Indicators: Prospects and Problems,' *Studies in Personal Psychology*, Spring.

WEICK, K.E. 1969. *The Social Psychology of Organisations*, Reading, Addison-Wesley.

———. 1976. 'Education Organisations as Loosely Coupled Systems,' *Administrative Science Quarterly*, March.

WERTHEIMER, MAX. 1945. *Productive Thinking*, New York, Harper and Row.

WILLIAMS, TREVOR. 1982. *Learning to Manage Our Futures*, New York, John Wiley.

WINTHROP, H. 1978. *Foreseeing the Future: Roadblocks and Difficulties*, Delhi, B.R. Publishing.

240   *Alternative Designs of Human Organisations*

WODDIS, JACK. 1972. *New Theories of Revolution*, New York, International Publishers.
YANKELOVICH, D. 1974. 'The Meaning of Work,' in J.M. Rostow, *op. cit.*
YANOWITCH, MURRAY. 1979. *Soviet Work Attitudes*, Oxford, Martin Robertson.
ZEITLIN, MAURICE. 1982. 'Alienation and Revolution,' in A.W. Finiter (ed.), *op. cit.*

Author Index

Subject Index